PRE-REFORMATION ENGLISH
SPIRITUALITY

PRE-REFORMATION ENGLISH SPIRITUALITY

Edited and Introduced by
JAMES WALSH, S.J.

FORDHAM UNIVERSITY PRESS

BRONX · NEW YORK

ד ׀ ד ׀

CUM PERMISSU SUPERIORUM

Library of Congress Catalog Card No.: 65-12885

PRINTED IN GREAT BRITAIN

CONTENTS

INTRODUCTION

"CONTEMPLATION cannot be achieved unless a man leave the tumult of the world and give his heart entirely to God; so that he finds his delight in desiring God in solitude."[1]

The term "English Spirituality" has become synonymous with the variety of contemplative experience and the written instruction on the contemplative life of four figures of the fourteenth century, Richard Rolle, Walter Hilton, the author of the *Cloud of Unknowing* and Julian of Norwich. Rolle is the very apotheosis of the hermit; Julian's mystical experience was received in her anchorhold at Norwich; Hilton wrote his main work for a recluse, and finished his life in the quasi-eremitical state, amongst the Canons Regular of St. Augustine at Thurgarton; whilst the author of the *Cloud* and the disciple whom he was directing by writing were both called to "that singular form of living called solitary."

Of the other personalities whose experiences and teaching are described in this book, practically all lived the solitary life, or wrote for solitaries. Nor are they to be considered as isolated representatives of the intensity and diversity of religious life in England, from its first articulate description in the writings of Bede the Venerable to the treatises of those exilic hermits of the English Reformation, Benet Canfield and Augustine Baker. They present, in substance, the history of English Spirituality for close on a thousand years. Of the three who have no immediate connection with the eremitical life, Edmund Rich "was by instinct a recluse" and "was happiest in retreat among his Cistercian friends at Stanley Abbey, where he often spent half the year";[2] Thomas More made no secret of the attraction which the Carthusian vocation had for him; and Margery Kempe could be described as a hermit on pilgrimage. The antagonism of ecclesiastical authority and organised religion to Rolle, the author of the *Cloud* and Margery Kempe and the constant criticism in *Piers Plowman* of the hierarchy and the religious orders of his day, also serve to substantiate the claim that one great characteristic of English Spirituality from first to last is independence of religious life as lived in the great orders from the days of Alfred to Henry VIII.[3]

Allied, however, to this independence is insistence on spiritual orthodoxy, which meant in practice fidelity to the principles of monastic spirituality. Rolle has no fundamental quarrel with monastic life as lived in its purity. When the author of the *Ancrene Riwle* tells

---

[1] Richard Rolle, *Super Mulierem Fortem*, cited in Hope Emily Allen, *Writings ascribed to Richard Rolle*, p. 160.

[2] *Infra*, pp. 105–6.   [3] Cf. *infra*, p. 17.

his recluses that if asked to which Order they belong, they are to say that they belong to the Order of St. James, he is not joining in a controversy between the relative merits of the eremitical and cenobitic ways of life; but he is making a simple distinction between "good religious who live in the world, particularly prelates and true preachers" and those others who keep themselves "clean and unspotted from the world" like the great hermits Paul and Anthony, who are to be counted amongst the founders of Western Monasticism.[1] The vows that bind the anchoress are those that bind the monk, when he is living perfectly according to his vocation: obedience, chastity, and stability of abode. When Aelred of Rievaulx is writing for his anchoresses, his outlook is the same as that of his fellow Cistercian, William of St. Thierry, in his famous letter to the Carthusians of Mont Dieu: "[The solitary life] is of the ancient religion and piety, perfectly founded in Christ; it is the ancient heritage of the Church of God . . . it was whilst the memory of the Passion of the Lord was still fresh in the hearts of men that they began to choose this solitary life, to follow poverty of the spirit, and to rival one another in that leisure which produces spiritual exercises and the contemplation of God."[2] All that William has to say in this letter on the Christian life and its goal, the perfection of contemplation, applies equally to the Benedictine or Cistercian and to the Carthusian solitary. Richard Methley, Carthusian monk of Mount Grace in Yorkshire, who translated the *Cloud of Unknowing* into Latin at the end of the fifteenth century, writes of the form of living to which the author of the *Cloud* and his disciple are called: "The ordinary degree is of lay people, the special of clerics or religious, and the singular of solitaries: that is, hermits, anchorites and especially Carthusians. Hence we may conclude that this book was written for a Carthusian, since in our day it is not customary, as it was in days gone by, to leave an approved religious order for a hermitage, but only for the Carthusians."

Whenever, then, in English spiritual writing, there is an awareness of conflict between the cenobitic and eremitical ways of life, this has to do, not with the substance of a common spirituality, but with accidental differences of place and circumstances. There will always be the feeling that hermits and anchorites are "against the Establishment," and they can expect to suffer for it. When the Orders devote themselves to learning, the anti-intellectualism which the hermit manifests, whether explicitly as preached by the learned Rolle or the author of the *Cloud*, or implicitly in the illiteracy of a Godric, or a Margery or in Julian's lack of schooling ("because I am a woman should I therefore believe that I ought not to tell you about the goodness of God?"), is a reproach to those whose love of God grows cold because of their

[1] Cf. *The Ancrene Riwle*, ed. Salu, pp. 4–5.   [2] *Epistola Aurea*, PL 184, 310.

love of learning for its own sake. The learning that these illiterates display, mastery in spiritual direction and the discernment of spirits— "the art of arts" as Hilton calls it—emphasises the defects of those clerics and religious who should possess it. It prompts them to ask the question that was asked of Christ, "How came he by this learning?" and suggests the answer, "he casts out devils by the power of Beelzebub." Book-learning is not an essential for contemplative living: "a man who leans on faith, hope and charity, and has a firm grasp of them, does not need writings except perhaps for the instruction of others. And thus many with these three can live in solitude without books."[1] And Thomas More will quote the great humanist Pico Della Mirandola: "Alas, how mad of us to keep seeking by knowledge that which love alone can reach and grasp."[2]

If there is a distinction to be made between the cenobitic and eremitical ways of life, it is that the monk is the apprentice, whilst the solitary should be the skilled craftsman in the work of contemplation. A contemplative life demands interior silence in hermitage, anchorhold and monastery alike. But the hermit's cell provides the best circumstances in which to achieve it. When William of St. Thierry writes to the Carthusians of Mont Dieu: *Aliorum est Deo servire, vestrum adhaerere*—"It belongs to others to serve God, your task is to cling to Him . . . this is indeed your profession, to seek the God of Jacob; and not in the ordinary manner of men but to seek the face of God,"[3] he is stating the ideal common both to monk and hermit. The real dichotomy, in England as in Europe generally in the Middle Ages, was between the contemplative and the active life; or, as the author of the *Cloud* puts it, between perfection and salvation. It is worth remarking that the very real contribution that English writers have made to the doctrine of the Mystical Body—one thinks particularly of the teaching of Julian, Hilton and the author of the *Cloud*—is given by way of answer to the common objection that contemplatives, in their preoccupation with the love of God, neglect the love of their fellow-man.

The English solitary's preparation for contemplative graces is wholly orthodox and traditional: reading, prayer and meditation, with the accompanying *ascesis* of progressive self-renunciation. The hinge here is the simple form of mental prayer in which the whole man is engaged, the imaginative contemplation of a particular mystery of the incarnate Christ. We see this contemplation in embryo in Bede's second homily on the Nativity;[4] its development in the West is owed principally to Aelred; it is more or less the constant occupation of Christina of Markyate and Margery Kempe; it established itself firmly in later

[1] William of St. Thierry, *Speculum Fidei*, PL 180, 367.   [2] *Infra*, p. 228.
[3] *Epistola Aurea*, PL 184, 311, 313.   [4] Cf. *infra*, p. 9.

Western spirituality by way of the *Life of Christ* of the Carthusian
Ludolph of Saxony, and the *Spiritual Exercises* of Ignatius Loyola. It
depends from the prayerful study of the Gospel text, often through
learning by heart in repeated listening, and with the help of pictures,
sculpture and dramatic representation. This contemplation is the
knowledge-in-love of Christ in his sacred humanity. So Rolle propa-
gates devotion to the holy name of Jesus, and the Monk of Farne to
the Sacred Heart. The self-renunciation which adherence to the divine
Will demanded of Christ is seen particularly in the Passion; so that it
is only to be expected that affective writing on the Lord's sufferings
will be another characteristic of English spirituality.

The movement from this imaginative contemplation to a purer
form, expressed in the Bernardine *per Christum Hominem ad Christum
Deum* is epitomised in the contemplative exegesis of the text from
Ephesians, "May you be able to comprehend with all the saints what
is the length and breadth and height and depth of the love of Christ,
to know what is beyond knowledge," which both Hilton[1] and the
Cloud[2] take over from St. Bernard's *De Consideratione*.[3] The English
devotion to our Blessed Lady is similarly recognised as a way to
contemplation, as Julian notes: "I was taught that every contemplative
soul to whom it is given to behold and feel God, shall see her [our
Lady St. Mary] and pass unto God by contemplation."[4]

It must be conceded that the atmosphere of English spirituality is,
for the most part, far removed from the field full of folk of the
Ploughman's Vision. Whenever the world is glimpsed, it is always in
the pejorative sense in which Christ uses the word: all in human
nature and living that is opposed to him. It is true that there is a vivid
consciousness of "fellow-Christians," those for whom the contemplative offers himself; and there is also a constant effort to hand on the
fruits of contemplation in the sort of preaching and teaching of devout
living which an imitative liturgy affords.[5] But the primacy of the
contemplative life remains absolute. The perfection which actives can
achieve is always in terms of approximation to contemplation.[6]
William of St. Thierry's dichotomy between those who serve God
and those who cleave to him is constantly seen as a conflict of opposites.

The English writer who first perceives that a resolution of the
antinomy is feasible, and one which the spiritual theologian must
work towards, is Walter Hilton. Hilton, by any standards, is one
of the great spiritual theologians of the West. And, as Miss Joy
Russell-Smith shows so clearly, his success in reducing the gap between
action and contemplation, his insistence that the two should comple-

[1] Cf. *infra*, p. 181.   [2] *Cloud*, ch. 38.   [3] Chs. 13–14.
[4] *A Shewing of God's love: the shorter version of the Revelations*, ed. Reynolds
(London, 1938), p. 38.   [5] Cf. *infra*, pp. 26–7.   [6] Cf. *e.g.* the *Cloud*, ch. 21.

ment one another, puts him above his peers. One feels that when the
author of the *Cloud* makes a rather grudging exception for men of the
active life at the end of his *Prologue*,[1] he is reluctantly following in
Hilton's footsteps. We can see Hilton's teaching in practice in Thomas
More, the great friend and benefactor of the London Charterhouse
and the student of the *Scale of Perfection*. It is in Hilton, therefore, that
we see the final justification of the ideals of monastic spirituality: the
inculcation of the virtues of humility and obedience which are the
true mirroring of the incarnate Christ, and which lead to the consummate charity of St. Thomas More.

It is often maintained that the Counter-Reformation spirituality,
with which most of us are familiar, is un-English because it seems to
conflict so radically with the ideal contemplative spirituality of which
we have been speaking and which is the predominant theme of this
book. But it is worth noting that one of the most famous exponents
of the new spirituality is the founder of the Society of Jesus, Ignatius
Loyola; Ignatius, who spent so many years in the hermit garb of a
Richard Rolle; who rivalled Margery Kempe in the importance he
attached to the gift of tears; whose mysticism was trinitarian like
Julian's; who, through his sons, has taught the method of prayer
practised and developed by Christina, Aelred and so many others in
this book, a method now known universally by every religious order
and pious layman as meditation, but which Ignatius called contemplation.

Ignatius ends his *Spiritual Exercises* (the manual of "Ignatian"
spirituality) with a contemplation for obtaining divine love—the goal
of every solitary. He directed that his novices, after making these
exercises, should be sent into the hospitals, on eremitical pilgrimages,
to teach the catechism to the poor and the ignorant, in order to give
the proof of the love they had obtained in contemplation. There is
not a whit of difference between Ignatian spirituality, whose ideal is
contemplation in action, and the words of Walter Hilton: "Many
seek after Christ by withdrawing and fleeing from all men, in the
belief that he cannot be found except in that way. But it is not so, if
you would be a spouse of Jesus Christ and would find him whom you
seek, I shall tell you where Jesus your spouse is, and where you can
find him—in your sick brother who is lame or blind or afflicted with
any other disease. Go to the hospital and find Christ there."

We should not forget, either, the immense weight that Ignatius
lays on orthodoxy, on loyalty to Mother Church; or how exactly in
his "Rules for the Discernment of Spirits" he echoes the teaching of
Rolle, Hilton and the author of the *Cloud*. It would, of course, be
foolish to press too far this relationship between the thought of

[1] Cf. *infra*, p. 171.

Ignatius the Spaniard and the soldier and the English Spirituals. But the comparison does indicate the essential continuity of Western Spirituality before and after the Reformation, the danger of laying too much stress on the epithet "English" and indeed of thinking in terms of "schools" of spirituality at all.

It is often said that in our day we have need of a completely new spirituality; that the old monastic spirituality should be left to the professional contemplatives, and that revolutionary spiritual thinking is required to meet the needs of the multitudes of religious and lay-folk in the active apostolate in the world. It is true that the life of the Church demands a growth and development in her spirituality, even as much as in her dogma. What is said of dogma, that it must be re-thought and re-formulated to suit the needs of each succeeding age, is equally true of spirituality. In Augustine Baker and Benet Canfield we see that the traditional spirituality of England seemed to become that of the exile and the ghetto. But what we must not forget is that for both these authors the English Church *was* in exile, in "anchorholds" in France and the Low Countries. In discarding the ghetto mentality, we must not discard those traditional principles that union with God in the perfect fulfilment of his divine Will is the ideal of every Christian, and that in every situation a working synthesis of action and contemplation must be found. It may be said with real justification that the synthesis between action and contempla- tion, which is the crown of English pre-Reformation spirituality, is expressed anew and more deeply in the call to a closer participation for all the people of God in the liturgy: "It is of the essence of the Church," says the Constitution of Vatican Council II on the sacred liturgy, "that she be both human and divine, visible and yet invisibly equipped, eager to act and yet intent on contemplation, present in this world and yet not at home in it; and she is all these things in such wise that in her the human is directed and subordinated to the divine, the visible likewise to the invisible, action to contemplation, and this present world to that city yet to come, which we seek." Now, as never before, the deep and constant desire of the Church is being expressed that in the holy sacrifice all the people of God should come together to perfect that divine praise which Rolle saw as the perfection of contemplation in this life, a participation in the song of angels. Here there is no longer any dichotomy between action and contempla- tion; all are called to be contemplatives in the moment of the sacred action.

I wish to express my thanks to all the contributors to this volume, especially to the Reverend Edmund Colledge, O.S.A., for his constant advice and help; to the Editor of *The Month*, the Reverend Ronald

Moffat, S.J., in whose periodical these chapters first appeared; and to Mr. Ronald Browne, the Farm Street Librarian, who was responsible for drawing up the bibliography.

JAMES WALSH, S.J.

1. ST. BEDE

Donald Nicholl

MANY SAINTS, from the moment of their conception, are the occasions of pious prophecy and miraculous visions; for the rest of their lives they are the subjects of spectacular graces and astonishing intuitions. Their writings and sayings are organised into systematic guide-books to the heights of spirituality, and their treasured relics become the means of wonderful cures, dramatic conversions and terrible punishments. None of these things happened to St. Bede. No fuss seems to have been made of his birth; even his parents' names are unrecorded. We are not told of his being favoured by visions; nor did he work miracles—though it is, perhaps, typical of him that he should be the beneficiary of one which he mentions casually, almost shyly.[1] After his death no cult of him swept the country; not until 1899, in fact, some twelve hundred years afterwards, did the Church officially recognise him and grant him the title of doctor. On the face of it, Bede is not the most promising subject for study in a series on the mystical tradition.

Yet one wonders how many of the older saints are so likely as Bede to make spiritual life intelligible to men of our day, for his is the spirituality of the technician; the man who serves his apprenticeship quietly, steadily and conscientiously mastering the necessary skills and only revealing his consummate achievement in the last decade of his life. Our contemporaries who are rightly sceptical of short-cuts to wisdom and look doubtfully on youthful lyricism might well be reassured as they glance at the titles of Bede's early works: *De arte metrica*, *De orthographia*, *De schematibus et tropis*, etc. Like a craftsman bending over his last, Bede applies himself assiduously to the dry details of learning, to getting his quantities right and mastering his references. With each fresh treatise he perfects the chief tool of his trade, his

[1] *Vita sancti Cuthberti* (ed. W. Jaager, Leipzig, 1935), p. 57.

Latin prose style, which becomes ever more exact. As he frees his Latin prose from all those superfluities and adornments upon which his contemporaries prided themselves, so when incorporating the work of other men into his own he cuts out all irrelevant material and goes straight to the nerve of the subject. As a result the story of his spiritual growth does not tell of how a youthful vision had to be clung to despite the dark clouds which came with the realities of experience; on the contrary, the darkness and incomprehension are dispelled with the years, so that the note of youthful joy grows stronger, his mind moves with increasing ease and flexibility, until at the last he can say: "It is time for me, if it be His will, to return to my Maker, who formed me, when as yet I was not, out of nothing. I have lived long, and my merciful Judge has well disposed my life. The time of my departure is at hand, for my soul desires to see Christ my King in His beauty."[1]

There is an economy in these dying words of Bede that befits the manner of his living. Only a boy of seven when he was entrusted to the monastery of Wearmouth, he spent the next fifty-five years until the day of his death (25 May, 735) either there or in the house at Jarrow. Fifty-five years of monastic duty, the office, manual work and teaching, a routine scarcely ever broken. There was the journey he made once to Lindisfarne and, not long before his death, the journey to York. Otherwise he worked away unceasingly at his scientific treatises, his hagiographies, biblical commentaries and the *Historia Ecclesiastica*. It is upon the latter, quite rightly, that Bede's fame is based, for it is in the proper sense of the term an epoch-making study of history. But one feels that Bede would be pleased if at least one or two of the thousands who read his history would turn sometimes to the "mystical" aspect of his teaching—to what he himself regarded as of highest importance.

However there is a sense in which it is misguided, and even in a measure an offence to the memory of Bede, to speak of *his* mystical teaching at all. For though he was a teacher he was at every instant conscious of being a Catholic teacher, whose duty it is to come ever closer to the mind of the Catholic Church: whoever wishes to be united to God must first become united

[1] The eye-witness was Cuthbert, afterwards Abbot of Wearmouth and Jarrow, cf. *Baedae Opera Historica* (ed. C. Plummer), p. lxxvii.

with the Church, learn its faith and be imbued with its sacraments.[1] Then when a person, in fear and trembling, assumes the
office of teacher and begins to announce Catholic truth to the
unlearned, he must above all things avoid giving to that teaching
some special interpretation of his own—that would be to ape
the pagan oracles.[2] It is, in fact, this habit of sullying the purity
of Scripture with human fictions that made heretics so detestable
to Bede:[3] for him, heretics are the little foxes referred to in the
Song of Songs who destroy the vines, that is, who lacerate the
simple minds of faithful Catholics; it is the duty of Catholic
teachers to seize them before they can do much damage.[4] His
burning zeal for the purity of the Catholic faith accounts for the
one outburst of real anger from this usually serene man, on the
occasion of his own orthodoxy being called in question by the
"babbler" David.[5] And for the same reason it is most inaccurate
to cite him, as frequently happens, as a representative of "Benedictine spirituality" for there is not the remotest suggestion in
his writings that he recognised any schools of spirituality—
the very notion would smack to him of conventicles rather than
of the Church.[6]

Of course, all Catholic teachers bring out fresh treasures from
the inexhaustible stock of Catholic wisdom, according to their
own times and their own temperament, but if one is not to con-
fuse the proportions completely and be unfaithful to Bede, one
must stress that the main body of his writings consists of a conscientious repetition of basic Biblical texts and the standard
comments of the fathers. Rarely does he venture an opinion of
his own; his was not a brilliant, original, speculative mind—
the theology of the Incarnation, for example, or of the Trinity,
receives no exciting development at his hands—and his own
attitude is frequently only to be inferred from the way he treats
his authorities. When one finds, for instance, that he omits
from his rendering of Adamnan's De locis sanctis the disgusting
story of the Jew who threw an ikon of Our Lady into the

[1] Opera 12 (ed. Giles), p. 271.   [2] Opera 7, p. 244.
[3] Opera 12, p. 267.   [4] Opera 9, p. 247.
[5] Bedae Opera de Temporibus (ed. C. W. Jones, 1943), pp. 132–5. Jones points
out that Bede is here criticising St. Wilfrid, also, in whose presence the accusation
was made without rebuff.
[6] St. Benedict himself is scarcely ever referred to by Bede.

B

privy, one can infer something about Bede's temperament. His omission of the story is the silence of a fastidious spirit. But such aspects of his temperament are usually to be inferred rather than demonstrated.

Fortunately we do not depend upon inference to realise that it was Bede's close attachment to tradition that led him to the Scriptures as the beginning and end of a Catholic's spiritual life, for he says as much quite plainly. How, he asks, can anyone boast of being a Christian who does not, to the limit of his capacity, devote himself to study of the Scriptures in search of Christ?[1] The very first thing a Christian must do, if he wishes to arrive at contemplation of the divine majesty, is to seek strength from those two breasts of the Church, the Old and the New Testaments.[2] Everything he receives there will be a source to him of peace and charity,[3] for the will of God is our peace and only in sacred Scripture can we be sure at all times of discovering God's will.[4] At the same time let no one imagine that he can arrive at an understanding of the Scriptures if he reads them hastily and negligently—Bede has severe things to say of gifted men who harbour this illusion—they must be studied constantly and diligently.[5]

So faithful was Bede to his own advice, so close was he to the Scriptures, that it would be inadequate to speak of him interpreting the world in the light of them; it would even be inadequate to describe the Scriptures as the spectacles through which he saw the world, and nearer to the truth to say that Scriptures were the eyes with which he beheld it. And if one wishes at a glance to see that world for oneself one can scarcely do better than to look long at the illuminated pages of the Lindisfarne Gospels, the gospels produced by the community at Lindisfarne which Bede himself visited, for which he wrote his life of St. Cuthbert and which, in return, inscribed his name in its Book of Life. The words *"In principio erat verbum,"* for instance, are *seen* when they appear in the Lindisfarne Gospels to contain depths of meaning which they are not seen to contain when they appear in the clipped, efficient form of modern type, devoid of any penumbra of suggestion. Within the initials one finds trumpet

---

[1] *Opera* 11, p. 380.   [2] *Opera* 12, p. 212.   [3] *Opera* 8, p. 326.
[4] *Opera* 8, p. 27.   [5] *Opera* 11, pp. 68-9, and 9, p. 254.

patterns, whorls, triangles and lozenges, and birds and animals interlaced, as though foreshadowing the whole wealth of forms and life that was to issue from the Word; and this whole microcosm is highlighted by the interplay of colours used for the illumination, green, mauve, yellow, red and pink. In a similar fashion the world revealed by Scripture was for Bede full of many layers of meaning, literal, allegorical and tropological. And just as the purpose of the illumination was to ensure the greatest impact of the words upon the eye and mind of the reader so the purpose of biblical study, for Bede, was to allow the interior, or mystical, meaning of Scripture to make its full impact upon the heart of the devout reader.

The images used by Bede to characterise the relationship between the literal and the spiritual[1] meanings of Scripture are remarkable; the literal is a veil which has to be drawn aside to reveal the spiritual sense;[2] it is the bark one must strip off to come to the pith;[3] it is the shadow of the allegorical truth.[4] When one translates the literal sense into the spiritual it is like the change of water into wine,[5] like rolling the stone away from our uncomprehending hearts.[6] Or again:

A honeycomb is wax containing honey; but the honey in the wax is the spiritual sense of the divine words in the letter, which is properly described as a dripping honeycomb. The honeycomb is dripping indeed since it has more honey than its waxen cells can contain; for such is the fecundity of the sacred Scriptures that a verse which is usually written down in one short line would fill many pages if one examined it more closely and tried to bring out how much sweetness of spiritual understanding it contains within. Let us give an example:—the psalmist says, Praise the Lord, Jerusalem. In the literal sense, the psalmist is urging the citizens of that city, in which stands the temple of God, to sing the Lord's praises. In the allegorical sense, Jerusalem, the Church of Christ, is spread throughout the whole world. Tropologically, that is, according to the moral sense, each holy soul is rightly named Jerusalem. Anagogically, that is, as signifying the highest

---

[1] For the sake of brevity I might say quite baldly that I do not think that one can *literally* maintain that Bede was consistent in his use of the terms, mystical, allegorical, anagogical, etc.; but the *spirit* of the distinctions is clear enough.

[2] *Opera* 7, p. 108. [3] *Opera* 8, p. 360. [4] *Opera* 8, p. 153.
[5] *Opera* 9, p. 13. [6] *Opera homiletica et rhythmica* (1955), p. 247–8.

things, Jerusalem is the habitation of the heavenly kingdom, which consists of holy angels and men.[1]

From these examples the danger of Bede's approach is obvious: that just as the wealth of colours and patterns in the illuminated initials of the Lindisfarne Gospels may distract the eye from the words themselves, so Bede's zeal for the spiritual sense may deflect our attention from the literal meaning. Indeed, his references to the literal meaning are almost slighting[2] and as a result he sometimes denatures an event of scriptural history. The story of Christ raising Jairus' daughter, for instance, he takes as an allegory of the fate of the synagogue represented by Jairus, the leader of the synagogue; and not once throughout his commentary on this incident does he betray any sense of the time and place of the incident, of the anguish in Jairus' heart, the sickening delay in getting to his home and, finally, the tender solicitude of Christ over the girl, telling her parents to give her food.[3] The personalities of the drama, and the drama itself, melt into the moulds of allegorical types.

This by no means isolated example of Bede's manipulation of the literal sense[4] is the kind of scriptural exegesis which makes modern scholars dismiss his allegorising as a quaint aberration he shared with his age. But to shrug off such a large proportion of Bede's work in this way is to fail to grasp that for Bede the Scriptures are primarily the means of spiritual edification rather than a field for historical expertise. The latter should not be neglected, certainly, but it remains secondary. Convinced that all the Scriptures, even the names and locations of places that occur there, abound with spiritual significance,[5] Bede impressed the names and places, numbers, colours and shapes of Scripture so deeply upon his heart that his heart itself became Holy Land, filled with the spiritual significance of the places and events that occurred there. It has been pointed out that the word "sacrament" is a favourite word with Bede in this connection, and that for him it means, not "the outward and visible signs of an inward and spiritual grace," but rather the inner and spiritual meaning

---

[1] *Opera* 9, p. 283.
[2] In addition to the references already given cf. *Opera* 9, p. 242 and p. 365.
[3] *Opera* 11, pp. 81–9.   [4] Cf. *Opera* 11, p. 186.
[5] *Retractatio in Actus Apostolorum* (ed. Laistner, 1939), p. 125.

of an external fact, or narrative, or name.[1] Consequently Bede
traces out upon the hearts of his readers a kind of spiritual
geography derived from the geography of the Holy Land:
Ephra, Beth-horon and Seboim, for instance, the three vulnerable
points of the Israelite position attacked by the three companies
of the Philistines are the concupiscent, wrathful and rational
areas of man respectively;[2] again, the building of the temple of
Solomon[3] is the external event corresponding to the transforma-
tion of the soul into the temple of God, and the four-square
stones of the temple, the measurements of it, the kind of wood
used for the beams, the decoration with gold and silver, the
vestments of gold and violet and purple and scarlet twice dyed,[4]
all this wealth of form, number and colour has its corresponding
inner and spiritual meaning. Or, as he puts it in another
passage:

> If our conscience, once it is purified of its vices, rejoices in having
> God dwelling there, then it is truly to be called Jerusalem. What
> are the gates of this Jerusalem except the senses of our body, that
> is, sight, hearing, taste, smell and touch? . . . These on the Sabbath
> day we are ordered to shut so that we may take our leisure with
> God, occupying ourselves in psalms and prayers.[5]

But nowhere does the "wondrous sacramental concord"[6] of
nature and history achieved by Bede's allegorical method strike
such an immediately authentic note as in that chapter of his
Reckoning of Time which he devotes to the typical or mystical
significance of Easter time.[7] Coming at the end of a long scientific
work, of great technical complexity, this chapter fuses the external
and internal into one so that we see at a glance what Bede on
another occasion described as "the fair harmony of things."[8]
For the events of Easter time in the heavens and upon earth

---

[1] Plummer in *Baedae Opera Historica*, pp. lvi–lvii.
[2] *Opera* 8, p. 49.   [3] *Opera* 8, pp. 262–9.
[4] *Opera* 7, pp. 324–5. From his commentary on the tabernacle.
[5] *Opera* 9, pp. 50–1.   [6] *Opera* 11, p. 21.
[7] *Opera de Temporibus* (ed. Jones), pp. 286–90. This chapter is described by
Levison (*Bede, His Life, Times and Writings*, ed. Hamilton Thompson 1935,
p. 122) as "sublime devotion." It should certainly be studied by all who wish to
understand why the Easter controversy raised such strong passions in the seventh
century.
[8] The translation is Plummer's (*Opera Historica*, p. lxi.)

bespeak the Easter mysteries enacted once in the Holy Land and re-enacted each year by the Church in her Easter rites. We have the token for entering upon the Easter ritual when the spring equinox assures us that God's Son has opened up for man the paths of light and destroyed the powers of darkness, as the sun itself gains the victory over the shadows of night. This is the first month of the year's cycle, the same month in which the world was created[1] and in which man was set in Paradise; the same month in which man who has strayed from Paradise is made anew—for now the Lord makes all things new. Thus the great sacrament of Easter is celebrated at every level of Creation, in the mounting power of the sun, reflected by the waxing moon, in the renewal of vegetation on the face of the earth, and in the renewal of life within the souls of the faithful, that is, in the Church. This is already a participation in the great Eighth Day of the world when the souls of the just will enter into that eternal rest won for them by Christ their King, whom they now behold in His beauty.

There we have the climax of man's spiritual life envisaged by Bede. Inevitably the question arises, are these heights of mystical perception within the reach of everyone, or only of a few? Certainly Bede held that only a few are capable in this life of penetrating into the secrets of heavenly contemplation, and he issues a warning to those who have not achieved consummate virtue at the human level: they should not presume to meddle in divine things lest they come to harm, falling into heresy, for instance, or into despair.[2] But the context of the warning makes it quite clear that it was to those who wish to know God's particular secrets that his warning applies and not to those who seek the normal means of perfection. In fact there is not the slightest trace in Bede of spiritual snobbism, of any suggestion that there is a special way of spirituality for a few specially gifted people; the categories of fragmented individualism underlying such an assumption are totally foreign to him. So intimately shot together are all members of the Church that it is virtually impossible to say when the virtue of one begins and the virtue of another ends. Each of us is in the same position as a stone in

---

[1] Cf. *Opera* 7, p. 13, "It is clear from these words of God that it was in springtime that the adornment of the world was perfected."
[2] *Opera* 7, pp. 419–20.

the building of the temple, resting on some and supporting others.¹ Even those who are least polished (are, indeed, rather insensitive and mule-like)² have their part in furthering the work of edification and redemption when they humbly and patiently offer their shoulders to bear the burden of fraternal charity.

It is true, of course, that Bede holds to traditional teaching on status, and that the orders of the married, the continent and the virgins are to be placed in an ascending order of dignity;³ it is also true that there is a select group of men who achieve such perfection in the active life, and the virtues it demands, that they are granted the grace of divine vision.⁴ But of this latter grace, as of what are usually termed "mystical experiences," Bede has little or nothing to say.⁵ And considering the monastic audience he was usually addressing it is notable how rarely he alludes to the special privileges of the monastic status, whereas he is constantly reminding them of the part which the simple faithful, the laity, have to play in the Church. They are all aware, he remarks, how many people of lay status are leading lives of outstanding virtue whilst many dedicated from childhood to the religious life are seen to have fallen into sloth. Again, he says, all the faithful are truly priests,⁶ and in a heart-warming sermon preached on the Nativity of Our Lord he speaks of how the title of pastor is not confined to bishops, priests and deacons or rulers of monasteries but is rightly applied to all the faithful who keep watch over their tiny homes.⁷ Such a delicate sense of the sanctity of everyday duties was rare amongst Bede's contemporaries and rarer still was the ability to express it as he did: "We must aim, then, by good living to hasten to behold the face of our Creator in such a way that we never in any wise desert our neighbour who is running along with us, but let us

¹ *Opera* 8, p. 289. ² *Opera* 8, p. 379.
³ *Opera* 11, pp. 66–7. In the same commentary (p. 257) he cites Job as the type of married goodness.
⁴ *Opera* 7, p. 229. From the context it seems that Bede considers this grace to be limited to certain prophets and patriarchs.
⁵ Except, of course, in his hagiographical writings where he is simply following his authorities.
⁶ *Opera* 7, pp. 365–6; 10, p. 37.
⁷ *Opera homiletica et rhythmica*, p. 49.

take care to appear before the face of the Lord all together with him."[1]

No one, therefore, whatever his status or however limited his talents, need fear that Bede's spiritual teaching is too rarefied for him. Indeed the diffident especially might find in him the ideal teacher. To begin with, he is always ready with a word of encouragement: he assures us, for instance, that we need not despair if, through ignorance and weakness, we fail to achieve the good we aim at, so long as our actions are rooted in good will.[2] Similarly with the involuntary thoughts which distract our minds; they are to be treated as a nuisance, like flies that keep on buzzing around one, but we can take comfort from the fact that though they take the edge off our vision they do not blind us.[3] We must bear in mind, moreover, as Bede is never tired of reminding us, that growth in the spiritual life is not sudden; it is a slow growth, like that of a young tree;[4] also like a young tree, it is a tender thing, with most of its strength underground in the darkness, hence we must hesitate before revealing our spiritual aspirations lest the tender shoots become corrupted and wither.[5] At the same time we must be sensitive to every touch of grace and ready to respond at the crucial moments of growth.[6] And it is absolutely essential to root all our spiritual aspirations in hope[7]—the unshakable hope that we shall achieve our desires with the help of God. There is nothing more execrable than lack of hope, for without it our courage in the fight of faith is completely sapped away.[8]

The importance that Bede attaches to hope needs to be insisted upon because it explains a feature of his writings that has puzzled, and even shocked, some scholars: the severity with which he condemns Pelagianism. But this is not surprising, even in so tranquil a soul as Bede, when we recognise that Pelagianism, with its teaching that man of his own goodness can do good, drives

---

[1] *Opera* 7, p. 273. It may intrigue the reader to learn that this exhortation occurs in Bede's comment upon Exodus XXVI, 5: "Every curtain shall have fifty loops on both sides, so set on, that one loop may be set against another loop, and one may be fitted to the other."

[2] *Opera homiletica et rhythmica*, p. 45.   [3] *Ibid*, p. 266.

[4] *Opera* 10, p. 141; 11, p. 188.   [5] *Opera* 8, pp. 51–2.

[6] *Opera* 7, p. 195.   [7] *Opera* 9, p. 1.

[8] *Ibid*, p. 144. I should point out that these last five notes represent a sharp telescoping of Bede's observations.

men to despair. When they find out that unaided they do evil, instead of throwing themselves upon divine grace, they tend to give up hope. Scholars are agreed that the Pelagian controversy was a live one in the England of Bede but have tended to speak of it as though it affected only the men of learning; Bede's vehemence against Pelagius and his joy over those of the faithful who were brought back from "heresy and despair" suggest that it may even have been an immediate pastoral issue. The hope of men hung upon it.

We have now shown how even the humblest of men have their role in the common work of building the temple and seen how dependent each one is upon the other even for doing his own work. It remains to describe the means that the individual must adopt, according to Bede, if he is to be made perfect. It goes without saying that he constantly recalls us to the central Catholic teaching that to be perfect means to love God and one's neighbour—love of one's neighbour coming first in the order of time, and love of God being prior in dignity. It also goes without saying that the traditional teaching on asceticism is repeated over and over again: prayer, fasting, vigils are indispensable aids to spiritual growth. All this is common to the tradition that Bede absorbed so thoroughly, and has to be taken as read. But a striking feature of his teaching which gives it a peculiar nuance—and a very English one at that—is the emphasis he lays upon practical moral behaviour as a means of purification.[1] And amongst these injunctions of practical morality there are three which recur so persistently in Bede's writings that they give his spiritual teaching a character of its own; these are, the need to control one's tongue, the need for mutual correction amongst the faithful, and the need to give alms.

Presumably as a result of living for so many years in a monastic community Bede had come to realise vividly that the tongue is the greatest source of discord[2] in the human community. From

[1] An instructive comparison may be found in the commentaries upon the *Song of Songs* which Bede and St. Bernard composed. St. Bernard's is "mystical" in a later sense of the word than that familiar to Bede: he delves into the recesses of the individual's psychology with truly poetic intuition. Bede's commentary is "mystical" in his own sense, as signifying interior, but it is the interiority of moral behaviour rather than of psychological experience.

[2] Cf. *Opera* 9, pp. 83-4, on the grave crime of sowing discord by which "unity and fraternity, which is welded together by the grace of the Holy Spirit, is dissipated."

the use of the tongue for purposes of detraction almost the whole human race lies in danger;[1] so we should bear detraction patiently and try not to provoke those who malign us,[2] because the tongue is a fire, and the abuse of it can burn down the carefully planted woods of virtue—its corrosive effects are to be felt in almost all aspects of human behaviour.[3] We should not, for instance, quickly start talking after a time of prayer since that is to dissipate the fruits of our devotion,[4] and such promiscuity is destructive of chastity—a virtue of the tongue no less than it is of the body.[5] How strongly Bede felt that the control of the tongue is a *sine qua non* of purity may be sensed not only from the number of occasions when he cites "idle words" as illustrating aspects of sinful behaviour—and the number is enormous—but also from the fact he even speaks approvingly of a pagan philosophical discipline in this regard. This was the Pythagorean practice of making the master's disciples keep silence for five years.

But there is a time to keep silent and a time to speak out, as Bede notes, and the time to speak out is when we see one of our brethren committing sin. For a person who holds his tongue when he sees one of his brethren sinning is no less a sinner than the man who refuses forgiveness to a penitent sinner. In fact, failing to correct and refusing to forgive are but two sides of the same coin, since a person cannot be forgiven until he has been corrected and is penitent. Similarly forgiveness should not be indiscriminately accorded, but only when the sinner is ready to do penance.[6] Bede himself, as we have seen, demanded public restitution of his own good Catholic name from his detractor David, nor did he hesitate to demand that his own diocesan bishop, Wilfrid, should join in the restitution since he had tacitly shared in the detraction,[7] Bede's action is totally misunderstood, moreover, unless it is seen as arising from his charity towards the two transgressors, because the duty of correction is not one that he allowed to be undertaken lightly. Above all we must make sure that we do not undertake it out of hatred—which is so much more deadly than, for instance, anger: anger may be a motive for genuinely wanting to correct a person but

[1] *Opera* 9, p. 146.   [2] *Opera* 12, p. 326.   [3] *Opera* 12, pp. 182-3.
[4] *Opera* 7, p. 358.   [5] *Opera* 10, p. 341.   [6] *Opera* 11, p. 239.
[7] Cf. p. 255 of this article.

hatred never can be. Again, before pointing out some fault in one of our brethren, we should examine ourselves to discover if we ourselves have never been guilty of the same fault: if we never have, then let us reflect that we also are men, and might well have been guilty in that way.[1]

What a magnificent corrector Bede must have been, with his quiet penetration into human self-deceit. Equally penetrating and bold are his observations on the third of the practical issues which we have claimed as characteristic of his teaching, that is, the need for alms-giving. And the boldest of these observations are to be found in his commentary on Nehemias, where the extortion wreaked upon the poor by their governors gives Bede the opportunity to tell the secular and ecclesiastical leaders of his own day[2] some uncomfortable home-truths. Here he is even prepared to abandon his beloved allegorising entirely and insist that Nehemias' threats against the rich for oppressing the poor are to be taken quite literally: anyone who makes exactions of the poor in their time of distress will be shaken out of the lap of God: even our just claims at such a time must be waived if we ourselves wish our Father to forgive us our debts.[3] Once more he is prepared to insist upon the literal meaning, a little later in the same commentary, when he tells his monastic readers that they must make sure on feast days of putting aside some portion of their food to be given to the poor and to pilgrims.[4] For nothing is more apt than generous alms-giving to cure a person of spiritual aridity and sterility.[5] And unless a man stretches out his hand to give to the needy it is in vain for him to stretch out his hands to God in search of forgiveness for his sins.[6]

This image of the hands stretched forth, giving and forgiving, may well stand in our minds as typical of Bede's spiritual teaching, bringing home to us how all events in this world—even the humble movement of the hands—are charged with intimations

[1] *Opera* 11, pp. 30–1.
[2] The commentary was written between 725 and 730, a period when Bede's discontent at the condition of Northumbria was mounting.
[3] *Opera* 9, p. 22.   [4] *Opera* 9, p. 29.
[5] How reminiscent are Bede's words of the advice on this very subject given by Gerard Hopkins to Robert Bridges in his letter of 19 January, 1879: "It changes the whole man, if anything can; not his mind only but the will and everything."   [6] *Opera* 11, p. 7.

of that divine order wherein "all things are double one against another."[1] Bede did not have the quick fluency of some other saints in speculating about the secrets of that order, but he did know what contribution to it was demanded of his particular talents. It was, for the most part, a craftsman's contribution of regular attendance upon the everyday moral demands of the work. He knew that his own hands were but a shadow of the divine craftsman's hands—for God is the ultimate craftsman.[2]

---

[1] Cf. Plummer (*Opera Historica*), p. lxi.   [2] *Opera* 10, pp. 83–4.

2. EARLY ENGLISH
RELIGIOUS LITERATURE—I

Edmund Colledge

IN HIS LAST afflicted months at Littlemore, Newman was burdened, among his other sorrows and preoccupations, with much tedious correspondence about *The Lives of the English Saints*. The title was not his: it, and the consequent diminution of his original grand design, was the work of his publishers, and when we read the printed prospectus of 1843 and the careful plans which he drew up, we can see that what he wanted was not limited by any considerations of national history. Although he always disclaimed knowledge or appreciation of the Middle Ages, his disciplined scientific mind had perceived, as he worked through the Bollandist *Acta* and the other sources to which he went, that devotion to the founders of English Christianity could best be promoted (for the promotion of such devotion was his object, much to the disquiet of some of his correspondents, including W. E. Gladstone) by acknowledging our debt to every saint who had brought the Gospel to the British Isles and had preached it here in no matter what tongue. Deeply versed in the history of the early Church, Newman must have seen the same processes of evangelisation at work in seventh-century Britain as in the Mediterranean countries five hundred years before; he must have seen that the faith which the English received from Rome was strengthened and enriched by their links with Gaul, with the Empire, and with the Celts to their west and north, and that the saints of England and Ireland brought gifts and benefits to one another's lands. The Irish who returned from Lindisfarne and Jarrow taught their countrymen to follow the stricter Roman uses in which Augustine had been schooled; and the Irish of Columba's family taught the English, and then all the West, their modes of prayer and their devout ways, the piety which at first appeared outlandish and extravagant, which yet established itself as a simple and natural offering of the human heart to God. There is no need to sentimentalise or falsify the truth: there was discord and hostility between the English and Irish Churches to the end of the Anglo-Saxon period and long after; yet even Bede, usually a most intransigent nationalist, could praise Ireland as a God-fearing people who had wished us nothing but good. If we read his *History* with attention, we can see that he recognised that the English Catholics owed a certain debt to the Irish Church.

The legend which England had inherited was different. When St. Thomas More stood before the judges who had condemned him, and urged upon them, mildly, reasonably, charitably, the enormity of the crime which was being committed against their land, he reminded them that they were helping to end nearly a thousand years of history, which had begun "when we received baptism from Gregory." These are the words of every good English historian after Bede, and they presented matters so because that seemed to them to be the truth; but we know now that in rejecting Rome the Reformers were destroying an inheritance even more ancient and more precious than More knew.

It is not easy to describe the derivations and the accumulation of that inheritance in England before the Norman Conquest. At first sight, the differences seem so great between the forms and expressions of spiritual life from the twelfth century onwards and what we know about prayer and contemplation in Anglo-Saxon times that we are tempted to believe that with the coming of the French a wholly new way of life was introduced, that had it not been for such changes later English spirituality, culminating in *The Cloud* and the writings of Hilton and Julian, might never have been. Those who wished to promote such an attitude, to argue for the imperative necessity of a twelfth-century cross-fertilisation of Germanic with Romance culture, might point to the relative spiritual poverty of the Scandinavian countries until the end of the Middle Ages, might argue that so too would the English Church have become, had it not been reshaped by Norman hands. But if we look at the evidence, we shall see that this is not true.

The evidence is usually hard to find, but just because the seeking is so laborious, its discovery can sometimes be revealing and illuminating beyond ordinary measure. To stand dwarfed

and silenced by the majesty of the great crosses at Bewcastle and
Ruthwell, to turn the fantastic pages of Chad's Welsh gospel-
book at Lichfield, to read *The Dream of the Rood* and savour the
subtlety with which the thoughts and the language of Roman
and African and pagan Englishman are blended in it, is to be
arrested across the ages by a civilisation Christian, international,
sophisticated. Only because it had already assimilated so fully and
readily what it could learn from the Mediterranean lands and from
the British Church was it possible for England so to respond to
the new movements of the twelfth and thirteenth centuries; and
in the end the Norman conquerors were conquered, much as
the Danes before them had finished by becoming good sons and
servants of our Church.

What, then, are those characteristics of later medieval spirituality for the origins of which we must search in Anglo-Saxon
times: what shall we find, and what will seem to be missing?

If we look at the manifestations of English religious life round
about the year 1400, we at once see two characteristics which
make it different from what was happening on the Continent.
There was no one spiritual writer or teacher tainted or associated
with heresy, and most of them were virtually independent of
organized religious life. In Europe the tendency was usually
towards coalescence, towards the absorption of individual talents
into religious orders, and to the promotion by the orders of
characteristic patterns of devotion and enthusiasm; and this was
as true of women as of men. Hadewijch was a Beguine, very
conscious of her place in an international movement, Mechtild
of Magdeburg ended her life as a nun in office, Bridget had established her own Rule, Catherine of Siena lived as a Dominican,
albeit of the Third Order; and there are few among the great
men who enriched and transformed spiritual life in the thirteenth
and fourteenth centuries who were not religious, whose orders
did not promote the knowledge of their teachings. Only Walter
Hilton in this country lived so; Richard Rolle and Julian were
solitaries, and the author of *The Cloud*, whoever he may have
been, seems to have produced his works in defiance of the dis-
approval of members of his community, whichever it was.
Among the minor figures, too, it is striking how many of them
had chosen an anachoritic way of life: Godric of Finchale,
Christina of Markyate, William Flete, the Monk of Farne. This

seeking for isolation is surely a trait for the beginnings of which we should look to Anglo-Saxon times.

Then, next, we have no figure in England whom we can compare with Eckhart, and there is virtually no evidence of English interest in his type of mysticism, whether it be represented by the lives of the German and Netherlands lunatic fringe, with their false passivity, false deification, false beliefs concerning the birth of the word, or by Eckhart's teachings as they were purified and redirected by Tauler and Ruysbroek. Richard Rolle and Margery Kempe were our only two genuine enthusiasts, and though what they taught and did was harmless enough, they have left us their own accounts of how little their extravagances were to the taste of their fellow-countrymen.

The great religious orders, in contact with the European centres of intellectual life and with their own internal organisations for higher studies, seem to have made very little direct contribution to English mysticism. This is particularly true of the mendicants, who appear to have been largely indifferent to what their saints overseas had done and written. Only the Carthusians can be shown to have made it their policy to import and translate modern spiritual classics; and the Carthusians themselves were aware that this was one of several characteristics which made them unique in English religious life. We must not dispraise the constant work of instruction of the laity to which every order, as well as the secular clergy, made its own contribution, a part of which was always the renewing for each generation of the teachings of the fathers and the great doctors of the Church; but very soon after the Norman Conquest this was supplemented by the emergence of a great body of vernacular devotional literature which nourished and guided the spiritual life of the country in remarkable fashion. Not even Italy or the Netherlands can in this respect be compared with England, and particularly in the wealth of religious poetry which has survived we have witness to the depth and fervour of medieval English piety, especially for the Passion and the mysteries of our Lady. Here again, even though post-Conquest Mediterranean literary forms and conventions helped to fashion these divine songs, their true stuff, England's love for the suffering Christ and His immaculate Mother, had been made long before.

We can find the seeds of almost every flowering of later

medieval devotion in Bede's great homily for the Nativity. Though he is preaching to a monastic community, his message is for everyone. It was simple, humble shepherds who first brought the angels' good tidings, and every Christian must be a shepherd. They had been keeping watch at their appointed task, and so too must we watch and long for the perfect vision of God, not in false idleness but doing our proper work. We too must hasten to Bethlehem, to adore Him, the Word Incarnate, the image of God in which all men are formed; and there we shall also find and praise His Mother, rod of Jesse, daughter of Sion, tower of David, seat of wisdom.[1] Bede's scholarly restraint is in great contrast to, say, Anselm's romantic exuberance, but they are alike filled with deep love for the Incarnation, and they are seeking to make it live for ordinary folk through the language of affection and devotion.

Such affective writing is not often found in Anglo-Saxon homilies. Usually a preacher is concerned with minimal essentials, the Creed, the sacraments, the Church's laws as they govern man's daily lives, the Gospel narratives. When the Normans took over, England was still missionary territory. Aelfric and Wulfstan had been striving to complete the work begun under Alfred, to reassemble Christ's scattered flock and to give it wise and faithful shepherds. To such men, the days of Bede must have seemed a fabled, vanished golden age; and it is difficult for us not to feel, as we read their desperate calls to repentance before it is too late, before Antichrist himself shall appear, that the long years of pillage and burning and murder and enslavement had hardened hearts and narrowed minds and fostered a way of life in which the sweetness of devotion might seem a reprehensible self-indulgence.

This may be why some of the great preachers of the age strike us as perfunctory when they come to deal with what we regard as the perennial topics of Catholic affective writing. In her sensitive study of Aelfric, M-M. Dubois seems wholly justified in suggesting that his Eucharistic teaching shows not lack of belief but lack of perception of the implications of belief. In his sermon for Easter Day on the Mass, it is clear that he is more concerned to answer doubts and to impart true faith than to promote devotion; yet even so at times he does foreshadow the great

[1] *Homilia II in Nativitate Domini.*

C

ages which were yet to come. The Blessed Sacrament is "that pledge . . . . to which we shall hold fast until we come to truth," it is "the sacrament of our peace and of our unity."[1] Indeed, those who have imputed to Aelfric lack of true doctrine here should consider the traditions in which he was reared. In Bede we shall find still less of such devotion, but his teaching on the Mass is unambiguous, as when he writes, in his Homily for the first Sunday after Epiphany.

> In the Apocalypse the Apostle John says "He loved us, and He washed us of our sins in His blood"; and He washed us of our sins in His blood not only when He shed His blood for us upon the Cross, or when each one of us is washed in the water of baptism through the mystery of His most holy Passion, but every day He takes away the sins of the world and washes us of our daily sins when the memory of His blessed Passion is renewed at the altar, when created bread and wine are changed by the sanctification of His ineffable Spirit into the sacrament of His flesh and blood, which are given, not into the hands of the faithless, to be slain and spilled to their destruction, but into the mouths of the faithful, to be received for their salvation.[2]

And in Bede's story, equally touching in his own Latin and in the Old English translation, of Caedmon receiving viaticum on his death-bed, there is no need for him to state the obvious, that this holy old man was filled with deepest reverence and love for the *sacramentum pacis*.[3]

At first sight, Aelfric seems to deal as cursorily with our Lady's mysteries as he does with the Mass. For his homily for 15 August, he contents himself with Augustine's exposition of the gospel for the day, and at the end he observes:

> If we say more about this feast day than we read in the holy books which were written as God commanded, we shall be like the heretics who wrote many lying tales out of their own fantasies or dreams; but orthodox teachers such as Augustine, Jerome, Gregory and others in their wisdom have rejected them. Yet such heretical books still exist, both in Latin and English, and they are read by ignorant men.[4]

[1] *Sermo de Sacrificio in Die Pascae* (Thorpe, *The Homilies of the Anglo-Saxon Church*, ii, 262-82).

[2] *Homilia* (15) *post Epiphaniam*.

[3] *Hist. Eccl. IV*, ch. xxii (Plummer i, 258-62).

[4] *Assumptio Sanctae Mariae Virginis* (Thorpe ii, 438-45).

Probably he has in mind such expositions as the Blickling Homily for the Assumption, which, Rudolph Willard has shown, is a mixture of wholly incompatible traditions, of so-called *transitus* texts teaching that Mary's body was translated, and of others which held that it was resurrected. Yet Aelfric points out that he has elsewhere translated "Jerome" (in reality Radbert, abbot of Corbie) on the Assumption, and Radbert begins his homily by deploring these conflicting traditions and rejecting the theory of translation.[1] We should be wrong in assuming from the laconic treatment of the subject on 15 August that Aelfric did not accept the Assumption: what he rejects is some of the legends of how the Assumption was effected, which are lavishly recorded in the extravagant Blickling conflation, and which he regards as erroneous.

Radbert had been one of our Lady's most fervent devotees, and no doubt inspired by Jerome's own praises of her virgin fecundity, he had seen no harm in dressing his work as an epistle sent by Jerome to two of his known disciples and correspondents. But Aelfric was only one of many who accepted *De Assumptione Beatae Mariae* as part of the Jerome canon (indeed, two extracts from this sermon are still so attributed in the Roman Breviary for 8 December), and he may have been moved to include his excerpts from it among the Catholic Homilies because he knew that in Carolingian France it figured largely in the office for the feast of the Assumption. And long before Aelfric there is evidence to show that pious legend, such as the account of the sorrows of Mary in the *Gospel of Nichodemus*, was stimulating the imagination of the English and working to produce the earliest examples of the *planctus Mariae* and the "meditations" on her life which in later centuries were to dominate English piety. Inserted among the majestic paraphrases of the monastic Advent antiphons which constitute the so-called *Christ I* of the Exeter Book, we find a poem, "O Joseph mine, O Jacob's child," a dialogue between our Lady and St. Joseph which has no reference whatever to the liturgy. It is inspired by St. Matthew i, 19, and it contains in embryo the matter of some of the most famous poems and plays which treat at the end of the Middle Ages of the childhood of Mary and of the Nativity. The Anglo-Saxon poet draws us a touching picture, simple and direct, of the bewilderment and

[1] *De Assumptione Beatae Mariae* (Thorpe ii, 446–54).

grief of a pious, chaste elder when the malicious gossip of his neighbours tells him that the dedicated virgin from the Temple whom he has taken into his home is with child; and Mary's reply is a hymn of praise to God for her own Immaculate Conception, for the Annunciation and for the coming Nativity:

> I am His Temple now
> built without blemish,   and in me abode
> the Paraclete.   So be at peace,
> cease from your sorrow,   to my Son give thanks
> that by His Father's might   I am His mother. . .[1]

Such a poem is fittingly placed among the Church's ancient Advent salutations, O virgo virginum and O mundi domina, and it tells us of an Anglo-Saxon devotion to the Mother of God to which Aelfric pays only a halting and partial tribute.

We also can find much evidence for the early growth and full development in pre-Conquest days of a parallel devotion to Christ's humanity. Wulfstan, for instance, can write:

> But Christ made Himself wonderfully humble when He for our needs accepted human nature, and in His humanity His divinity was so concealed that He humbly suffered as a man all that any man suffers, except sin alone. When He was a child, they fed Him just as other children are fed. He lay wrapped in a cradle just as other children do, and they carried Him until He could walk. He suffered everything in His humanity which was its lot: sometimes He was thirsty, sometimes hungry, He ate and drank, He felt the cold and the heat.[2]

Here again we have the appeal to our pity and tenderness and compassion which we associate with later ages. Writing of this temper is rare in Wulfstan. More often he represents Christ as the dreaded judge, the terrible avenger who will appear on Doomsday. In the Vercelli Homilies we shall also find such alternating appeals to our love and our fear. The first homily is an English narrative, of scholarly simplicity, of the Passion according to St. John, with singularly few additions either from the other evangelists or of later invention; and it ends with a brief and moving exhortation that we should every day be filled with love for Christ, who on the Cross redeemed us, and broke

1 Ed. Krapp and Dobbie, New York 1936, pp. 7-9.
2 The Homilies of Wulfstan, ed. Bethurum, Oxford 1957, pp. 152-3.

open Hell to lead out our forefathers, and has given us all the promise of eternal life. But the second homily is very different, a Dantesque vision of the Day of Doom when the Redeemer shall be seen as judge, dreadful to look upon as He was on Calvary, His Cross high in the heavens, streaming once again with blood and filling with terror the hearts of evil men. The preacher's excitement cannot in the end be contained in prose, and bursts out into a fearful "lay of the Last Day":

> See, this is the coming wrath of that Day of Judgment which we
> would not dread, day of wretchedness, day of suffering, day of
> sadness, day of wailing, day of weeping, day of anguish, day of
> sorrow, day of darkness.   On that day will be revealed to us
> The heavens opened   and the angelic host,
> mankind cast down,   the earth destroyed,
> faithless men fallen   and the stars all dimmed,
> the pealing thunder   and the tempest black. . . .[1]

We find this same terrifying figure, exhibiting the marks and instruments of His Passion on the last day as a condemnation of mankind, in the Blickling Homily for Easter Day and in Wulfstan; and a recent learned editor of Wulfstan has shown that it derives from ancient tradition among the fathers, who saw the prophecy, *Et aspicient ad me quem confixerunt*, and the vision in the Apocalypse, *Ecce venit cum nubibus, et videbit eum omnis oculus, et qui eum pupugerunt*, awaiting fulfilment at the last judgment.

But in all Anglo-Saxon writings upon the Passion, devotional or liturgical, there is nothing to equal the short English poem found in the Vercelli Book, *The Dream of the Rood*. It is difficult to determine the date of its composition. The Vercelli text, and the brief quotation inscribed on a reliquary now at Ste. Gudule in Brussels, seem to be of the late tenth century, but the longer excerpts in runic characters on the Ruthwell Cross, even though they are no part of the first sculptor's design, can be shown to be earlier by some two hundred years. It must have been written long before the famous rescue in Rome by English pilgrims of the desecrated relic of the True Cross and the subsequent presentation of a portion of it to King Alfred by Pope Marinus I. There is nothing to suggest that the poem is a commissioned piece, produced to honour some national event: it celebrates Calvary and the Crucifixion, and it bears the marks of an entirely personal

[1] Homily II, ed. Förster.

and immediate veneration of our redemption and its instruments. It is a Good Friday poem, with many subtle allusions to the liturgy of the day, the breviary lessons and the great hymns of Fortunatus. His paradoxes are repeated and expanded: the poet, in his dream, watches a mysterious transmutation, as a bloody, terrifying piece of wood, a stake for evil-doers to end their lives upon in misery, is transformed before his eyes into a gorgeous and solemn treasure, mounting and spreading till its arms extend to the ends of the earth and its glory illumines the whole world. When the Cross itself speaks to the dreamer (and the dialogue is entirely between these two, for it is part of the poem's art that we are made to see the Passion from a great distance, to accept the Cross as narrator, to watch a far-off, silent Christ, as the Cross itself once beheld Him), it begins in the dark, teasing style of the classical riddles:

> It was long years ago—   I can recall it yet—
> that I was felled   in a place in the forest,
> hauled away from my home.   Hostile hands seized me,
> made me lift miscreants up   for men to see their shame . . .

Yet when it is set upon the hill by its foes, it sees a young hero who hastens, like a victor, to mount upon it. It is the Cross which trembles, but Christ embraces it in love and commands it to stand firm (scholars who have explored the liturgical elements in *The Dream* have shown how this echoes the York Breviary lessons for the feast of St. Andrew—"Before our Lord mounted upon you, blessed Cross, you were filled with mortal fear . . . it was I who loved you, and longed for your embrace"). Step by step, the Passion story is unfolded, always as experienced by the Cross: Christ and it were both reviled by blasphemers, and when He has died and His body has been taken down to be laid in the nearby tomb of shining, unused stone, it is the Cross which is left to stand, deserted and sorrowing. Then all three crosses are cut down and hidden away, till the day comes when true servants of the Lord rediscover it and adorn it with gold and silver:

> On me the Son of God
> suffered for a season,   and so in splendour now
> I soar up to the skies,   and I can save
> each man who in his heart   has holy dread for me.
> I whom they made to be   most hateful to all men,

most dreadful of all deaths   do now make straight
the way of life   to every living man.
See how the King of Glory   has greatly honoured me:
no tree in all the wood   is dearer to Heaven's Lord,
me He has magnified   as was His Mother, Mary,
chosen from all mankind   by Him, Almighty God,
who made her richer far   than all the race of Eve.

Then, characteristically, the Cross passes from this hymn to its own greatness on to the work of instruction, to remind men of the coming doom, when few will not be filled with fear when the Saviour-Judge appears to ask where are those who have been willing to share in His Passion which He suffered for them; and the poem ends with an elegiac diminuendo, so typical of the Anglo-Saxon genius. Life is transient, this vision which was granted to him is the poet's one consolation in his solitude, as he longs to be with his departed dear ones who rejoice before the Lord. For a brief time He suffered, to bring us the promise of eternal joy: this is our hope and comfort, that He may one day call us, as once He called the holy souls out of the hell which He had harrowed, into that Paradise which is His own true native land.[1]

This incomparable poem is one of the glories of Anglo-Saxon letters, and though its language makes it incomprehensible except to the experts, even in translation into modern versions it has impressed scholars as one of the greatest gifts of Western Christendom to the literature of the Passion. It is, too, a singular monument to its age, to that antique world over which the Redeemer reigned from the Tree as on a throne, solitary, kingly, motionless in awful grandeur.

[1] Ed. Dickins and Ross, London 1934.

3. EARLY ENGLISH
RELIGIOUS LITERATURE—II

Edmund Colledge

I T IS INEVITABLE that we should think of *The Dream of the Rood* in searching for the origins of English vernacular poems about the crucified Christ, but it is much later in Saxon times that we see the emergence of the *imago pietatis*, the delineations of the suffering Son of Man whose humanity and griefs are stressed, to the exclusion of His divine kingship, so as to excite compassion in His brother men; and as the *imago pietatis* evolves we see, perhaps most clearly, the influence upon English prayer of those private devotions, of what Bishop called "the ejaculatory, litanic, asyndetic type," which seem beyond doubt to have been one of Ireland's chief contributions to English and Continental spirituality.

Such devotions are first found, as in their Irish archetypes, in manuals of private prayer, the Book of Cerne (which, it is now generally accepted, was written for Bishop Ethelwold of Lichfield in the early ninth century), the Winchester Nunnaminster Book and the comparable MS Royal 2 A xx. Then, later, under the influence of the monastic liturgical reforms inspired by Dunstan and his circle, we find them incorporated into the Church's Holy Week services.

Here is the *Oratio Sancta ad Dominum* from the Cerne Book:

> My Lord Jesus Christ, I adore You stretched upon the Cross and crowned with thorns. I pray You that this Cross may save me from the destroying angel. My Lord Jesus Christ, I adore You transfixed upon the Cross and given gall and vinegar to drink. I pray You that Your wounds may be healing to my soul.[1]

Here are two prayers from MS Royal 2 A xx:

> Most merciful Jesus, You who did extend Your hands upon the wood of the Cross, stretch out to me the hand of Your mercy.

[1] Ed. Kuypers, Cambridge 1902, p. 116.

With the spear of fear and love pierce my heart of stone, You who suffered Your holy and venerable hands upon the Cross to be pierced with nails. Heal in my hands and in my heart each wound of wickedness. . . . O Jesus who suffered Your breast to be pierced with a spear, open to me the gate of life, and when I have entered in I shall sing Your praises, O my Lord. By the wound in Your side, heal with the medicine of Your mercy all the wounds of my misdeeds.[1]

These two last prayers are copied as separate petitions in the Book of Nunnaminster, where also we find that which begins "O right hand of God, giver of healing, who stretched Your arms upon the wood of the Cross . . . "[2] which, Thomas Symons has pointed out, seems to be the source of the third of the public prayers to be offered on Good Friday during the Veneration of the Cross as prescribed by the *Regularis Concordia*:

Almighty God, Jesus Christ, who placed Your spotless hands upon the Cross for us, and with Your Precious Blood redeemed us, make me to feel and know how I may have true penitence and good perseverance all the days of my life.[3]

It should be observed that the *Concordia* specifies that whilst these prayers are being recited, the Veneration is to be performed by the abbot, his community, the clergy and the laity; and Lilli Gjerløw, in her recent study of fragments of such liturgical manuscripts which have survived in Norway, has shown how widely the rites and prayers formulated by the *Concordia* were disseminated, and not only in monastic uses, in the eleventh and twelfth centuries. We can also see beyond doubt a similar spirit of reform, working to provide vernacular aids for the laity in following or imitating religious liturgical observance, in the so-called *Benedictine Office*. James Ure, the most recent editor of the *Office*, remarks that "it is not an office, nor is it specifically Benedictine"; he considers it to be an adaptation of the monastic liturgy in "a form to be celebrated by the secular clergy in the presence of the laity." In it we find affective vernacular devotional writing which is the more striking because it is so rare. Here, as one example, is the meditation which is to substitute for Matins:

At daybreak one should praise God as David said: "My God, I

1 Quoted Bonetti, *Le Stimate della Passione*, Rovigo 1952, p. 88.
2 Ed. De Gray Birch, p. 72.
3 Ed. Symons, London 1953, p. 44.

watch for You from early light"; and again he said: "At daybreak I pondered upon You, because You were my help." Christ is the help of all the human race, the helper of the whole world. It was at daybreak that through the power of God Moses led the people of Israel all unscathed out of the land of Egypt across the Red Sea, and then at once the same sea overwhelmed and drowned God's enemies, Pharaoh and all his host. And it was at daybreak that Christ rose from death and led those whom He wished for out of hell; and His enemies, the devil himself and all his host, He plunged into the torment of hell. So at daybreak we should joyfully praise God, and ever thank Him for the mercies that He performed for man, when He set him free from the devil's power and the pain of hell, and opened then the straight way to the kingdom of heaven for all who do His will here in this life.[1]

Though this "meditation" ends with a quotation from the *Te Deum*, the middle section, the praise of daybreak which resembles the praise of the night in the *Exsultet*, may owe something to the invocations, Irish or Irish-Northumbrian in origin, of the Book of Cerne. The final Cerne invocations, to the Passion, were destined, as Lilli Gjerløw has said, "to go on forever as a separate prayer"; but the earlier ones, "Lord Jesus Christ, I adore You when You said before the world was made 'Let there be light' . . ." "Lord Jesus Christ, I adore You when You called Adam at midday . . ," "Lord Jesus Christ, I adore You when You sent the flood and struck all mankind, and spared the righteous man Noah . . ," "Lord Jesus Christ, I adore You when You drowned Pharaoh and set the children of Israel free. I supplicate Your greatness to set me free from my sins,"[2] though they did not survive elsewhere as popular devotions, seem to have been the inspiration of this meditation in the *Office*.

It is manifest that the *Benedictine Office* was intended to go beyond the scope of the Breviary, and to furnish those who used it with prayers which would serve as repertories of the Faith and recollections of the sacraments. We can see this in part of the poetic meditation upon the *Our Father*:

> *Panem nostrum cotidianum da nobis hodie*:
> Give us this day,   Lord of mankind,
> great king of heaven   that bread for us
> which You did send   to save men's souls

[1] Ed. Ure, Edinburgh 1957, pp. 81-2.
[2] Ed. Kuypers, pp. 114-5.

> into this habitation   of the human race,
> Christ undefiled,   our Lord, our God.[1]

This may not be Eucharistic devotion as we today know it, but it is the plainest enjoinder to the laity that they should have daily recollection of the memorial of Christ's Passion, of the *panis angelorum*.

It is today a commonplace that the great flood of devotional fervour which overwhelmed Western Europe in the late twelfth and early thirteenth centuries had as one of its springs the refusal of the laity, the Latinless, the illiterate, to be excluded from the apostolic life of the Church; but though the historians usually show the Church as at first hesitant, repressive, reluctant to meet these demands, it must be remembered that it was in and from the Church that the laity learned to ask for more than they had yet been given. It is in such texts as *The Benedictine Office* that we can see early encouragement being given to the people to take a more active part in daily liturgical life, and, to that end, formal vernacular prayers being furnished for them. And although the *Office* is probably unique in Anglo-Saxon writings as a precursor of the "little offices" and primers of the later Middle Ages, it must be placed in its setting, and seen as only one of many aids towards fuller lay participation in worship and devotion.

There are some few other works also inspired directly by the liturgy, notably the Exeter Advent Antiphons, already mentioned. There is, too, a long tradition of Scriptural translation, beginning with the now lost version of St. John on which Bede was working at the time of his death, and culminating in the highly competent and scholarly Late West Saxon Gospels; and it may be that in the oldest fragment of English Christian poetry which we have, Bede's quotation in the *Historia Ecclesiastica* of the beginning of the song which the illiterate oblate of Whitby Abbey, Caedmon, was inspired to compose, we have the first example of this tradition. N.F. Blake has not long ago suggested that the standard critical response to Caedmon's Hymn—that it completely invalidates Bede's exegesis by displaying no trace of originality, presenting merely a collection of tags and clichés from the repertory of the bards—is entirely misconceived. Instead, Blake tellingly argues, we should see the hymn as a layman's *Laudate Dominum*, a series of ejaculatory praises of God the Creator

[1] Ed. Ure, p. 86.

derived from the thought and the Latin of the Psalter. Bede tells us that after the Hymn was composed, the abbess Hilda put Latin scholars at Caedmon's disposal, to familiarise him with Biblical texts so that he might compose further divine songs to serve as a compendium of Scriptural knowledge in English verse; but if Blake's well-reasoned interpretation of the Hymn is sound, it would seem that Hilda, herself of the first generation of converts from paganism, whose zeal for the provision of monastic learning Bede several times praises, had ensured some understanding of the Divine Office even for the lowliest of her family. If we read the Hymn in its whole context, the story, the more edifying because it is so reverently and lovingly told by one whose learning and Latinity were the admiration of Christendom, of a poor stuttering dolt so ashamed of his ignorance that he preferred the company of dumb beasts who could not make him feel a fool, who yet became a matchless singer of all God's mercies, and whose sanctified spirit was escorted to Heaven by the choirs of angels, takes on a new meaning. Bede's account of Caedmon is in reality a very early prelude to the praises which we shall so often read from the pens of great scholars (St. Thomas and Tauler, to name only two) of a *sancta simplicitas* measured by which their own graces of erudition and gifts of tongues seem to them impoverished.

If Caedmon was not the plagiarist but the initiator of traditional Christian narrative poetry, it is the more to be regretted that most of what has survived in this genre falls so far short of the inspiration which Bede admired in his work, now, alas, lost except for the Hymn itself. For those searching for evidence of a personal, individual devotion, deeply experienced and expressed in living language, performances such as *Christ* and *Elene* are sad stuff, and there is no reason for not saying so. One no longer feels convicted of inferior taste or of insensitivity after one has read the tepid appraisal of Cynewulf's achievement which is the most afforded to him by such a connoisseur as Sisam. Such verse has most of the demerits of the secular heroic poetry of the epoch, sprawling, ill-organised narrative, intolerable verbosity and a high rhetorical style which centuries of repetition have robbed of potency; and too rarely does it reflect the virtues of such poetry. It is only occasionally, as when a falling Lucifer shrieks his blasphemous defiance, or a pious empress proposes unspeakable torments for the Jews whom she cannot bend to her devout will, that we are stirred, as we are by the duels and blood feuds and hauntings of the epics. The Christian poems for the most part are far too formal and too proper, and only employ the old language because it has lost its power to startle and illumine: one feels suffocated, as if by hour upon hour of genteel *Unterhaltungsmusik*. It is very different when the great Byrhtnoth goes down fighting to the last beside the ebbing river, gasping out his life in words of thanks to God for all the joys that he has known, in prayers for his soul's safe journey from among the spectres of hell who are crowding around him; but Byrhtnoth and his nameless bard were singing about life and its good fight, about the straight race that men run towards Heaven, they were not merely turning out a few hundred edifying lines to soothe an abbot at recreation.

The Battle of Maldon is the only great English poem which we can compare with the many Irish and Scottish laments for the brave dead who fought with no hope of an earthly victory, whose martyrdom ensured life for their country. Its resemblances to the old pagan lays are merely superficial: the spirit which quickens it is wholly and profoundly Christian. Though less easy to discern, much of the same spirit moves in *Beowulf* itself; and Dorothy Whitelock has most rewardingly explored a new field of study of the so-called "heathen poetry" of Anglo-Saxon times in her survey of the practices of individual Christians and the precepts of the Church concerning some of the topics most essential to the plot of *Beowulf*, particularly the blood-feud. She has shown us that for the right understanding of this poem, we need the expert help not only of the archaeologist and anthropologist, but also of the ecclesiastical historian and of the theologian; and in the stimulating controversy which in these last years has been conducted about the real meaning of *The Seafarer*, Ida Gordon has directed our thoughts in the same direction and with the same extension of our critical sympathies. It would seem that she is right in her argument that this poem is neither, as it long was regarded, a nature-poem depicting the miseries and glories of life at sea, with a few Christian pieties tacked on, probably by another hand, nor an allegory of the soul's pilgrimage towards eternity, but a factual account of the hardships, the rewards and the theology of *peregrinatio*, of the way of life of those who, in the words of an English chronicler recording the appearance on our shores of one of the many groups of Irish *peregrini*, "wanted to live in exile for the love of God."

Perhaps too much emphasis has been put, in the interpretation of *The Seafarer* and in other connexions, on the possibility of specific and exclusive Celtic inspiration for Anglo-Saxon learning and spirituality. Those who claim that the anachoritic life is a peculiarly Irish phenomenon, that its growth and plenitude in seventh and eighth-century Ireland originated not in a recognition of the need for monastic reform but as a protest against the new, Romanising ways imported after Whitby from England, seem guilty of special pleading. Before we can estimate the significance of any one *peregrinatio*, we need to enquire why the pilgrim went abroad or into solitude, and where, and what he did when he arrived; and the evidence is very diverse.

Sometimes, it seems, he went solely out of obedience, and was sent overseas as a punishment. Bede says that there was a certain Irishman, namesake of the great abbot of Iona, Adamnan, at the double monastery of Coldingham, then ruled by an English abbess, living a life of extraordinary penance originally enjoined upon him by his spiritual director, who had then returned to Ireland and died without releasing Adamnan; and Marianus the Irishman, who in the mid-eleventh century was in Germany, visited at Paderborn the cell of his countryman Paternus, who had died in the fire which had destroyed the town rather than break his vow of enclosure. Marianus says that Paternus had been banished from Ireland for a minor infraction of discipline, and that he himself had been sent abroad for an equally light fault.

It would seem, too, that not all who set out on such travels (whether we call them, as Leclercq would have us do, *pérégrinations*, "journeys in search of a life-long exile," or *pèlerinages*, "pilgrimages" in the modern sense) were thought to leave for weighty reasons or seen to attain desirable ends. Boniface begged the Archbishop of Canterbury to check the mania for pilgrimages among his flock, especially nuns, and said that there were few Lombard, Frankish or Gaulish cities without English whores who had set out as pilgrims; and the same sad stories were told of Irishwomen. It was an Irishman of the ninth century who wrote "To go to Rome is great labour, little gain," and Bede had said of Benedict Biscop, who went there six times, that he never returned profitless and empty-handed, "as is the custom of some." Aldhelm at the end of the seventh century is seen complaining about the hordes of young Englishmen migrating to Ireland for study, "when they could get just as good instruction from the masters at Canterbury."

There can be no doubt that the predominantly Celtic communities of the early days at Lindisfarne under Columba, Aidan, Finnan and Colman, protected by Oswald and his successors in Northumbria who had received an Irish education, and at such enduring centres of Anglo-Irish contact as Glastonbury, provided constant and fruitful intercourse between the two civilisations. Some of the fruits we have already seen, in Latin devotional manuals which are probably of Irish inspiration; and in one case, that of Dunstan, we are told that in his years at Glastonbury he profited greatly from the learned and pious books brought there by Irish pilgrims to the tomb of "beati Patricii junioris." But there were probably few others so proficient as Dunstan: it is noteworthy, for instance, that Aelfric did not recognise that the ascription to Jerome of the homily on the Assumption which he translated was impossible, because Radbert, its real author, included in it excerpts from Abbot Adamnan's *Holy Places*.

There is one further piece of evidence, negative, it is true, which deserves to be weighed in this connexion. Had Celtic influence upon English Christianity been so strong as is often suggested, we should find it hard to explain why so few words of Irish or Welsh derivation are found in Old English, not merely in the speech of ordinary men, but also in the learned glosses and the language of the multiplicity of sciences and skills which were fostered in the monastic houses. Probably the last scholar genuinely competent alike in Irish and English linguistic studies was Max Förster, but his classical examination of this matter presents us with a very clear picture, much the same as we derive from Cuthbert and Bede, of two hostile civilisations which refused to learn from one another. Half a dozen trading terms, three or four words to do with hunting and agriculture, two or three names of features of the landscape, and *dry*, "wizard": these exhaust his list, apart from two specifically Christian expressions, *staer*, "history," and *cross* itself. All later scholars have followed Förster and his authorities in agreeing that "cross," which is a

late borrowing into Old English, was brought here by Christian-
ised Northmen (its first recorded use is *c.* A.D. 1000, in a place-
name, "Northmen's Cross"), and the probability is that it first
gained currency in the technical language not of theology or of
devotion but of architecture. Even if we include those Latin
names learned from the Christian Welsh for the shrines desecrated and the religious murdered or enslaved by the heathen
English, words such as *Eccles, minster, minchen* ("nun"), it still
remains a very short list, showing a situation no different from
that depicted in the *Historia Ecclesiastica*, in the account of the
thirty or so English monks, *peregrini*, whom Colman took back
to Ireland with him from Lindisfarne and settled on Inisboffin,
whence they had to be withdrawn to a separate English house at
Mayo, still flourishing in Bede's time, still famous for its sanctity
and austerity, yet established because they and the Irish monks
could not live together in peace.

To argue that marks of cultural intercourse such as borrowings
need not be sought, because Latin would be the common tongue,
is no argument. Latin was the common tongue through which
England learned from Italy and Gaul, and the vocabulary of
any educated Englishman of the seventh century and onwards
included hundreds of anglicised Latin words which show, by
their sounds and forms and meanings, that they travelled here
westwards and not from the West.

Though "cross" is an Irish word which in the end prevailed,
during four centuries the English had found their own native
"rood" adequate, and when they searched for synonyms they
had drawn them from sources such as Venantius Fortunatus,
his *signum* becoming the *beacen* of *The Dream, lignum triumphale*
appearing as *sigebeam* on the Bewcastle Cross inscription. There
is little reason to suppose that the early Anglo-Saxon devotion
to the Cross, any more than the language of such devotion, did
not come to us from Latin sources, and it is merely frivolous
to put forward contrary suggestions without evidence. A recent
instance of such irresponsibility is the statement that there are
parallels between the epilogue to *Elene* and the tenth-century
Irish poem, *Christ's Cross*, ascribed to Mugrón. This has been
said to fortify the assertion, often found elsewhere, that "the
Celtic emphasis on the veneration of the Holy Cross lies behind
... *The Dream of the Rood* and all that led up to it, and also ...

Elene." But when one consults Gerard Murphy's modern English translation of *Christ's Cross*, one finds that there are no such resemblances. Mugrón composed a *lorica*, very like the Old English Cross-periapt in MS Corpus Christi Cambridge 41, and they merely ask the Cross for daily protection of the body against physical dangers and afflictions, an idea worlds removed from *The Dream's* salutations of the Cross as the *spes unica* of the soul. All these poems, certainly, must have been composed by men who had devotion to Christ's Passion and veneration for the True Cross; but what Christian had not?

Indeed, in Aldhelm's complaints about the superfluous studies in Ireland of his young men, we see a problem which persists today in our attempts to evaluate Irish influence upon English learning and spirituality. Gougaud, for instance, has amassed much evidence to show how many great figures in the Anglo-Saxon Church, men such as Ecgbert, Chad and Willibrord, had learned in Ireland from men "steeped in the sacred Scriptures." But so were Gregory and Jerome and Augustine steeped in the Scriptures, and they were not neglected in this country, as Bede's collections of Jerome on the Prophets, Augustine on Paul testify.

It will be long before final judgment on such matters can be made. We need a new generation of scholars, equally competent in Latin, Celtic and Germanic philology, and we need also their evaluation of many more texts than are now available. Then, too, we must take account of the trends of scholarship in recent years in tracing the origins and growth of Western spirituality. The older view, taken by such men as Rousselot, that devotion to the mysteries of Christ's humanity, and particularly to the Passion, was "the great discovery and the incomparable merit of the late Middle Ages, beginning with St. Bernard and St. Francis," has been questioned by Vernet. Thurston showed that St. Francis was not the originator but the populariser of the ecstatic devotions associated with him; and he reminded us that there were Syriac fathers of the fourth century writing tracts on the Crucifixion which might have been composed by thirteenth-century Franciscans. We have thought of Anselm and Aelred as early exponents of the type of "meditations" which the unlearned laity were to adopt and use so widely; yet it was Abbot Piammon, seven centuries before them, who wrote "My soul went to a place where I saw St. Mary the Mother of God weep at the foot of the Cross." Wilmart proved that devotions to the humanity and sufferings of Christ were familiar in the eleventh century, Berlière traced their origins to ninth-century Benedictine spirituality, Bishop, Symons and Bonetti have all pointed to the early Irish strain in the prayers and worship of English monastic houses not long before the Conquest. Especially when we remember how much of the evidence needed is irredeemably lost, we must see that it is mere imprudence to claim any teacher as an innovator, when his teaching may be the only example surviving to us of what in his own age was widely received and derived from yet earlier sources. Bede perhaps was, as has been asserted, the first to teach that Christ chose to retain in His glorified body the wounds of the Passion, to show to the blessed the marks of the love which redeemed them, to the damned on the Day of Judgment with what justice they are condemned; but we have seen that part at least of this teaching, which is repeated in later Anglo-Saxon homiletic and poetic tradition, corresponds with what we can find in Scriptural commentaries older by far than Bede.

There is probably little harm in our reading still in our missals that one of Christendom's greatest prayers is "The Petitions of St. Ignatius to our Holy Redeemer"; the Missal is not the place for the erudition displayed by Wilmart and Bonetti, when, in their separate studies of *Anima Christi*, they demonstrated how little we know of the centuries through which these aspirations to the Passion were added lovingly one to another, until they reached their last perfect shape. We can see that they were known, in some form, to the author of the *Ancrene Riwle*, several decades before the earliest texts identified by Wilmart; and in that petition which inspired one of the Riwle's finest passages, *In vulneribus tuis late me*, we have a most instructive example of how erudition and sanctity can beget a piety which lives and grows long after its originators are forgotten. The author of the *Riwle* knows that this petition derives from an interpretation of the verse in Canticles, "Hiding as a dove hides in the clefts of the rock," and he may have learned this either from Bernard, or from the "other expositor" whom Bernard cites, who is Bede. But Bede himself seems to have borrowed this spiritual interpretation, in which the "dove" is the soul of man and the "clefts" are the Sacred Wounds, from Spain, from Justus of Urgel writing in the sixth century. Such are the origins, themselves complex, of this supplication, the gift of Spain and England and France to the common heritage of the universal Church.

It is to the Church's universality that we owe it that Christian faith and Christian practice came as they did to our country, by the many paths which divine providence directed, and that the English were in their turn able to give to other lands what they had so richly received.

BIBLIOGRAPHY

Texts

The Homilies of the Anglo-Saxon Church, ed. B. Thorpe, London, 2 vols., 1844 and 1843.

The Blickling Homilies, ed. R. Morris, London, 2 vols., 1874-80.

An Ancient Manuscript (the Nunnaminster Book), ed. W. De Gray Birch, London, 1889.

Bede, Historia Ecclesiastica, ed. C. Plummer, Oxford, 1896.

The Book of Cerne, ed. A. B. Kuypers, Cambridge, 1902.

Die Vercelli-Homilien, ed. M. Förster, Hamburg, 1932.

The Dream of the Rood, ed. B. Dickins and A. S. C. Ross, London, 1934.

The Exeter Book, ed. G. P. Krapp and E. van K. Dobbie, New York, 1936.

The Battle of Maldon, ed. E. V. Gordon, London, 1937.

Regularis Concordia, ed. T. Symons, London, 1953.

Bede, Homilies, ed. D. Hurst, in Corpus Christianorum Series Latina 122, 1955.

Gerard Murphy: Early Irish Lyrics, Oxford, 1956.

The Homilies of Wulfstan, ed. Dorothy Bethurum, Oxford, 1957.

The Benedictine Office, ed. J. Ure, Edinburgh, 1957.

The Seafarer, ed. Ida Gordon, London, 1960.

Lilli Gjerløw: Adoratio Crucis, Oslo, 1961.

Studies

E. Bishop: Liturgica Historica, Oxford, 1918.

N. F. Blake: Caedmon's Hymn (Notes and Queries 207, 1962, pp. 243-6).

I. Bonetti: Le Stimate della Passione, Rovigo, 1952.

Anna Dorothee von den Brincken: Marianus Scottus (Deutsches Archiv für Erforschung des MA 17, 1961, pp. 191-238).

M-M. Dubois: Aelfric, sermonnaire, docteur et grammarien, Paris, 1943.

M. Förster: Keltisches Wortgut im Englischen, Holle, 1921.

L. Gougaud: Christianity in Celtic Lands, London, 1932.

J. Leclercq: *Monachisme et pérégrination du ixe au xiie siècle* (Studia Monastica 3, 1961, pp. 33-52).

K. Sisam: *Studies in the History of Old English Literature*, Oxford, 1953.

F. Vernet: *Mediaeval Spirituality*, London, 1930.

Dorothy Whitelock: *The Audience of 'Beowulf,'* Oxford, 1951.

A. Wilmart: *Auteurs spirituels et textes dévots du moyen âge latin*, Paris, 1932.

4. GODRIC OF FINCHALE
AND
CHRISTINA OF MARKYATE

C. H. Talbot

THE FASCINATION which the solitary life has held for people of every age is one of the phenomena which we find it difficult nowadays to understand. The tendency at the present time is for people to live more and more in communities, to become members of corporate bodies and to avoid any form of behaviour that might be construed as singular or individual. It is felt that life in solitude, withdrawn from ordinary human contacts, is unnatural, eccentric and odd. Yet the suspicion persists, even amongst the most gregarious, that anyone embarking on the solitary life will enjoy a spiritual experience, an intimacy with God and a depth of wisdom attainable by very few. For this reason solitaries are and have been held in the highest esteem.

Yet the Church has not always been sympathetic to the withdrawal of the Christian from the world. The dangers attendant on the solitary life were considered to be too great to be faced except by those who had been tested in the crucible of coenobitic life. Most spiritual writers, therefore, counselled aspirants to submit first to some form of discipline in the cloister, whilst the ecclesiastical authorities stipulated that no one should embark on the eremitical or solitary life without special licence from the bishop of the diocese.

In spite of these restrictions there were always considerable numbers of hermits and recluses. Every county in England could boast of its holy men and women and we have the names and abodes of over seven hundred and fifty of them. They established themselves in the depths of the woods and forests, in caves on the hillsides, in marshes and fens, on lonely islands, on bleak headlands facing the sea, anywhere, in fact, where they could pursue their vocation undisturbed. But, whenever possible, they attached themselves to some church or monastery, where their spiritual needs could be satisfied and their material subsistence assured. Here, pledged to obedience to an abbot or prior, they were given spiritual direction by one of the monks or canons, and in return they served the community by writing books, illuminating manuscripts, guarding shrines, keeping bridges or roads in repair or simply by edifying the neighbourhood by their austere and holy lives.

The motives which prompted them to undertake this form of life were ultimately reducible to a desire for the contemplative life. But the immediate reasons for seeking solitude varied from individual to individual according to temperament and circumstance, so that among hermits and recluses we find extraordinary differences. This point is clearly illustrated in the lives of the hermits, Godric of Finchale and Christina of Markyate, who are the subjects of the following remarks.[1]

Godric was born towards the end of the eleventh century, the child of a poor family living near the banks of the river Welland in Norfolk. He was by nature shrewd, self-reliant and tenacious, but completely illiterate. As a boy he spent most of his time scouring the shores of the fenland country for the wreckage of ships, finding it more profitable than tilling the soil. Later he became a pedlar and sold his wares in the outlying villages, gradually extending his movements to markets farther and farther afield. Eventually, he took to the sea and sailed with his bundles of goods to Scotland, Denmark and Flanders. Then, when he had amassed enough profit from these voyages, he bought a share in a ship and because he had an unrivalled knowledge of the winds and tides, he acted as steersman. He was, at that time, a sturdy, robust man, with broad shoulders, blue eyes, black curly hair and long beard. On his journeys across the sea he visited many churches and the shrines of saints, but the ones he loved best were the island of Farne, where St. Cuthbert had lived as a solitary, and Lindisfarne where Cuthbert had held his episcopal see.

---

[1] These remarks are based upon the following books: *Vita Godrici Eremitae*, Surtees Soc. 20, 1845; *Christina of Markyate*, ed. C. H. Talbot, Oxford, 1959; *The Liber Confortatorius of Goscelin of Saint Bertin*, ed. C. H. Talbot, Studia Anselmiana, XXXVII, Rome, 1955, pp. 1-117; *De Institutis Inclusarum*, ed. C. H. Talbot, Analecta S.O. Cist. VII, 1951, pp. 177-217.

After sixteen years of seafaring this tough and seasoned mariner decided to follow in St. Cuthbert's footsteps. But before settling down in a hermitage he made several pilgrimages to the Holy Land, Compostella and Rome, under the impression, as his biographer points out, that one becomes holy by going to holy places. But eventually he sought solitude at Carlisle and, after a series of false starts found his way to Durham, where he attended a school for small children so that he might learn how to read, recite the psalms and sing. In this way he prepared himself to carry out the liturgical side of his vocation. Then one day, hearing two shepherds speak of a place called Finchale, he gave one of them a halfpenny to show him the way, and finding it to be almost inaccessible because of the briars, he chose it as his final abode. Here, on a level plot of ground in a bend of the river Wear, hidden by the steep, densely wooded banks and protected from intrusion by the rushing waters, he fixed his hermitage.

At first he practised every kind of physical austerity, wearing hair-shirts, eating herbs, acorns and roots, sleeping on the ground with a stone for his pillow, plunging into the icy waters of the river and remaining there the whole night through. These extremes were dictated partly by his ardent temperament, partly by his meditations on the pains of hell. Though he mitigated these rigorous practices later in life as he learned that excessive mortification has less value, from a spiritual point of view, than the exercise of certain virtues, he never succeeded in wholly divesting himself of this urge for penitential exercises. The idea that God would punish the least defect by torments of unimaginable ferocity was never far from his thoughts and any suffering or inconvenience that he underwent was always alleviated by recurrence to this theme.

Though he never expressed any views about the hermit's life, his practical teaching was that it should not be subject to whims and fancies, but should follow a strict and rigid discipline, alternating between work, prayer and silence. Theoretically, the work undertaken by a hermit could be anything that occupied the hands for a certain portion of the day, such as making baskets, mats, rugs, tools, or even pursuing more artistic activities such as copying manuscripts, illuminating, or carving images. All these things had been prescribed by early writers on the solitary life. But Godric chose heavy agricultural work, digging the rough and uncultivated ground, planting and grafting trees, feeding and milking cows, in fact, anything that taxed his strength and at the same time provided food for himself and the poor who visited him.

Manual labour, however, no matter how heavy and fatiguing it may be, can often be easier than prayer. Perhaps it was for this reason that Herrad of Lansperg depicted the hermit's garden in the *Hortus deliciarum* as being his chief stumbling-block to perfection. Godric understood this also and, as a precaution against neglecting prayer for the sake of his crops, he hung a small bell in his oratory which could be rung at the appropriate hours of the day to call him back from work. In this way he forced himself to conform to a strict pattern of prayer and meditation. What the prayer was did not matter. As he was illiterate he could not follow the breviary, but he had a small prayer book from which he read, and he also composed his own prayers as he went along, sometimes reciting the creed, sometimes the Lord's Prayer, but at all times fixing his mind on God. Simple as these kinds of prayer seem to have been, they raised him to a high degree of contemplation, in which he had visions of Our Lady and the saints and in which he was taught to compose hymns and musical sequences.

But it is silence which is the guardian and nurse of prayer. Godric, therefore, restricted not only the times at which he would speak, but also the people with whom he would hold conversation. On four days of the week, Sunday, Monday, Tuesday and Friday, he did not speak at all. From the first Sunday of Advent until the fifth day after Christmas and during the whole of Lent he observed absolute silence. To visitors he spoke but little. Only when they brought from the Prior of Durham a small wooden cross in their hands, (a prearranged sign between them), would he relax a little of his wonted austerity. But when he spoke, St. Gregory's dictum that "silence is the mother of preachers" was fully proved. Those who sought his help and counsel found him a well of wisdom, whilst even monks of tried experience and holiness listened to him with rapt attention as he interpreted the scriptures and explained the mysteries of faith. St. Aelred of Rievaulx and St. Robert of Newminster, both abbots of large and important communities, sought his company for the sake of profiting by his spiritual teaching. But

what the themes of this spiritual teaching were it is difficult to
say. Since Godric could not write and was unable, perhaps even
unwilling, to consign his thoughts to parchment, and since his
biographer was more concerned to describe his visions than to
give an outline of his views on the spiritual life, we have to
extract what we can from the disparate remarks recorded by his
biographer.

One of the basic ideas which lies at the root of Godric's conduct and teaching is the danger of idleness. He taught that every
moment of the day should be occupied by work or prayer or
reading and meditation, and that none of these activities should
be interrupted or suspended through weariness, discomfort or
even for social obligations. This constant keeping of the mind
and body at full stretch was, he admitted, a difficult and irksome
task, but it could be made easier by varying the routine of one's
life. Much as he feared idleness, which left mind and body open
to every form of temptation, he feared even more the boredom
and fatigue which could invade the spirit through too great a
concentration on any single activity, be it prayer or reading or
manual work. For this reason he counselled frequent changes of
spiritual exercise. Godric himself even had two oratories, one
dedicated to Our Lady, the other to St. John the Baptist, so that
he could pass from one to the other and vary his surroundings
for meditation and contemplation.

For warding off temptation, alleviating his physical sufferings
and making bearable the irritations and inconveniences of everyday life, Godric had constant recourse to the cross. The cross, he
used to say, was his treasure. As it hung on the wall of his small
chapel or greeted his sight as he opened the pages of his prayer-
book, it recalled for him the Passion of Christ. It was therefore
the symbol *par excellence* of obedience. This was a theme that
was ever on his lips. He realised that disobedience was the cause
of all man's unhappiness and that submission to God's commands
was the surest and shortest way to spiritual perfection. Godric
repeatedly complained of the failure, even of good people, to
submit unquestioningly to the divine precepts and contrasted
their behaviour with that of the wild animals, the deer and the
hare, who when warned by Godric not to invade his garden and
eat his plants, respected his prohibition and fed themselves in
the woods.

These simple and rather elementary, yet essential ideas, are the sole basis for any assessment of Godric's contribution to teaching on the contemplative life. Yet sixty years spent in solitude, eight of them on a bed of sickness, must have yielded a more fruitful harvest of ideas and practical advice than is contained in these bald statements. It is not improbable, however, that Aelred of Rievaulx, Godric's friend and frequent visitor, may have incorporated some of the hermit's teaching in the *Rule for Recluses* which he wrote for his sister. When we examine the contents of this Rule, we shall, perhaps, find the hidden springs of his spirituality there.

Very different from Godric, in almost every respect, was Christina of Markyate. She came of a rich and influential family which could boast of powerful connections both in the secular and ecclesiastical sphere. Her father was head of the merchants' gild at Huntingdon, whilst her mother was related indirectly to Ralph Flambard, Chancellor of the Kingdom. Christina's life, therefore, unlike that of Godric was sheltered and well ordered, and, had she so wished it, could have been pampered. But at an early age she became aware of her religious vocation through a chance visit to the abbey of St. Albans, where the architectural beauty of the buildings, the solemn chanting of the divine office and the grave demeanour of the monks made an indelible impression on her mind. She resolved there and then to become a nun, and scratched a cross on the wall of the abbey church as a sign of her decision.

When Ralph Flambard, now become bishop of Durham, made his journeys to London, he stayed with Christina's aunt at Huntingdon. On one of these occasions, when the rest of the family was celebrating the arrival of their distinguished visitor, Flambard had the unsuspecting girl brought to his private chamber and, after dismissing the servants, foisted his attentions on her. By pretending to close the door to keep out intruders Christina managed to escape. But Flambard, furious at being repulsed, determined at all costs to have his revenge, and suggested that Christina be married to one of his acquaintances. To bring this about every form of flattery, threat, and physical violence was employed, and when Christina would not agree, her parents resorted to the most discreditable tricks in order to extort her consent, attempting to make her drunk, introducing

GODRIC OF FINCHALE 45

men into her room when she was asleep, bringing her before
ecclesiastical courts where the judges had been bribed. And
when all these means failed, they stripped her of her clothes,
drove her out naked into the night and then beat her and tore
out her hair.

For Christina there was only one way out of her difficulties:
flight. In the locality lived a hermit named Edwin, who had many
contacts with people in authority. By bribing her keepers
Christina was able to speak to the hermit and ask him to find her
a place of refuge. And Edwin, after consulting the archbishop of
Canterbury who decided that Christina had right on her side,
arranged with Alfwen, a recluse at Flamstead, to receive her and
give her shelter. A day was fixed on which a boy with two horses
should wait for her in the meadow near the river at Huntingdon;
and whilst her parents were visiting another hermit six miles
away, Christina, disguised in man's apparel, mounted a horse,
set spurs to his flanks and galloped hard to cover the thirty miles
that lay between Huntingdon and Alfwen's hermitage at Flamstead. There she was warmly welcomed, clad in rough garments,
given a cell and allowed to live in peace. For two years Christina
remained at Flamstead concealed and unknown. And then,
perhaps because of some dissension between the two women,
Christina made her way at dead of night to the hermitage of
Roger of Caddington, and there, cooped up in a cramped space
that would allow her neither to stand up nor to lie down, forbidden to speak or disclose her presence by any sound, she lived
under Roger's authority. For four years she endured this rigid
seclusion, suffering pangs of thirst and hunger, unprotected
against the heat and cold, free only in the evening to leave her
cell to answer the calls of nature. And then Roger, her director
as well as protector, died, leaving her the sole occupant of the
hermitage.

One again she became the object of persecution, but thanks to
the intervention of the archbishop of York who would willingly
have set her over one of the convents in his diocese, she was
allowed to live in peace. Soon she was joined by kindred spirits
and, with the generous co-operation of the community of St.
Albans, a small convent was built, the house was placed under
the jurisdiction of the abbey and Christina became the first
prioress. How long she ruled the community we do not know,

but she was still alive in 1155 when Henry II made a grant of fifty shillings to her support.

Christina, unlike Godric, was not illiterate. A remarkably beautiful psalter, which has survived the ravages of the Reformation, is known to have belonged to her and in it there are entries relating to her family and friends which must have been added at her express wish and under her supervision. It is obvious that she was quite capable, if called upon, of writing down her spiritual doctrine, and it is no less obvious that as prioress and founder of a community she had every opportunity of instructing her nuns in the principles of the contemplative life. It is to be regretted that she never did so. But women at that period do not appear to have regarded writing as their province and, with the exception of St. Gertrude and St. Hildegarde of Bingen, they were content to have their spiritual treatises written for them.

Fortunately, we have two remarkable treatises, written expressly for women who followed the life of a recluse, which contain all the spiritual doctrine available to religious of Christina's mould. One is the *Liber Confortatorius* written by Goscelin for a nun from Wilton, who had fled to Angers to become a recluse there: the other is the *Institutio Inclusarum*, drawn up by St. Aelred of Rievaulx for his elder sister.

Goscelin's work, which is of considerable length and substance, is remarkable for the little concession it makes to what one imagines to be the more sensitive nature of women. From beginning to end there is an assumption of virile, almost masculine fortitude in his client which one associates normally with people like St. Teresa of Avila. Though he knows that Eve, an aristocrat from the royal convent at Wilton, must feel her isolation at Angers where she has neither her abbess, St. Edith, nor Goscelin, her spiritual director, to encourage her, he wastes no time on misplaced sympathy. You have come thus far, he says, in your single combat and so there is no return. You must fight or die. "Often," he recalls, "when I have come with the bishop to London by the river Thames, I have noticed that when we reached the narrow passages where the water was turbulent, the sailors shouted and plied their oars with greater violence to keep us afloat, conscious that if they slackened their efforts, the wind and the waves would surely send us to the bottom. And at those times the thought struck me: So must heaven be reached; we must exert all our energy or die." So too must the recluse, without repining, face all the difficulties that beset her path.

In the same way she must use violence to rid herself of the temptations that will inevitably attack her. The devil will try to entangle her with his wiles, but she must be bold and burst out of them like a criminal breaking out of prison. The martyrs of the early Church were not spineless, timid or gentle creatures: their temptations and their trials were seemingly insuperable. Yet they triumphed over all by summoning up all their strength, by acting promptly, by meeting violence with fortitude and answering flattery with vehemence. Nor must this exercise of fortitude be short lived; it must be backed up by tenacity and perseverance and a determination not to submit. To point this advice Goscelin recounts the story of the hermit at Bury St. Edmunds, who preferred to be burned to death rather than forsake the cell which had been set on fire by pirates.

When the obvious temptations and dangers have been overcome, there still remains the monotony of the recluse's life. To be always in the same place, reciting the same prayers, performing the same spiritual exercises, to follow, in short, a routine that seems endless and that shows no tangible result is painful to nature. To make things worse, the human spirit is fickle and yielding, like a sea in constant movement, so that at one moment it is elated, and at another depressed. What must be achieved at all costs is stability. Even St. Peter lost confidence and began to sink as he walked these waves, but he was saved by grasping the hand of Christ. The recluse grasps the hand of Christ by meditating on the scriptures, by reading the commentaries of the Fathers and by studying the teachings of the saints. This reading must not be merely something that passes the time: it must involve real intellectual exercise:

Read Augustine on the City of God, Orosius on the History of the World, Boethius on the Consolation of Philosphy: then you will learn that there is nothing more miserable than this changing world, nothing more satisfying than the peace of Christ. These studies will soon banish boredom and make the days seem short; your solitude will bring you pleasure and render unnecessary any exhortation from others. And if at times you fail to understand the sense of a passage, do not skip over it, but pore over it, turn it over in your mind, read it again and again, and do not leave it until you have thoroughly understood it, for there is nothing that cannot be solved by hard work, whilst the Lord opens to all who seek and knock.

Goscelin was not a believer in rustic simplicity and ignorance. Though knowledge and learning might have its dangers, its advantages for the spiritual person far outweighed any possible drawbacks. And just because Eve was a nun, it did not release her from the obligation of using her brains or of studying solid, profound, theological works. She was expected to know scripture as well as the monk in the cloister.

Further to ward off the monotony of the recluse's life, Goscelin counselled the consecration of each hour of the day to some facet of Christ's Passion:

> At midnight meditate on his capture and imprisonment: at dawn on his scourging: at nine o'clock on his sentence to death: at noon on his nailing to the cross: in the afternoon on his death: in the evening on his burial.

Each day of the week could also be employed in this way, though Friday was particularly suitable for such devotion. And when these had been completed, five psalms could be recited in honour of the five wounds in the hands, feet and side of Christ. And if the recluse was still beset with thoughts of discouragement, by a feeling that her life was aimless, that her efforts were useless, she was to unite her actions to that of the whole Church:

> Think how many are the chambers in the house of Christ; think of the patriarchs, the prophets, the apostles, the martyrs, the confessors, the virgins, the widows and all the elect: think how they are all related, men with angels, angels with archangels, archangels and thrones, thrones and dominations, dominations and principalities, principalities and powers, cherubim, seraphim and even the Lord, king and emperor himself, ruling every creature with justice, love and benignity . . . . Never think of yourself alone when you have the companionship of so many denizens of heaven. Never complain of dreariness, torpor, sadness and tedium when you can share in the joys of such wonderful souls.

The most certain method of driving away these feelings of languor and inertia was, said Goscelin, to thank God for His ineffable mercies. For there are many in monasteries and in the world who would grasp at the opportunity of enjoying a peaceful life of contemplation, but who are, like Martha, "troubled about many things." Above all, receive if possible "the viaticum of the heavenly banquet" every day, for by sharing in the body and blood of the Lord, the Christian becomes one with Christ.

It is impossible in these few lines to compress the contents of more than one hundred pages, but these fragments and disconnected ideas will have to suffice to convey the atmosphere and flavour of Goscelin's teaching. It was common-sense, well-informed, sound teaching, the product of traditional monastic spirituality, untinged by sentimentality and strictly theological. It possessed that "gravitas" which was well adapted to fostering in those who practised it a sobriety and moderation which are the hall-marks of solid piety.

Goscelin wrote his book for Eve about the year 1080. Aelred's treatise was not composed for another seventy or eighty years. But both have much in common, not merely the pedestrian details which regulate the external activities of the recluse, but also that substratum of psychological teaching culled from the early monastic legislators and a certain amount of traditional lore, the source of which is not easily definable. All this appears in the introductory part of Aelred's Rule for Recluses. What is completely new is his detailed method of meditation.

One of the grave preoccupations of medieval spiritual writers was the control of the imagination. Aelred himself has described the disorders to which the imagination, left untrammelled, could give rise, and one of the tasks he set himself was to use it constructively by directing its powers into useful channels. Ailred was under no illusions about the dangers run by a recluse, left alone in her cell, but visited from time to time by garrulous, scandal-mongering old women; but he knew that a mere warning against these dangers would have little effect. And so, after prescribing certain exterior regulations on prayer, reading, fasting and manual work, he suggested for the recluse a threefold form of meditation, dealing with the past, the present and the future "in order that the sweet love of Christ may grow in your heart."

The meditation on the past consisted in recalling the chief mysteries of Christ's life: meditation on the present consisted in recalling all the benefits received from God: meditation on the future consisted in bringing to mind the four last things, death, judgment, hell and heaven.

The particular value which Aelred gave to this spiritual exercise lay in the use he made of the imagination. Nowadays this has become an accepted element in Christian spirituality, but in the twelfth century it was a complete innovation. This is how he begins this section of his treatise:

When you have cleared your mind of all extraneous thoughts, cast your imagination back to the Blessed Mary and entering with her into the inner chamber read with her the books of scripture which foretell the birth of Christ. Wait there the coming of the angel, so that you may see him enter and hear him offer his salutation. And then, in your turn, in a burst of joy greet your sweet lady with these words: 'Hail, full of grace, the Lord is with thee, blessed art thou among women.' And repeating these phrases gaze upon this fullness of grace in which the whole world has shared, since the Word was made flesh and dwelt among us, full of grace and truth. Contemplate with astonishment the Lord who fills heaven and earth, now enclosed within the womb of a young maiden, whom the Father has sanctified, the Son has made fruitful and the Spirit has covered with his shadow.

Each of the mysteries of Christ's life was depicted in this manner, followed in most cases by a few words of prayer and a moral lesson. It brought vividly before the imagination not merely the characters and events of the gospel story, but also the emotions aroused at each scene. In this way the recluse was meant to follow almost in the footsteps of Christ, to see His face, to hear His voice, to touch His garments, to feel horror at the scourging, to undergo something like torment when He was nailed to the cross. This vivid representation of events was intended to have a powerful cathartic effect on the memory, which, according to St. Augustine, is the most profound of the spiritual faculties. In his view the memory lay at the foundation of the spiritual life, because its ability to recall the facts of Christ's Passion was an assurance of the presence of the beatific vision in the future.

There is no doubt that with this original contribution to the spiritual ideas of the Middle Ages Aelred assured himself of a place among the great directors of souls. When we recall that he was friend and confidant of Godric of Finchale, we may be justified in thinking that some of these ideas had been discussed between them, and that what Aelred advised his sister to practise may have already been known to the hermit of Durham.

Beyond this, there is in the Rule for Recluses a certain amount of teaching on mystical prayer. We do not pretend that there is an explicit and systematic doctrine such as we find in the writings of St. Bernard: but by examining the scriptural texts, the allusions to types and experiences ordinarily associated in the mind of his readers with mystical prayer, it is possible to discover a complete outline of his ideas on the contemplative life.

The ideal that Aelred places before the recluse is none other than a life of contemplation. He allows no external occupation, such as the teaching of girls, the care of the poor and infirm or the administration of property, to interrupt her life of prayer. Her vocation is to seek the embrace of Christ. She should not be like Martha, distracted by many things, but like Mary, sitting at the feet of Christ and allowing herself to be filled with His grace. Like Mary at Bethany she should spend herself in love, devotion and desire, allowing nothing to distract her, for she must fill the role of penitent and contemplative, not of an active worker: "Martha ministers, Lazarus sits, but Mary anoints the head of Christ. This is your vocation."

Here we have the two kinds of life, the active and the contemplative, taught by the traditional masters of the spiritual life, Augustine, Gregory and Bernard. The recluse is obliged to imitate the attitude of Mary, or to imitate St. John, who leaned his head on the bosom of Christ and became inebriated with the knowledge of his divinity.

Such a life demands great asceticism as a preparation. The recluse must not waste time in gossiping or idle conversation. The day should be spent in prayer, fasting and silence. This corresponds to Cassian's "active life" and to the observance of all the regulations taken by Aelred from the Rule of St. Benedict and adapted to the circumstances of the recluse. These spiritual exercises, which Aelred abridges into the stoic precept: "keep still, be silent, endure," comprise what we would call today the purgative way; but some of them, such as silence and prayer, are intimately linked with the contemplative life. Centuries before Aelred wrote, Cassian had remarked that the first step on the path to mystical prayer was the practice of silence, and all the masters of the spiritual life who followed him, including St. Benedict, had considered it as a corner-stone. Aelred was no exception. He told his sister: "There is nothing you should cultivate more assiduously than silence."

E

The reason is not difficult to find. Idle conversations, especially when they are prolonged, weaken the spirit, fill the imagination with dangerous images and arouse useless desires. This makes the raising of the mind to God almost impossible. "After such talks, the recluse goes back to her cell, but she stumbles like a drunken man over the psalms, and falls down completely over her reading." Hence the necessity for complete solitude and silence. Far from the noise of the busy world the recluse "should sit in silence, listening to the words of Christ and speaking to Him. And let her be convinced that, when she is by herself, she is not alone, for then she is with Christ."

Such a silence is not merely an exercise in "taciturnity" counselled by St. Benedict, nor is it an empty silence where thoughts as well as words are suppressed. It is a true interior silence, such as the mystics love to describe, a silence of the heart, a silence of the imagination, a silence of all earthly desires. It is a silence already filled with God, in which God addresses Himself to the soul, and in which the soul is free to converse with Him. It is a silence which has already progressed beyond the bounds of pure asceticism and has become a constitutive element of mystical prayer. This interior silence is a treasure to be jealously guarded and to preserve it the recluse must be prepared to sacrifice all. "You must see that the mind is rid of all temporal cares and freed from the burdens of worry."

According to the psalmist, the abode of God is peace. The recluse, therefore, must cultivate this peace of the soul with great intensity. "Above all things she must study to preserve tranquillity of spirit and peace of heart in order that she may have as the eternal guest of her breast him of whom it is written: In peace is his place." This profound peace and unruffled calm of the faculties which accompanies the divine presence is called by St. Aelred, "the most holy state of the soul."

Here we see the recluse then, enjoying mystical prayer, contemplating God in the depths of her soul and enjoying this silence of the faculties which follows the concentration of the spirit on one single and supreme object.

Yet one might fear that all the prescriptions relating to vocal prayer recommended by St. Aelred might contradict or upset the state already attained by the recluse. For, apart from the daily recitation of the divine office imposed by the Rule of St. Benedict, he obliges the recluse to recite the Office of Our Lady with commemoration of the saints, and to repeat frequently throughout the day the *Our Father* together with other prayers and psalms. Is so long a list of vocal prayers compatible with the mystical state he envisages? If there were a contradiction St. Aelred would certainly have noticed it. But his insistence that vocal prayer is not necessarily in conflict with his ideal of the contemplative state is taken from Cassian who had said that contemplation is not attached exclusively to mental prayer: one can reach contemplation, and in fact it is frequently reached, by vocal prayer. Hence his advice to the recluse to repeat at all hours of the day the Lord's Prayer, a practice which Cassian had assured him led inevitably to the most sublime degrees of contemplation. Hence also his recommendation to make frequent ejaculatory prayers, which, because they are short, tend to fix the mind continually on God without fatiguing the faculties of the soul.

All prayer, says Aelred, should be short, unless he who prays is unconsciously moved by devotion to prolong it. According to these words it would seem that vocal prayer develops under the inspiration of the Holy Spirit into true mystical prayer, a prayer which St. Benedict had called "pure prayer." This pure prayer is definitely mystical in character in so far as all words cease, the tongue fails and all sensible impressions are left behind: the recluse would no longer be conscious that she was praying, *ipso nesciente qui orat*, a remarkable phrase that evidently alludes to St. Anthony's aphorism, "that all prayer in which the monk is conscious that he is praying is not perfect, that is to say, is not contemplative."

According to Aelred, then, there will be occasions when the recluse will enjoy this "incorruptible prayer," when there will be no utterance of words, no use of images and when the spirit, transported beyond all sense, will give itself to God with ineffable sighs. This is the state in which the soul, leaning on the breast of Jesus like the contemplative St. John, will become inebriated with the knowledge of his divinity, the highest degree of prayer, the sublime end of the contemplative life.

It will be impossible, however, for the recluse to remain always in the embrace of the divine spouse. The instable nature of the soul itself prevents it, apart from the fact that in the designs of Providence man cannot give himself exclusively to the delights

of the spirit. So she must turn from her contemplation to meditation on the humanity of Christ: "*Si ad potiora non potes, dimitte
Johannis pectus, ubi eum vinum laetitiae in divinitatis cognitione
inebriet: tu currens ad ubera humanitatis, lac exprime quo nutriaris.*"
All the mystics mention this common experience of the tran-
sitory nature of the act of contemplation: it is good to be with
Christ on Mount Thabor, but the apostles must come down to
the humbler tasks of earth, even to the sufferings of the Mount
of Olives. So must the recluse return from time to time to the
labours of the active life where she can give to others the fruits
of her contemplation, just as Mary Magdalen left the presence of
Christ to announce the Resurrection to the Apostles. The in-
stinctive reaction of the soul is a feeling of resentment against
these interruptions. But she need have no fear: nothing will be
lost. "This good is not taken from you: it is merely deferred."
And so, having obeyed the injunctions of Christ, she can return
to the feet of her master: "Then shall be given to you what was
earlier withheld."

Here we have the classic doctrine of the relationship between
contemplation and good works: here is the repeated insistence
on the obligation of the contemplative to interrupt her converse
with God to attend to the needs and interests of her neighbour.

As has been remarked already this teaching of Aelred's is not
explicit, but has to be elaborated from allusions, passing remarks
and scattered phrases. This should not surprise us, because the
Rule, written as it was for his elder sister, is expressed with a
certain familiarity and lack of formality which takes for granted
that she will understand from indirect remarks what he is really
aiming at. As a result we possess in this Rule a document which
is very original, profoundly spiritual and full of common sense:
furthermore it is a Rule which is remarkable not only for its
breadth of spirit but for the sublimity of its aim.

What is common to Goscelin's work and Aelred's Rule has
been derived, as we have already mentioned, from traditional
monastic spirituality. There was an immense fund of experience,
of discipline, of spiritual maturity on which all monks could
draw and on which generations of saints and ascetics had been
nourished. This was available to all the members of the Church
and, no matter where they might be, whether in the north at
Durham or in the south at St. Albans, the spiritual ideas and

outlook produced by centuries of monastic endeavour would
be at their disposal. It is not to be expected, then, that there would
be great differences in the teaching either of a hermit like Godric
or a recluse like Christina. They might have widely differing
attitudes to certain devotions, lay greater or lesser emphasis on
penitential exercises, show indifference or enthusiasm for certain
aspects of church discipline. But these would be personal idio-
syncrasies deriving from temperament and character rather than
fundamental differences about the teaching and practice of the
spiritual life. For this reason, we can assume that though neither
Godric nor Christina produced any spiritual writing of their own,
the Rules for recluses composed by both Goscelin and Aelred
would have given ample expression to their ideas, their experience
and their aims. This must be the justification for describing at
such length two treatises which, at first glance, seem to have no
connection whatever with the title of this chapter.

5. ST. AELRED OF RIEVAULX[1]

Aelred Watkin

WHEN we hear him, we see him. Aelred of Rievaulx is one of those rare characters who seem to have transcended the limitations of their own epoch and to have crossed the icefloes of the centuries between ourselves and him. Nevertheless, we cannot pick upon any one quality in him to which we can attribute with confidence the immediacy he has for us. As a thinker and writer he has little of the originality and force which makes St. Bernard's voice still sound a trumpet call; as a stylist he was very unequal, eloquent and moving at times, he lacked unity of thought and expression; as an historian he ranks far below some of his contemporaries, and as an administrator his activity and efficiency, considerable as they were, were offset by a naïve optimism in regard to the goodwill of others which events were to show was unfounded. And yet, when all this has been said, we still feel drawn in an especial way to his memory, and he has exercised an influence so deep upon some of his admirers as almost to drown all critical faculty. Even the casual reader of his works wishes to know more about this quiet author who speaks to him as if he were in actual fact talking to him in the wooden hut under the steep cliffs with their dwarf oaks.

To speak in terms of charm is not to tell the whole tale. That Aelred possessed this indefinable quality in abundance is quite certain: it comes to us even through the ill-printed pages of Migne; we do not have to rely upon the evidence of contemporaries to recognise its presence, we can feel it for ourselves. It is, however, his courageous self-revelation that brings Aelred

[1] The life of St. Aelred has been dealt with magisterially by three writers in recent times: by Sir Maurice Powicke in the Introduction to his edition of the *Life of St. Aelred of Rievaulx*, by Walter Daniel; by Dom David Knowles in *The Monastic Order in England*, pp. 243–5, 258–66; and by Mr. Edmund Harvey in his *St. Aelred of Rievaulx*. Unfortunately I have not seen Dom David Knowles's paper in *Studies* on *The Humanism of the Twelfth Century*.

of Rievaulx so close to ourselves. Few of the arduous battles of the soul's path to God are hidden from our eyes. In autobiographical passages Aelred speaks of his earlier hesitations and doubts, his sins—he is even open enough to speak of habitual and humiliating sin—his difficulties in disciplining his affections and his need for affection. His sermons, also, are full of passages based undoubtedly upon deep personal experience. There is, for example, a vivid portrait of the ambitious and critical monk:

> He describes and, as it were, paints before the eyes of the brethren what type of person the abbot should be: so modest, so holy, so lovingly-disposed towards his subjects, so compassionate to them in their labours, so condescending to the weak; next, how the refectory should be organised and how the infirmary should sympathetically be run he confirms by the authority of scripture, so that his hearers respond in their hearts: "Oh if he were abbot, how wise, how eloquent, how kind, how human, he would be!"[1]

The voice of this critical monk comes back to us very vividly across the centuries. And it is, perhaps, this gift of vivid presentation of experiences common to the lot of man that is Aelred's distinguishing quality. He was, of course, not alone in this; indeed, the twelfth century was an age of self-revelation, but in Aelred's case this sense of intimacy is expressive of a personality of singular charm and of a mind where peace and order reigned supreme. Aelred assuredly possessed that "silent heart" of which we speak in the martyrs' hymn.

Aelred was born in 1110 in the shadow of the Roman wall at Hexham. The progress of clerical celibacy had been slow, especially in the north, and Aelred was descended from a long line of married priests who were the guardians of the church of Hexham with its relics of early saints and the crypt built by St. Wilfrid of inscribed Roman stones from Corbridge. Aelred soon left home and was taken into the household of the Earl of Huntingdon who became King David of Scotland in 1124. For ten years Aelred lived at the Scottish court with its memories of St. Margaret and its traditions of Saxon and Hungarian royalty. His schooling was brief, as Jocelin of Furness tells us, and, early involved in administration, he was eventually appointed to the position of steward of the royal household. A close friend of the king and of his son, Aelred had enemies who

[1] *XVII Serm. de Oneribus.*

were jealous of his influence. Given, as he tells us, to close friend-
ships ever since his school days, he seems always to have preserved
an inner self which never wholly capitulated to others. This was,
doubtless, a strength; but it is certain that some found this
quality intensely irritating. To the superficial it appeared to
manifest intellectual pride and aloof self-sufficiency.

These years were not happy. Aelred was in high favour at
court, he was one whose career seemed to stretch out with
measureless possibilities of position and prestige; to outward
appearances all could not have been going better. Inwardly,
however, Aelred felt more and more frustrated and anxious. He
was caught in the toils of sin,[1] resolution faltered in a milieu
where a thousand chains kept him from giving himself wholly to
God in whom alone he could find peace. When, as he himself
tells us, others remarked upon his good fortune, Aelred felt
oppressed, not only by the sense of what he was and of what he
would wish to be, but also by the knowledge that he was not
understood even by those closest to him. Like the young
Augustine he longed to make a new start, but no voice called
out to him in the garden.

In 1134 Aelred was in Yorkshire on business. Two years before
he had heard of the new order of Cîteaux and the fervour of
its early monks; now he was told that they had settled close to
where he then was. It was within two days of hearing this that
Aelred visited the new foundation of Rievaulx, and at once he
was violently attracted by everything he saw. That evening he
spent at Helmsley Castle, two miles away. It was a night of
conflict. Interiorly he was drawn first one way and then the
other; at one moment he yearned to throw in his lot with the
Cistercians, at another this seemed beyond the bounds of possibility, held as he was by the links he had forged in Scotland and
fearful of leaving all that was familiar for something so austere
and so unknown.[2] By the morning he had more than half made
up his mind, and at dawn he set out for Scotland with his companions. But the road he followed went past the brow of the

---

[1] This experience made a profound impression upon him. He refers over and
over again in his sermons to the shackles forged by a *consuetudo peccandi*.

[2] This is how I interpret Aelred's two visits to Rievaulx after a close reading of
Walter Daniel's description and of Aelred's own remarks. Daniel does not quite
seem to have understood all that was taking place in his abbot's mind at that
moment.

hill above the monastery and the steep track which led down to it. In every sense it was a parting of the ways and Aelred hesitated. Even now he could not make up his mind. He asked one of his servants if he would again like to go down and revisit the abbey. Had the servant preferred to have gone on northwards, Aelred would not have pressed the point and would, perhaps with relief, have followed the Scottish road.[1] The servant, however, contrary to what might be expected—for the hill was steep and he had seen the place only the day before—was all for going down. And Aelred did not return.

Aelred's inner history for the next ten years is largely hidden from us; as far as external events are concerned, the saint early became the companion of Abbot William on several important journeys and in 1141 was sent as the abbot's representative on a mission to Rome. Of the effect of this journey upon Aelred it is hard to judge. He did not, like St. Bruno and St. Ambrose, see the landscape with a poet's eye, and nowhere does he give any hint as to the impact of a scenery and a life which were utterly unfamiliar to him. At the same time there can be little doubt that he became completely captivated by the personality of St. Bernard, whom he must have met on this occasion or possibly earlier on. It is hard to overestimate the effect upon Aelred of the impact of this dynamic personality. It is clear that Bernard stamped an impress upon the saint's thought and writing which lasted for a decade at least, though in his later years we see it gradually disappear and Aelred's own personality and outlook come more clearly into their own.

St. Bernard, like many another great and original genius— Hilaire Belloc and Eric Gill in other spheres may be cited as recent examples—tended to create a school of second-rate imitators. The torrid eloquence, the pointed allegorical phrase, the devastating assurance and the trumpet-calls for reform, all these were, with St. Bernard, but the instruments by which he proclaimed an intense awareness of the overriding claims of God in language stamped with the hall-mark of a highly individual and powerful personality. In the hands of Bernard's imitators it was only too easy for eloquence to turn into rhetoric, allegory into undisciplined fancy, assurance into infallibility and asceticism

[1] Aelred tells us this himself. Daniel puts the saint's request down to humility, but I think he has failed to understand the significance of the incident.

into puritanism. And Aelred did not altogether escape from the impact of a personality far more powerful than his own; some of his earlier writings seem almost to have been written by two persons—the real Aelred, direct and simple, and the disciple of Bernard attempting to reproduce the thoughts and diction of the abbot of Clairvaux, but speaking uncertainly in a tongue and a manner foreign to him.

On Aelred's return from Rome in 1142, he was appointed novice-master and wrote his first book, the *Mirror of Love*. For the reasons which we have given it is a curiously disintegrated work. Composed originally from short meditations sent to his friend Hugh in the form of letters and as a kind of testament to his friendship with Hugh himself and with a young monk called Simon, who was now dead, the original simplicity and directness suffers not only from the rather feeble echoes of Bernard, at whose command the whole was first put into book form, but from an attempt to put the whole composition into a logical framework inspired by what Aelred doubtless thought was the language of the Schools which he had not attended. This latter attempt comes more to the fore in the second book where Aelred first asks and then answers feeble objections to his teaching. This method, when used by a genius such as St. Thomas Aquinas, can illuminate and clarify, but as anyone who has explored the by-paths of scholasticism knows, in inferior hands nothing can be more tedious. And it was not Aelred's *métier*.

Nevertheless, the *Mirror of Love* is a book which lingers in the reader's memory. Not only does Aelred display that gift for summing up a whole truth in a pithy sentence which seems to have been the especial gift of the most profound English spiritual writers,[1] but his own charm is always visible below forms of expression which do not always do it justice. The *Mirror*, also, contains two autobiographical passages which must always leave a haunting impression upon the reader. The description of the life and death of his friend Simon is intensely moving, even after the passage of eight centuries, and Aelred's account of his interview with a novice who found the Cistercian life almost too hard to bear shows a sympathy and a patience in dealing with personal

---

[1] Especially is this true of the author of the *Cloud* and of Julian of Norwich. Fr. Augustine Baker, despite all his prolixity, sometimes does it with immense effect.

difficulties which can only be the reflection of his own experience.

In 1143 Aelred became abbot of Revesby and in 1147 that of Rievaulx. By now Rievaulx was by far the most important Cistercian abbey in England and, for a variety of reasons—geographical and personal—it had become a centre of spiritual force and influence in the north. Part of this pre-eminence was certainly derived from the personality of her abbot. St. Aelred was industrious, tactful, easy of approach, a fluent speaker and a pleasant person to meet. He was called in to preach sermons at important functions, for he could be counted upon to say the right thing on the right occasion, he was selected as arbitrator in disputes. He already numbered among his friends the members of the royal house of Scotland, the canons of Hexham, the monks of Durham, the Cistercian Archbishop of York, the Bishop of London and the Abbot of Westminster. He kept up a close correspondence with the most powerful in the land.

Yet it was influence rather than power which he wielded. He was no Henry of Blois, to mention one famous contemporary. He had not the qualities of mind or taste which give distinction to almost every word that Henry wrote. But, equally, Aelred never suffered from the eclipses and reverses which marked Henry's path from ambitious striving to peace. Fragments of carved blue lias, flawless in their beauty as the Elgin marbles, are today dug up at Glastonbury to remind us of the cloister built by Henry of Blois; but it is Aelred himself who still lives for us in the ruins of Rievaulx.

Of his capabilities as abbot it is hard to judge. He certainly felt keenly his responsibilities and composed during these years a very beautiful prayer begging for God's help in carrying them out. He in no way neglected his duties and, indeed, it is clear that he found a quiet satisfaction in moulding the religious life of a growing and flourishing monastery. He was tireless in journeying on visitation, in supervising the erection of buildings, in preaching to the brethren and in coping with those day to day problems of administration which can form so stern an ascetic discipline for the conscientious. Nevertheless, granting all this, it remains hard to assess his qualities as an abbot, for it is impossible to tell how far his influence for good was offset by a leniency of rule of which some at least took advantage. Aelred gloried in opening wide the doors of Rievaulx to all comers, for he possessed a serene optimism which saw the possibilities of good in all. Yet, there was a danger here. It was from mature experience that St. Benedict in his rule emphasised the *difficultas ingressus* and the searching tests to be given to the novice. Rievaulx was to find, as many an abbey and religious order has found, that subjects unfitted by nature or temperament for the religious life cannot permanently be "carried" by the charm or holiness of one man, no matter how great or impressive. Such influence usually diminishes with time—for maturity lessens the capacity for hero-worship—and it tends quickly to disappear with the death of him who has called it into being. So it was at Rievaulx, and the alarming apostasies from religion which occurred in the early years of Aelred's successor may directly be traced to this policy of making Rievaulx a place of refuge for all who would come, many of whom, as the saint's biographer notes, Aelred did not even know.

It may be that this leniency came from a certain *naïveté*[1] which made Aelred, good judge as he was of problems where he was not personally involved, less sure in his judgment of persons. Thus, in one of the autobiographical passages in his book on *Spiritual Friendship*, he describes himself going round the cloister garth at Rievaulx and seeing the brethren sitting there. "I found," he continues, "no one in that multitude whom I did not love and by whom I was not confident that I was loved." The latter part of this statement was an illusion. Aelred had enemies both within and without the walls of Rievaulx. Some said that he had worked for his election as abbot and, to quote Sir Maurice Powicke, "Walter Daniel's Life was written in part as a passionate refutation of the suggestion that he was ambitious, a wirepuller, fond of luxurious living, a successful prig who in his time had been no better than he should have been."[2] That these insinuations were totally without foundation is obvious to any student of Aelred's life and works; that Aelred should have been, as far as we know, unaware that they were being made, shows, perhaps, a certain simplicity in him which could, and doubtless did, render him the catspaw of the unscrupulous and the adroit.

[1] We find occasional examples of it in his writings. Aelred's astounding treatise on the *Nun of Watton* does more credit to his heart than to his head or, indeed, sensibilities.

[2] *Life of Aelred of Rievaulx* by Walter Daniel, ed. Powicke, p. lxvi.

As the years went by the saint's health deteriorated. He suffered from the stone, to which later were added arthritis and attacks of asthma.[1] A small hut was constructed for him and it was here that he spent a great deal of the last few years of his life. These years of illness, which he bore with marvellous patience, were those in which Aelred finally became what he was. Pain and illness accepted with resignation work powerfully in the soul. More and more, as time went on, his reserves gave way to a complete simplicity, the derivativeness of style of much of his earlier work becomes less and less apparent and he speaks of God and of men with much more directness and sureness of touch.

Confined as he was to this hut for long periods, Aelred had now greater opportunity for that slow meditative reading which St. Benedict so stresses in his Rule. There is nothing that can deepen the mind so much as daily reading and pondering upon all that is best in the spiritual thought of the past. If a knowledge and love of the Classics lie at the back of all that Europe has meant by education from the fifteenth century to the recent past, equally it was the love and knowledge of the Fathers of the Church which created and sustained all that was best in the life of the monasteries of the early Middle Ages. Indeed, it may well be considered that it was the abandonment of this store of mature and calm wisdom, unprofessional but deeply pondered, in favour of the more spectacular, but more speculative (and therefore less in touch with life and experience) thought of the Schools which did more than anything else to kill the spirit and influence of early monasticism. Circumstances, however, had enabled Aelred to read more often and to ponder more in peace; we therefore notice a calmness and poise in his later writings which is sometimes absent from his earlier ones.[2] The Gospel of St. John and the pages of St. Augustine and St. Ambrose seem to have been much in his hands, but he does not merely re-echo them, he transposes them into the key of his individual thought.

It was during these years that St. Aelred wrote his dialogues on *Spiritual Friendship*. The use of dialogue and the portrayal of real persons do much to make the book live. The shy and sen-

---

[1] Which malady he shared with St. Augustine and the Venerable Bede.
[2] This can easily be seen if Aelred's works are read in their chronological order.

sitive Ivo of the first book lives on after his death in the pages of
the second and third; Walter Daniel, the saint's biographer, with
that mixture of impatience and incomprehension which is so
peculiarly his own, appears in the second and third books, where
he is joined by Gratian, an extrovert who is eager to love and to
be loved by all.

But it is not so much the vividness of the dialogues, nor their
content—which, indeed, contains little that is novel—which
claim our attention; it is the fact that they were written at all.
Other monks had written on the same subject—notably Cassian
—but Aelred fearlessly sets to work to establish the place of
human affection in the context of the early years of a drastic
monastic reform. There is an optimism and serenity about his
approach before which the morbid and the feverish shrinks away,
the calm faith of the author reaches beyond the hesitancies of
the scrupulous and creates an atmosphere in which self-indulgence
is not so much overcome as transcended. To those whose outlook
is coloured by the tortured introspectiveness or the popular
psychology of a later age, Aelred's view may seem suspect, if
not dangerous. And though it is true that in certain quarters
Aelred has been used to justify an unpleasing and self-conscious
"cult" of friendship, we must remember that—in the words of
the *Cloud of Unknowing*—"the nigher we are to truth the nigher
we are to error." In the end, as Aelred shows, human and divine
love are one, and the common enemy of both is sin. It is the
calmness and clarity with which the conviction is expressed
which makes this particular work of Aelred something of an
epoch in spiritual writing. We must try not to be too alienated
by the rather unpleasing use which has been made of it in certain
hands.

So the years went by, years of considerable literary activity
and of a large correspondence which has, unfortunately, perished.
Of Aelred's historical works—of which he wrote several—little
needs to be said. They are vivid in style and presentation but
not of importance in content. The saint's *De institutione inclusarum*, a work on the religious life for anchoresses, is not in
his best vein. He seems to be obsessed by the fragility of woman's
resolution and tends to lose the poise and optimism of the
de Spirituali Amicitia which was written about the same time.

Of his directly spiritual writings we have yet to mention his sermons—including a series on the "burdens" of Isaiah and an early work on the "Child Jesus at the age of twelve years" which has all Aelred's charm. His sermons differ widely in character: some are really eloquent and moving, while others are turgid and involved. Aelred may well have been one of those preachers who are at their best when speaking spontaneously, but lose all force and point when they prepare a sermon too carefully, and especially when they base it directly upon the writings of others. Of all Aelred's sermons, the Homilies on Isaiah are the most consistent and still repay careful reading.

The saint's final work—unrevised, if not unfinished—was a treatise on the *Soul*. Again, there is nothing original or profound, but in many respects it is the most pleasing of all his writings. Composed, again in dialogue form, with the awareness of his own approaching death much in his mind, this book exhibits a simplicity and directness which must make any reader feel that the author has finally arrived at that complete maturity of mind which is the reward of patience and suffering. Its philosophical ideas are of the simplest and it is markedly reminiscent of St. Augustine's *Soliloquies*. Nevertheless, it is pure Aelred. The tumultuous echoes of Bernard are now completely hushed, and the work proceeds with all the quiet movement of the seasons. Its final words mark the passage between Aelred's life and his death: "for without doubt [the saints] have care for us and pray for us with the more earnestness because they know that without us they cannot be fulfilled." He was soon to take his part in this consummation of the saints.

St. Aelred's death has so often and so well been described that there is no need to dwell upon it here. His illness and infirmity increased and, as he lay on his bed, he begged for Christ's coming, saying in English over and over again "*Festinate*, for Crist luve." His last intelligible words were: "Into thy hands I commend my spirit." He died on 12 January 1167.

Dom David Knowles has warned us against letting our historical judgment be lulled by "the siren voice of romanticism," and we should, perhaps, be even more upon our guard against being captivated by personal charm. Aelred had this in abundance and he is able to reveal it to us across the dead wastes of the centuries. We must, therefore, not be swept off our feet by the extravagant claims that have sometimes been made for him.

He was no original thinker, he said little that had not been said as well or better by others, his works are unequal in thought and content and when—as in his earlier writings—he is derivative he is unconvincing and uncertain. Yet, when we have said all this, we cannot escape from the recognition of a sanctity and a simplicity which is, because personal, in its own way unique. Beyond all that charm which still seems to haunt the ruins of Rievaulx and is displayed in almost every line he wrote, we are aware that we are in the presence of a soul given wholeheartedly to the search for God. Perhaps the most moving page in Walter Daniel's biography is that in which he sums up Aelred's behaviour as a novice: "At all times he submitted the preference of his own will to that of another . . . a sort of miracle, indeed, a sort of martyrdom." Here, Aelred steps across the centuries from the cloisters of Rievaulx to those of Lisieux.

6. THE ANCHORESSES' GUIDE

Peter Hackett

IT MUST BE ADMITTED at the outset that the *Anchoresses' Guide*[1] is not an ideal source of mystical teaching. In the first place, our ideas of true mystical writing are likely to be compounded from Spanish, Flemish and English classics of later date; and the *Anchoresses' Guide* was composed long before the building of interior castles in England. In the second place, it is quite quietly and firmly a rule of life, in spite of the somewhat less assuming title we have adopted here.[2] You will look in vain for elaborate, poetic descriptions of mystical states; look in vain, too, for that definite call to contemplation as the all-important ideal. Rules are by nature pragmatic, down-to-earth affairs, which order the limited aim and object of the beginner and sketch the background for God's spiritual initiative in the advanced.

This is not to say that the *Anchoresses' Guide* is irrelevant to the history of English mysticism. It is indeed a document of the first importance. It links traditional and up-to-date continental spirituality with the later English mystics; it has its own light hints of mystical possibility. How this is so we shall attempt to show in three stages: by characterising the work and its importance; by underlining the author's own preoccupations; and by relating these to more general teaching.

Not much can be said with absolute certainty about the circumstances of the *Guide's* composition. Scholarly opinion dates it as belonging most probably to the early thirteenth century,[3] assigns the West Midlands as the place of composition,[4] and considers that the unknown author was likely to have been a secular priest. This last is a good guess, based on the likelihood

---

[1] It is now easily available in the modern English version of M. B. Salu, *The Ancrene Riwle*, Burns and Oates, London, 1955. All page references are to this edition.

[2] A rendering of *Ancrene Wisse*, the title of the most acceptable manuscript.

[3] The evidence is the date of the manuscripts and a few hints in the text.

[4] The evidence is partly the provenance of the manuscripts and partly linguistic.

(almost certainty) that a member of a religious Order would betray his origins before he had been writing long; based too on the impatience with which the author tells his Sisters to disregard all distinction of "Black" and "White" and knuckle down to their proper task in the Order of "St. James"—the keeping of themselves unspotted from the world.[1]

There have of course been efforts to identify both the author and the young ladies for whom he wrote. Of particular interest is the attempt of Fr. Vincent McNabb, O.P., to prove that "(1) the *Ancrene Riwle* was written by an English Dominican Friar and (2) that the English Dominican Friar was probably Friar Robert Bacon, O.P." Though his theory is ingenious and closely argued, later scholarship has not been kind to it, largely because its nodal point, a reference to the practices of "our brothers," could be shown to exist only in one manuscript. Another guess made Gilbert of Sempringham the author; but this too is unlikely. Among other objections raised by the late Professor Chambers is this, that the author's "Wash wherever you need to as often as you like. . . . Dirt was never dear to God,"[2] accords ill with the Gilbertine warning: *Caveatur ab omnibus nostris balneum, cum sit libidinis fomentum.* Hope Emily Allen tentatively "proposed to identify the three maidens for whom the treatise was composed, with the *tribus puellis, Emmae, videlicet, et Guinildae et Christinae,* to whom . . . the hermitage of Kilburn was granted by the Abbot and Court of Westminster sometime between the years 1127 and 1135." The trouble here is place and date, particularly date.

How then to characterise the author and his work? He was a cultured man, with the culture of breeding and letters, provincial perhaps, but courtly in mind and manner. The distinction between the anchoresses and their servants appears quite clearly as a distinction also between the well-born and the ill. Courtly analogies abound, as when the Sisters are told to follow their true knight, Christ. He was kindly and gentle, as far as the somewhat relentless spirituality of his time would allow. "Although the flesh is our enemy," he says, using the common conceptions of the day, "we are told to support it. We must punish it as it often deserves, but not destroy it completely, for however weak it is, yet it is so coupled and so closely linked to our precious soul, which is God's own image, that we might easily destroy

[1] pp. 4 ff.   [2] p. 188.

the one with the other."[1] As a spiritual writer he combined two invaluable gifts: sanity and responsibility. He was sane in that he had no ready-made plan for the spiritual life, no short answer to its problems, no war-cry in response to all difficulties, no contemplative or active axes to grind. He was responsible in that he regarded his task—the helping of his anchoresses to holiness—as better fulfilled by a broad presentation of straight Christian asceticism, than by any personal quirks of his own. He was, however, no die-hard conservative. He was modern enough in his own age to be dated in ours.

A cultured man, then, and one working in a cultured tradition. He owed something to the literary tradition of the West Midlands of England and something to the history of Christian spirituality. At the contents of his library we can only guess (so much of his material remains unidentified), but he shows knowledge of all the approved authors, of Bernard, Augustine and Gregory, Origen, Cassian and the Victorines. This knowledge may not be direct. We know that in giving St. Bernard's doctrine in the section on penance, he is more likely to have been using Geoffrey of Auxerre's *Sententiae Excerptae*. A general impression is that, if all his sources were traced, the residue of originality might be slight indeed.

This is by no means to discredit his work. There was a real alchemy practised by the middle English translator, compiler and adapter which could, with surprising economy, transform even the sow's ear of an average Latin homily into a silk purse. A good example is the related *Sawles Warde*, a quite lively rendering of a rather inferior Latin homily attributed to Hugh of St. Victor. The gift, often little more than a gift for homely illustration, the author most certainly had; and he knew, too, how to take charge of his material and weld it into a whole.

His work, and this does not always seem to have been sufficiently realised by some critics, was a rule. It was not a treatise on prayer or mortification, a thoughtful commentary on life in general or religious life in particular, but a rule. It is singularly unembarrassed by spiritual phenomenology or spiritual theology; it had to be lived and therefore had to be liveable. This is clear if one considers the somewhat unlikely event of two or three young ladies asking to-day to be set up as anchoresses.

[1] p. 61.

You could not give them the *Cloud of Unknowing* as the basis of their life of prayer, penance and work, but you could give them the *Anchoresses' Guide*. And in this sense it is hardly to be judged by the ordinary criteria of the spiritual book; it answers so much more thoroughly the question: "What do *I* do?"

The two qualities of soundness and liveability at once popularised the work. It was translated into Latin and French (thereby hangs a tale, for it took much argument to get the English version accepted as the original). It was adopted by and adapted for other religious and layfolk. This popularity has left its mark. All the extant manuscripts show traces of editing, particularly in the sections on temptation and confession. It would not, however, be correct to assume that it is all to be laid at the door of revisors; a good deal of it, even where it leads to seeming inconsistency of purpose, might well be brought home to the author himself.

The *Anchoresses' Guide* also made its mark on subsequent spiritual writing. In tracing its influence, Hope Emily Allen was the chief detective. She found its ideas in other rules, the Dublin Rule for instance, and in other spiritual literature. The sixth comfort against temptation seems particularly to have appealed:

> Our Lord, when he allows us to be tempted, is playing with us as a mother with her darling child. She runs away from him and hides, and leaves him on his own, and he looks around for her, calling, "Mama! Mama!" and crying a little, and then she runs out to him quickly, her arms outspread, and she puts them round him, and kisses him, and wipes his eyes. In the same way Our Lord sometimes leaves us alone for a while and withdraws his grace.[1]

This is found in the *Chastising of God's Children*, the *Poor Caitiff* and Rolle.

Our examination of the author's spiritual teaching may best begin with a short account of the content of the *Anchoresses' Guide*. This is necessary, because the author is orderly in that only sense almost that a chain is orderly; one link follows another. Further, his own headings to the various sections do not always underline sufficiently their precise content. The work is composed of an introduction and eight books. Of these the eighth is not of outstanding importance to us (we have his own word for it), though it does give a background in which many details of thought and illustration become intelligible. Thus the rarity of

[1] p. 102.

the anchoresses' sacramental communions explains in part the importance attached to spiritual communion; a thoroughly well-bred way of life explains the thoroughly well-bred analogies with which the text is sprinkled.

The author's purpose in his introduction seems, wisely, to be to create a sense of proportion. He wants a relatively clear notion of what is important and what is not, what is obligatory and what is not. To this end he first distinguishes two rules, nicknamed characteristically the lady and the handmaid: God's inner rule of a pure heart, and changeable, man-made, external observances. His Sisters are not to muddle the two. Next, he will have no additions to the ordinary monastic vows of religion, Obedience, Chastity and Stability, for further vowed obligations might lead to scruples; the rest is to be left to the generosity of an open heart under the guidance of a good confessor. Thirdly, he is concerned that the anchoresses understand the part they are to play in the Church of God. Religion, for them, is to keep themselves unspotted from the world in a manner different from that of active friars and priests.

The first book of the rule proper is concerned with the more formal prayer of the anchoresses. Their day is to be built round the recital of the Office of Our Lady and a vast number of semi-liturgical and other devotions. The purpose is obvious: to provide the Sisters with a framework of prayer into which their private meditation will fit and out of which it will gradually grow. The devotions suggested are surprisingly rich for a thirteenth-century collection, but they are just what one would expect from a writer in the Bernardine tradition. They recommend and instil tremendous devotion to Our Lord and Our Lady in the Incarnation and the Passion. Although the accent on liturgical worship is maintained, the anchoresses are exhorted to "think of Him most intently during your hours,"[1] there is some evidence of that shift of emphasis from devotion to Christ's sacramental, as opposed to his sacrificial, presence at Mass which modern liturgists are inclined to make so (too?) much of. Alongside the elevation prayer: "Behold the salvation of the world, the Word of the Father, a true sacrifice, living flesh, the whole Godhead, true man,"[2] which preserves the balance, we can read the important:

[1] p. 20.   [2] p. 13.

"When the priest communicates .... embrace your beloved who has come down from heaven into your heart's bower."[1]

The second book of the *Anchoresses' Guide* introduces the ascetical teaching on which it insists so much, and is concerned with the guarding of the senses. Its teaching is on the whole, in so far as it is purely ascetic, fairly commonplace; though a modern reader is likely to take scandal that so much time should be spent in the discussion of the preservation of chastity. Common-sense suggests the explanation: first, the author supposes the young ladies to be much more at the mercy of so-called friends and relations than is conceivable to-day; second, they had to make their safeguards and did not receive them ready-made from a long tradition of post-Tridentine security; third, the contemplative life is liable to face the religious with problems hitherto unsuspected; fourth, good practical pedagogy often exaggerates. However, and this is much more important, what is said about custody of the senses is meant to lead to custody of the heart and thence to spiritual sensibility. He says:

> Holy men who have experienced [spiritual sight] know that every earthly happiness is by comparison worthless. "It is a hidden manna. And I will give him a white counter: and in the counter, a new name written, which no man knoweth but he that receiveth it." "It is a secret, healing draught," says St. John the Evangelist in the Apocalypse, "known to none who has not himself tasted it." This tasting and this recognition follow on spiritual insight, spiritual hearing, and the speech of the spirit, things which those people shall possess who, for the love of God, forgo the sounds of the world, the conversation of earth, and the sights to be seen by the eyes of the body.[2]

The passage, surely, could have come straight from William of St. Thierry.

The object of the third section is less easy to define; it would appear to be nothing more than the consideration of some virtues of the contemplative life, loosely put together by means of the exposition of certain texts in the psalter which mention birds. The author is concerned that the anchoresses be reconciled to the life they have chosen and live it to the full. Hence, in unavoidably random illustration, the pelican of the wilderness leads to the consideration of anger and gentleness, the sparrow

[1] p. 14.   [2] p. 41.

to the discussion of silence and chattering, the night-raven under the eaves to the examination of the whole quality of the contemplative life. The author is perhaps in this section at his most characteristic, playing quietly and colloquially with his ideas.

"The birds of heaven have their nests. . . . The nest should be hard on the outside, the heart within tender and sweet. Those who are bitter or hard of heart, and indulgent to their flesh, are making their nests the wrong way, soft on the outside and thorny within."[1]

The fourth section deals with temptations. Here the problem of an edited text becomes acute, for it is unnaturally long and gives the impression of being, in some of its pages, less directly addressed to anchoresses. Two layers of thought can be distinguished: the one a treatise on temptation and how to cope with it, the other a picturesque exposition of the seven deadly sins. There seems no good reason for supposing that another hand has been at work, so we must suppose that the author himself thought that a (perhaps previously composed) treatment of the deadly sins might be a useful addition to what he had to say about temptation.

The different quality of the two layers may easily be gathered from the way in which the more general treatment insists on the discernment of spirits:

At the beginning, it is all courtship, so that you are drawn into love. But as soon as ever He feels that you are accustomed to Him, He will be less patient with you. At last, after this trial, comes great joy.[2]

Or the warning about the deceptions of the devil:

"No," he says, "I cannot make this one sin through gluttony, but I will push her further to the side toward which she is already leaning, and then throw her on that side, and suddenly fall upon her when she least expects it."[3]

Or the passages containing the consolations against temptation, of which the "Mama" passage above is an example. On the other hand, in discussing the seven deadly sins, he takes to portrait drawing: "The man who is wrathful juggles with knives in front of the devil. He is his knife-thrower; he plays with swords,

[1] p. 60.   [2] p. 97.   [3] p. 99.

balancing them with the sharp point upon his tongue. . . ."[1]
His characters have been greatly admired, but one cannot help
reflecting that it is at this point, where the imagination of the
littérateur is most captured, that the author is perhaps at his least
useful.

Confession is the subject of the fifth section. Two layers are
again noticeable and in fact more obviously underlined. In the
more general exposition, which is nothing other than an account
of how to make a good confession, the author invites the penitent
to declare: "I am an 'anchoress,' or a 'nun,' or a 'married woman,'
a 'maiden,' or a 'woman who was very well trusted,' or 'a
woman who has been burnt by the same kind of thing before
and ought to better on my guard.' "[2] The second layer is introduced at the end with the words: "My dear sisters, this fifth part,
about Confession, has the same relevance for everybody; do not
therefore be surprised that I have not spoken, in this section,
especially to you."[3] He goes on to give more particular directions
to them:

> Confess at least once a week all common sins, for example sins
> of pride, a puffed-up or a haughty heart, sins of envy, anger, sloth,
> negligence, idle talk, undisciplined thoughts, listening to any idle
> conversation, any false joy or heavy sadness, hypocrisy, taking too
> much or too little food and drink, grumbling, looking miserable,
> breaking silence, sitting too long at the window, saying your hours
> badly or without attention of your heart, or at the wrong time,
> speaking falsely, swearing, being frivolous, shaking with laughter . . .
> etc.[4]

The formality and thoroughness of his treatment of certain
parts of the sections on temptation and confession has led Dom
Gerard Sitwell to conclude that they might be taken as making
a contribution to the literature on confessional practice which
was fast becoming popular around the time of the Fourth Lateran
Council.

The sixth and seventh parts treat respectively of Penance and
Love. Their characteristic is the way in which they switch from
the highest to the lowest: from the following of Christ crucified
to penitential bodily mortification, from the response to the
redemptive love of Christ to the avoidance of sin. The two

sections are complementary and provide the key to the whole work, as we shall see.

The author calls upon the Sisters to glory in the cross of Christ: "There are living on earth three kinds of men who are the elect of God. The first may be compared to good pilgrims, the second to the dead, the third to people hung with their own consent upon Jesus's cross."[1]

The Sisters are exhorted to follow the third, the highest:

> The dead man cares no more for honour than for shame, for luxury than for austerity, for he feels neither, and therefore he earns neither sorrow nor joy; but the man who is on the cross, and takes joy in that, turns shame into honour and pain into joy and therefore deserves a surpassing reward. . . . Dishonour and hardship, these two, as St. Bernard says, are the two sides of the ladder which go straight up to heaven, and between these sides are fixed the rungs of all the virtues by which men climb to the happiness of heaven.[2]

He expounds too, for their consideration, a courtly parable of love in which he demands that the ladies love their true knight, Christ, and honour his shield, the Cross.[3] We are then rapidly plunged back to earth again by the consideration of how the Greek fire of the love of God can only be quenched with urine (the stench of sin), sand (idleness) and vinegar (a sour heart).[4]

Field-Marshal Viscount Montgomery, in his Memoirs, makes much of the master-plan—the outline of action which states as simply as possible the objective and the broad pattern of the means by which it is to be achieved. A first necessity in breaking down the spirituality of the Anchoresses' Guide is to discover the author's master-plan. What, in this mixture of nature and grace, liturgy and personal devotion, action and contemplation, are the basic ideas?

A first consideration in the analysis is that any writer of a rule, however clear-minded he may be, must always confound four things: Christianity, perfection, the preoccupations of his own age and the particular form of religion he is describing. You would be practical on the subject of, say, temptation without too many "maybes" or "mights"; you cannot confine yourself to generalities and you must preach the highest. Hence you will

[1] p. 154.   [2] pp. 156-7.   [3] p. 172   [4] p. 178.

tend to expound what is good Christian conduct for this audience, living this life in these circumstances. So too the author of the *Anchoresses' Guide*. His strictures on anchoresses who appear too often at their windows will not make easy reading for a member of a secular institute:

> It was commanded in God's name in the Old Law that a pit should always be covered; and if an animal fell into an uncovered pit, the man who uncovered the pit had to pay the penalty. These are very terrible words for the woman who shows herself to man's sight. It is she who is represented by the man who uncovers the pit.[1]

The author is too intelligent not to have foreseen this difficulty, and so devoted, as we have seen, a considerable part of his introduction to creating a sense of proportion. What place, then, does he give in his rule to what may be called the decencies of religious life?

Here we must take into consideration another fact—that a writer on religious life will always tend to take some things for granted. Thus, if religious life is inconceivable without divine office in some form or other, or without monastic vows, they may not be stressed. And this is true of the *Anchoresses' Guide*. The author assumes an office, but deduces little from its presence; he introduces the three vows of religion largely in order to recommend that they should not be added to. He has no formal treatment of them, though considerations rising out of them appear throughout. It is immediately clear that, whether he expressly states the idea or not, the aim of religious life is, for him, the aim of a state of life. This gives the answer to the question about ordinary duties. They are important precisely as manifesting the quality of an anchoress's commitment to her chosen life. That is why, for instance, he requires such a detailed and regular confession. Perfection is the avoidance of sin in the state of perfection, religion, which imposes duties.

This notion explains much that is problematic in the *Anchoresses' Guide*. It shows why religion, for the author, can be expressed in the words of St. James, "to keep oneself unspotted from the world," why the emphasis on sin appears exaggerated. It puts in focus the chapter on the nature of birds compared to anchoresses. Why mention the avoidance of common sins and high virtue

[1] p. 25.

in almost the same breath? The anchoress, in a higher calling, has the light and duty for both. It soothes the disappointment that a modern reader may feel that the chapters on Penance and Love, having started with the highest, return to the lessons of common mortification and the avoidance of sin.

So much for the dominant theme of the *Anchoresses' Guide*. There is, however, a tonic theme too. It can be stated in a word as the following of Christ crucified. We have shown the statement of this at its boldest in the chapters on Penance and Love, but it may be followed throughout: in the devotions to Christ crucified, in the recommendation of custody of the senses, in the reasons to fight temptation and so on.

So we have the master-plan: the avoidance of sin in a state of perfection, the objective; the love of the Cross, the means.

It could, I suppose, be objected that all this is rather Pelagian. Why insist so much on human effort when perfection is the work of grace? Why be so preoccupied with human failing when to concentrate on holy aspiration would be more helpful? It is a point and one which is not easy to find an answer for. In the first place, the *Anchoresses' Guide* is a rule and of its nature deals with human striving. Another simple answer might be the author's own in discussing chastity:

> My dear sisters, although the cleanness of chastity is not to be bought from God, but is a gift of grace, yet ungrateful people who will not gladly endure hardship for it, resist it, and make themselves unworthy of a thing so noble.[1]

A deeper answer is that, if it be characteristic of the *Anchoresses' Guide* to be concerned with human effort, it is also characteristic that the whole work centres round the Sacrament of Penance.

Now, at the heart of the mystery of the Sacrament of Penance, hidden from the faithful in a Latin prayer, lies a truth whose fuller meaning has puzzled theologians. The prayer is the *Passio Domini*, and what it expresses is the truth that the penitent's whole life of virtue is relevant to his forgiveness, to his increase in grace. The *Anchoresses' Guide* contains a version of this prayer in a passage which reads:

> The priest need not give you any penance outside the life which you lead according to this rule, for any guilt, unless it is exceptional.

[1] p. 163.

But after the absolution he should say, "I enjoin and impose on you, for the remission of these sins and for the forgiveness of all your sins, all the good you ever perform and all the harm you ever endure for the love of Jesus Christ within your anchoresses' dwelling."[1]

This could, I suppose, just possibly be taken as excusing the anchoresses from graver canonical penances (for he goes on to mention light penances such as prayers and disciplines immediately), but the author clearly seems to mean something further, as the beginning of the next chapter shows: "All that you ever suffer, my dear sisters, all is penance. All the good you ever do and everything you suffer in such a hard order is martyrdom for you, for you are night and day upon God's cross."[2] It is here, it seems to me, that grace meets nature in the *Anchoresses' Guide*. One could have hoped for a little more about "the increase of grace," but as we have seen, the author is much more insistent upon the humble acknowledgment of failure in a high ideal.

It could be objected that the spirituality of the *Anchoresses' Guide* is too personal, too lacking in a sense of the world around. This cannot be maintained for a moment. We would not expect a great deal of insistence on such notions in a rule for solitaries, but we find it none the less. For instance, the Anchoresses are told that a Sister: "must also, by her example and by her holy prayers, give strength to other people and support them, so that they do not fall into the dung of sin."[3] Again, their prayers are to be like the prayers of Queen Esther, "life-giving prayers."[4] And to give but one other example, the author describes the hard physical penance of a certain man and woman known to him and adds:

> We can only thank God for the strength which He gives them and humbly acknowledge our own weakness. Let us love what is good in them and thus it comes to belong to us, for, as St. Gregory says, love is of such great power that it makes other's good our own, without any effort on our part.[5]

And what is the place of contemplation in all this? There is no formal treatment of the matter, and that for the very obvious reason that it is a side-issue in a rule of life. Further, the author was too conscious that he was writing for "young trees planted in God's orchard" to risk filling their minds with future possibilities

<hr>

[1] p. 153.   [2] p. 154.   [3] p. 62.   [4] p. 74.   [5] p. 169.

that depended on the free gift of God. He may well have thought the same way as the Mother Superior who forbade her Carmelites to read the *Interior Castle* lest it should lead to an unhealthy self-analysis. But this is not to say that contemplation is not considered by the author.

In the first place he insists upon the folly of the Cross. This is the very stuff from which the gift of higher prayer will rise; death to the world means life unto God. His rule lived as he intended it to be lived provides the very way of life into which mystics are born. Even its very insistence upon sin and the sense of sinfulness proves this, for there is no one more conscious of the horror of sin than your mystic. More than this, however, there are scattered throughout the text, hints of higher prayer and higher experience. The first of these is provided by the passage about spiritual communion:

> After the kiss of peace in the Mass, when the priest communicates, forget the world, be completely out of the body, and with burning love embrace your Beloved who has come down from heaven into your heart's bower, and hold him fast until he has granted all you ask.[1]

We must note too what the author has to say about spiritual sight in a passage which we quoted earlier. It clearly holds out the possibility of heavenly experience in this life, an experience in which William of St. Thierry says, "the soul already possesses a kind of kinship with and participation in heavenly realities." And not to multiply examples, there is the anchoress compared to the night-raven: "So shall an anchoress fly in contemplation, that is, with thoughts lifted up, and with holy prayers, to heaven, and gather by night the food of her soul."[2] We need look no further; the gift of contemplation will come as inevitably as it is taken for granted.

To read the *Anchoresses' Guide*, with its sound spirituality and styled (though not stylish) English is to reflect, first of all, how much it is to be recommended in these days when the first test of a spiritual book is not so much whether what is said is true, as whether anything is said at all. It is to reflect, too, how like the work of grace upon the soul is the work of the human mind upon language. Grace takes its own creature and disciplines it to love,

[1] p. 14.   [2] p. 63.

respecting it and raising it; so too the mind, language. Its own creature is formed, whose will is recognised as free, not to be forced into expression. The language of the *Anchoresses' Guide* is a language neither dominated nor dominating, ready to express what the author desires. Not only, like Shakespeare's, does it contain some interesting words, but it is strong and regular with a tradition of loving service; it is eager and earthy. The reader of Miss Salu's translation will grasp this, I think, if he remembers that modern English has become smoother.

7. ADAM OF DRYBURGH

Humphrey Pawsey

ADAM OF DRYBURGH, or Adam Scot, or Adam the Carthusian, as he has been indifferently called, was born in Berwickshire about 1150. After attending the Schools he entered the newly-founded Premonstratensian abbey of Dryburgh, near Melrose. Elected abbot in 1184, he held the office until 1189, when he transferred to the Charterhouse of Witham. This was three years after St. Hugh, his friend and patron, had been dragged from Witham to become Bishop of Lincoln. Adam died in Holy Week, 1212, after an illness of two years. At the end of a fourteenth-century copy of sermons of "Master Adam the Carthusian" (once the property of the old London Charterhouse and now in the possession of the new Charterhouse), there is an extract entitled *De vita et conversatione Magistri Ade Cartusiensis secundum quod habetur in chronica domus Witham.* The original chronicle, no longer extant, was written by a Witham monk who knew Adam intimately during the last ten years of his life. He says that Adam died "more like one falling asleep than passing away," that as a Premonstratensian his name and scholarship became widely known, that he was of medium height, good looking, with ready wit, gentle and cheerful in speech, with charming ways that made him welcome everywhere, and with a high reputation as a preacher. At the end of his life as a Carthusian he was a trifle stout, of cheery countenance, with a fringe of white hair relieving his baldness; but, adds the chronicler, "he was a man to awaken reverence".[1]

Adam's transfer from the White Canons to the Carthusians was not made without difficulty. He did not doubt the new direction of his vocation, but he had misgivings as to how it could be realised. He feared the opposition of Premontré, a fear that proved to be well founded. In his *De ordine, habitu et professione canonicorum,*[2] he had made a searching examination into

[1] "The Witham Chronicle Fragment", edited by Margaret Thompson, in *The Bulletin of the John Rylands Library*, vol. 16, no. 2, July 1932.
[2] P.L., 198, 497-507.

the reasons, good and bad, for and against a change of monastery, even of Order: "If your superiors are arrogant, alter them by humility . . . a sapling disturbed by wind and drought takes longer to fruit, but doubly so if transplanted . . . Discontent, rather than aspiration may be a man's real motive. But, should it be a true and burning desire for God, then neither good reasoning nor bad must withhold him from obedience to the call. Yet it is well to depart with the goodwill and approval of superiors and brethren".[1]

On a certain occasion Adam and the abbot of Premontré visited the Charterhouse of Val St. Pierre, his first meeting with Carthusians. Here he talked with Roger, a member of the community, who had been a White Canon himself, the first abbot of Dryburgh and Adam's former master. One may suppose that his leaning towards the Carthusians was intensified by this meeting. At all events, on his return from Premontré to Dryburgh, he made a detour to seek the advice of St. Hugh, who had been a Canon of the priory of Villarbenoit, near his family castle of Avalon. On a visit to Chartreuse, Hugh had felt an intense urge to remain there; but his prior opposed his wish and even prevailed upon him to take an oath not to follow it during his prior's lifetime. Later, Hugh considered that the oath was not binding, since it was sworn under pressure. He disregarded it, and never afterwards expressed regret for having done so. Adam opened his heart to Hugh, who gave him permission to enter Witham, over which he still retained authority as "provisor". Adam went to Witham and was accepted; only then did he report the step he had taken to Dryburgh. Premontré ordered him to return under pain of excommunication, but gave him twelve months' grace for appeal. About this time, Hugh came to Witham for the annual retreat he was accustomed to make there. He told Adam to set his mind at rest, and to leave the matter in his hands; and eventually Premontré gave way with a good grace. The honours and cares of his abbacy thus set aside, Adam was free to lead a life entirely given to God. From his first day at Witham, it is said, there was only one occasion on which he went beyond the outer gate of the monastery. The only path he trod for the next twenty-four years was that which led from his cell to the chapel. While a Premonstratensian, he had declared,

[1] Cf. *Adam of Dryburgh*, by J. Bulloch, S.P.C.K., London 1958.

in his *De tripartito Tabernaculo*,[1] the place of the anchorites to be
the Holy of Holies: "The secret and solitary conversation of the
anchorites may be called the bridechamber." In the spiritual
hierarchy hermits held the highest place, followed by the Orders,
canonical and monastic, such as the Premonstratensians, Carthusians and Cistercians. Elsewhere he claimed that Canons were
superior to monks, on the grounds that the priesthood was an
essential element of their way of life.

Until the coming of the Premonstratensians the monastic life
and the priestly apostolate had been regarded as incompatible
vocations. Adam presents their two-fold ideal under the image
of the tabernacle which Moses entered to commune in secret
with God, and from which he came forth to guide God's people.
"There are two ways of life, the contemplative life whereby we
enter the tabernacle, and the active life in which we leave it . . .
We enter within to know in some sort the divinity of Christ
through the pureness of contemplation, and going out we follow
his humanity in public by imitating his deeds".[2] But the note
that dominated Premonstratensian spirituality was recollection
and solitude of heart in a cloister usually far from towns. "*Multa
quies*", the statutes say, and Adam wrote in reference to it:
"*vigor claustralium quies eorum*".[3] The realization of their twofold
ideal became susceptible of bifurcation, either tending more
towards its cloistral contemplative element, as in France, or more
towards that of the active ministry, as in Germany.[4] In Adam's
own case the tension of the two attractions did not slacken as
long as he remained a Canon. In his *Soliloquia de instructione
animae* he envisages in particular, before transferring to the
Carthusians, the case of conscience raised by his vow of stability
in the Order of his profession. But in spite of all the objections
his "reason" advances he resolves it in the sense that his "soul"
dictates; "out of a wish for greater perfection and a more strict
order, he will amend his life and strengthen his conversion to
God".[5] Yet Adam remains the foremost witness to what Canons
regular as a whole and cloisterers of every observance had in
common.[6]

[1] P.L. 198, 609-792.
[2] *De tripartito Tabernaculo*, P.L., 198, 774.
[3] Cf. *La Spiritualité des Premontrés*, by François Petit, 1947, p. 218.
[4] Cf. Bulloch, *op. cit.* p. 104.
[5] P.L., 198, 861.
[6] Cf. *La Spiritualité du Moyen Age*; Aubier, 1961, p. 186.

It has been said that in becoming a Carthusian Adam joined an order totally unconcerned with the outsider or his welfare. When writing for his brethren about the active side of their vocation he had taught that such activity has two expressions, preaching and teaching the truth to one's erring neighbour, and succouring him in his bodily needs.[1] As an abbot he must have been actively interested in such welfare of those outside the monastery; and were he not he would have felt less attraction than he did to go to Witham. For there he would read in the rule, the *Consuetudines Guigonis*, a whole chapter devoted to almsdeeds and the poor, who were to be fed and cared for "as goodwill suggests and means allow".[2] But because the spiritual works of mercy are more important than the corporal ones "it is not to be wondered at if we make more welcome those who come to us for the sake of their souls rather than for that of their bodies".[3] "We beg and implore all priors to indulge in generous almsgiving, as far as the facilities of their houses permit; for nothing is more in keeping with nature than to do for others exactly what we would wish done by others for ourselves when in some need like to theirs".[4] In his *Meditationes* the same Guigo says: "Christ's name is Jesus; so, the moment, for no matter what motive, you lose the will to save no matter whom amongst men, you cut yourself off as a member of Christ".

Adam has also been taken to task in the matter of manual work: "since he showed so little interest in it as a Canon, it was not illogical that he should become a Carthusian". But as a Canon he held that manual work was most fitting for religious, not only for their upkeep, but as a needful relaxation of mind and body for those given to things spiritual: "It is very beneficial and most becoming for religious men to be at times occupied in corporal work, in season and as needs be".[5] In his Carthusian rule he would find a list of things each monk was to have, not only because each had to do his own chores, but for the making of books, for writing, copying and binding them: "as we are not able to preach the word of God in speech we do so with our hands. For it seems to us that with each book we write we are

---

[1] De tripartito Tabernaculo, P.L., 198, 775.
[2] Ch. xx; P.L., 153, 673.
[3] Ibid.
[4] *Statuta Ordinis Cartusiensis*, I, xx, 1.
[5] P.L., 198. 856.

creating a herald of the truth, trusting in God for a reward for all who through them will either be brought back from error or advanced in Catholic truth".[1] The last of the four exercises Adam treats of in his *De Quadripertito Exercitio Cellae* is *Diligence in useful work*. Here he endorses what he preached as a canon: "Who is there that is sound in mind and limb that cannot work some good task with his hands . . . for manual work taketh away that peevish feeling thou mayest have, and furnisheth thee with a sense of delight; it bringeth thee great good and alloweth not sloth, which is the enemy of the soul, to overcome thee".[2] He did not value manual work for its own sake merely; it "hath some ghostly profit" he says; but quoting St. Paul he says also that "Godliness is profitable to all things . . . bodily exercise is profitable to little".[3]

The Charterhouse of St. Mary at Witham in Somerset was the first Carthusian foundation in England (1178-9). It was part of King Henry II's penance for the murder of St. Thomas Becket. St. Hugh, the first Carthusian to be canonized, arrived at Witham about 1178, and in a few years under his leadership the monastery flourished and was fervent. The life St. Hugh had lived in the cradle of the order was that of the very first followers of its founder St. Bruno, and it was this life of poverty, simplicity, prayer and work, unchanged, that he brought to England. It pursued the solitary life, but somewhat moderated for the sake of the practical exercise of brotherly love, the foremost duty of which is to one's family, or group. In such an atmosphere Adam lived for the rest of his life, concerned with the prayer and devotions, and the theology of them, which he had cultivated and preached about as a Canon: to the Blessed Trinity, to Our Lord, to Our Lady, and to the Church.

Adam's devotion to the Blessed Trinity was that of the early Church: he adores the mystery rather than speculates about it. He seeks to grow in admiration and love of it, and thence to learn by what titles we may belong to the divine family. In the way of perfection he attributes to the Father the cure of the wounds of memory, to the Son those of the intellect, to the Holy Ghost those of the will.[4] The Blessed Trinity re-forms

[1] *Consuetudines*, c. xxviii, 2-4; P.L., 153, 693-694.
[2] *Eden's Fourfold River*, London 1927, pp. 90-91. This is a translation of the second part (cc. XXV-XXXVI) of the *De Quadripertito Exercitio Cellae*.
[3] 1 Tim 4, 8.
[4] P.L., 198, 770.

the soul, re-establishes it in all its splendour as Its mirror. In heaven the Father will give us a share in his Power, the Son in his Wisdom, the Holy Ghost in his Love.[1] Meanwhile, here on earth, the soul strengthened by grace is to run towards this divine likeness; we shall only be like to God in heaven in so far as we have tried to imitate him on earth.[2]

Throughout his works it is remarkable with what tenderness he writes of Our Lord, under the evident influence of St. Augustine and St. Bernard. For him the great motive of the Incarnation is the fall of man, who had overturned the divine likeness in himself. Humanity he compares to the traveller robbed and wounded on the way to Jericho. The Good Samaritan comes — the Word was made flesh. This is God's work par excellence, capable of dumbfounding the very angels. The Word, the only begotten Son of the Father from all eternity, wishing not to remain alone, has granted us the honour of bearing by grace the name he himself bears by nature.[3] The contemplation of Jesus is the proper exercise for all degrees of the spiritual life, for he is the way and the life: but in various ways, according to the measure of true progress. Adam explains this in a sermon for the feast of St. Stephen.

Let those who amongst us are spiritual and are fortified in purity of conscience, and in whom there shines the clarity of interior gaze, raise their eyes to the Son of man standing at the right hand of the Father, to see his glory so great, even inconceivable, and hear, none the less, words which it is not lawful for man to utter[4] . . . But those who aspire to such heights must shed the grossness of humanity, bowed down and dark, and assume the rarefied state of pure and limpid spirituality, all the more because to his boon companion, his beloved — not a servant but a friend — the Lord says: "man shall not see me and live".[5] Let those who are yet unable to raise their eyes to the splendour of this brilliant Sun gaze on the human nature assumed and glorified at the right hand of God. Let them, I say, look upon that nature at the right hand of the Father, which never once committed any fault whatever while dwelling with men on earth, yet bore the ignominious and cruel penalty of death, the death of the Cross. Now, if any there be so encumbered with fancies, or so torn with remorse for their wrongs, or so tortured by the

[1] Ibid, 821.
[2] Sermo IV De Adventu Domini, P.L., 198, 117-118.
[3] P.L., 198, 117.
[4] Cf. II Cor. 12, 4.
[5] Exod. 33, 20.

movements of the senses, that they cannot give themselves to one or other of these ways, let them still keep before their eyes him of whom we are speaking, the Son of man, as he goes about, here and there, healing all that are oppressed by the devil[1] . . . let them cry out "Behold the Lamb of God, behold him who taketh away the sins of the world".[2] And let them not imagine they will gain little from thus gazing on him; their gain will be very great, since in a sense they see with their eyes, hear with their ears, and touch with their hands somewhat of the Word of life.[3]

For Adam, devotion to the Holy Eucharist and to the Sacred Humanity of Christ are one and the same; its chief aspect was gratitude to Jesus as the victim of sacrifice.

His devotion to Our Lady is simply the overflow of his regard for her Son, because she gives him to us. It is seen most strikingly in his sermons for the feasts of her Purification, Annunciation and Nativity. He continually exalts her divine maternity and perpetual virginity. He does not mention her Immaculate Conception, and on the authority of St. Augustine he says in regard to her Assumption only that heaven was far more worthy than the earth to have her.[4]

Adam is of particular interest to us as he is one of the few who tell of cloistral life as it was in England and Scotland in the twelfth century, and because he bears the fullest witness of any English writer to the spiritual life of both White Canons and Carthusians. The most important of his works from the spiritual angle, and at the same time the most read and studied of all he wrote, is the *De triplici genere contemplationis*,[5] considered to be his masterpiece from the literary as well as the theological point of view. It treats of God incomprehensible in himself, following St. Augustine in the tenth book of his *Confessions*, of Hell, how God permits evil without participating in it, and of predestination. His *Soliloquia de instructione animae*,[6] the longest of his works and written while he was still a Canon, was formerly attributed to his namesake Adam of St. Victor. It is in the form of a dialogue between Reason and the Soul, showing how the trials of community life can serve one on the way to perfection; it explains in detail the Premonstratensian formula of profession.

[1] Acts 10, 38.
[2] John 1, 36.
[3] 1 John 1, 1. P.L., 198, 298-299.
[4] Petit, *op. cit.*, p. 113.
[5] P.L., 198, 705 sqq.
[6] P.L., 198, 843 sqq.

The *De Quadripertito Exercitio Cellae*,[1] which he wrote when a Carthusian, is the last of his writings and said to be "one of the most celebrated writings of the middle ages".[2] As a Canon he had simply divided the spiritual exercises of the cell under three heads, reading, prayer and work. Now he introduces a fourth exercise, meditation. He divides meditation into eight degrees, making contemplation properly so called to be its last and highest degree.

Adam wrote the *De Quadripertito Exercitio Cellae* during the lifetime of St. Hugh of Lincoln, whose close friend and disciple he was. It represents without doubt the Carthusian ideal, not only as Adam saw it, but as experienced and lived by Hugh at Chartreuse. After a fervent insistence on the blessings of the Carthusian General Chapter, Adam goes on to the general characteristics of Carthusian life: humility, mortification, perfect renunciation of the world, the life of retreat in the silence and solitude of the cell. He speaks of detachment from temporals, and of the practice of personal poverty: "external exercises are to be qualified by poverty in dress, austerity in wearing the hair-cloth and frugality in food. Such poverty and austerity suggest two great gifts of God, lowliness of heart and mortification of the flesh; the one represses uprisings of elation in the mind, the other destroys the dross of sinful corruption, for these are the two chief fetters with which, in evil-doers, the old Enemy binds mankind . . . frugality in food will beat the Prince of cooks [the Devil!]". Adam is as insistent as any of his Carthusian predecessors on remaining poor: all things are to be rugged and most simple: the monk's place is rather with the beggar at the rich man's gates than with him who dines plenteously within;[3] at no time is his lot to be better, often it should be worse. The substance of this treatise concerns the four means whereby the solitary may dwell profitably in his solitude and reap the fullest favours of a life dedicated entirely to God, following in the footsteps of Christ: "after Christ, in the strength of Christ, till he come to Christ himself".[4] Lest the monk imitate Dina,[5] the personification of indolence, driven from Bethlehem to Moab, his solitude must not be of the body, but of the mind

1 P.L., 153, 799 sqq., where it is attributed to Guigo I.
2 *Dictionnaire de Spiritualité*, t. I, col. 196, art. *Adam l'Ecossais*.
3 Luke 16, 19.
4 P.L. 153, 807.   5 Cf. Gen 30, 21; 34, 2.

and heart. He must live constantly as a stranger to the 'world' (Adam uses the word in the Lord's sense: cp. John 17), constantly on his guard against *acedia*, one of the most dangerous temptations of the spiritual life, which is a companion of weariness and discouragement (*taedium*).[1] Adam is well aware that his readers will be those who are still human while their aim is so high. He sympathizes with them when the burden of life in solitude seems to be unbearable; but he warns them that the spiritual quiet of their cell is not regained by leaving it, by satisfying idle curiosity outside. The longer one has lived profitably there, he says, the more dangerous it is to wander long and far from it; a cell-dweller can live spiritually out of his cell no longer than a fish can live bodily out of water.[2]

Adam likens the eremitical way of life to the ladder of which Jacob dreamed and to 'the better part' of Mary, at the Master's feet. He insists on the need of being alone to pray; it is the reason that justifies the solitude, a severe test, which renders the soul supple by weaning it from all but God: "the trial of solitude is decisive, for those who are unable to bear it leave it . . ."[3] Such teaching is useful for every Christian worthy of the name, in the world with Christ, but not "of it". Our Lord himself has told us that "when thou shalt pray, enter into thy chamber, and having shut the door, pray to thy Father in secret, and thy Father who seeth in secret will repay thee".[4] All need some atmosphere of solitude, and silence of body, mind and heart, to grow in the loving knowledge of God, as surely as they seek it to grow in intimacy with one another, with some one other. But, continues Adam, in the long lonely hours a voice to his heart may tempt the solitary: "this solitary life, is it meant for me . . . are other religious at fault for getting on without it, the Cluniacs, the Cistercians? Why such waste of talents that could be of service to souls and to the Church?". The talents which Adam mentions are in fact the very ones that had made him an eloquent preacher and an able administrator when he was abbot of Dryburgh. It is telling to see that he dismisses such thoughts as mere temptations. Today they might be taken as possible inspirations; at least they would indicate the need for a reasoned justification

[1] Cf. *Dictionnaire de Spiritualité*, fasc. I (1932), col. 166, art. *Acedia*; fasc. VII (1927), c. 214, art. *Cassien*.
[2] P.L., 153, 815.
[3] P.L., 153, 749.
[4] Matt. 6, 18.

of the alleged superiority of the purely contemplative life. Adam's answer to such doubting is that the solitary must delve all the more deeply into the meaning of the eremitical life and what it stands for.

Of the four exercises of the solitary life, reading, meditation, prayer and work, "the greatest is prayer".[1] It is the most frequent of the exercises. It is a gift, which depends on unction from on high rather than on learning; for the Apostle says "we know not what we should ask for as we ought, but the Spirit himself asketh for us, with unspeakable groanings".[2] When we pray, we remember in our hearts, for very little do we utter with our lips, "this people honoureth me with their lips, but their heart is far from me".[3] Quoting the *Regula Monachorum* of St. Benedict, Adam says that prayer should be short and pure, unless by divine inspiration it be prolonged.[4] But how should we appear before God in prayer? God himself will tell you within your own heart without whose giving your prayer is not pleasing to him, nor of profit to yourself: he whose only word achieves what it says. "If you wish to pray, think on these three things; the way you approach prayer, how in the time of prayer you offer yourself to God, how you behave when it is over; that is, how unaffected and undisturbed you are when you begin it, how pure and undivided you are while it lasts, how sober, and serious you are when it devoutly comes to an end".[5] "If you want to know how to pray as purely as you ardently desire to, reflect on these four points: on him to whom you pray, on him through whom you pray, on what you pray about, on him who prays, namely yourself. Your heart must be wide open to encompass all these four at once; that is, God whose unction[6] will teach you better than any human learning, the mediator of God and man, Jesus Christ, your mind and tongue pleading, with your sins and weaknesses before you, like the publican who stands afar off, who would not so much as lift up his eyes to heaven but struck his breast.[7]

By reading, Adam means the careful and prayerful study of Holy Scripture; it is meant to raise the mind to God, and provide matter for worthy conversation for when monks meet to talk. So, "servant of God, dwelling in your cell alone but never

[1] P.L., 153, 802.   [2] Rom 8, 26.   [3] Isai 29, 13.   [4] Ch. 20.
[5] P.L., 153, 868.   [6] Cf. 1 John 2, 27.   [7] P.L., 153, 879.

lonely, from your studious reading of the Scriptures a ray of truth shines forth, bestowing the light of knowledge, most clear mental insight, according to that saying of St. Peter: 'And now the word of the prophets gives us more confidence than ever. It is with good reason that you are paying so much attention to that word; it will go on shining, like a lamp in some darkened room'."[1]

Of meditation the matter is again Holy Scripture—*ruminatio sacrae scripturae*; prolonging and outstripping the reading, it reaches to the marrow of the meaning of what is read. Just as reading without understanding is loss, so too, to forget what was read and understood is nothing else than to forfeit what was gained by both. Meditation is indispensable; reading without it is dangerous, "vain science", says Adam. Meditation makes for lasting maturity of mind, by curbing excesses. It prevents the mind from becoming foolishly elated beyond its limits, and from sinking limply below them. By meditation a monk achieves that state of purity of soul necessary for prayer.

The reason why Adam, when speaking of the material for reading and meditations, speaks only of Holy Scripture, is because it is unique, with a meaning quite apart. "The dignity of Holy Scripture consists in this that, unlike all unsanctified writings, its events as well as its words have a meaning. All the liberal arts are subservient to it. By allegory is brought to light the present or future mysteries of the Church, hidden figuratively either in the phrases or the facts".[2] Thus Adam makes the careful reading and deep meditation of the Bible the indispensable basis of allegorical transference which leads on to a doctrinal order of things, to a symbolical theology.

Meditation, Adam continues, is of many kinds. It is the source of instruction, sorrow and fear, love and comfort, piety and compassion, discretion and humility, renewal and rebirth; admiration. Finally there is that kind of meditation in which the mind, sober, saintly, free, in a gaze that is not spiritual only nor rational but rather intuitive, perceives amidst spiritual truths Truth itself. In Truth all things, past, present and future are one. This intuitive gaze on Truth itself is no longer merely meditation: it may be called high contemplation. It concerns itself with things invisible, that is, with the soul, angels and the divine

[1] 2 Pet 1, 19.   [2] *De tripartito Tabernaculo*, P.L., 198, 697.

nature itself. Here the solitary learns to listen to three spiritual voices speaking to him: the voice of his own heart, of the angels and of Him who created the other two. Each voice has its own way of speaking. Man differs from the rest of God's creation in that he is spiritual, as well as fleshly, and can "bend all his mind thither where Christ sits at the right hand of God the Father"; and "alone his soul is made after the image and likeness of God". Further, the solitary, when he prays to his Father in secret, "in the inner sanctuary of his soul, paces with the solemn and persevering steps of his enlightened mind and warm affections, and surveys that mansion of blessed spirits who in heaven always see the Father's face". Finally, "in your cell without let or hindrance, you are on fire with love for God; you pray devotedly to him and desire to come into God's inmost heart". For Adam, it is love that plays the essential part in contemplation. Love is its cause: "Without love, sight is impossible".

Adam of Dryburgh plays a vital rôle in the history of medieval spirituality. It is not merely that his century is the golden age; but his writings reflect the spirit of two Orders which were responsible for promoting the two facets of the perfect life— the Premonstratensians, with their combination of cloistral life and priestly apostolate, and the Carthusians, with their uncompromising return to the predominantly eremitical mode of life. In his writings Adam retains the old liking for allegory and symbolism in the interpretation of Scripture, whilst preparing the ground for the more scholastic treatises of the thirteenth century with their tendency to analysis and manifold distinctions. By contrast he is less simple than his forebears, but less scientific than those who were to come after: more contemplative, less intellectual. When we read the *De Quadripertito Exercitio Cellae* we are aware that it represents a transition; but even though the work is expressly written for Carthusians as a guide for their interior life, we have not yet reached the period when we can speak with any certainty of a 'school' of spirituality. There is nothing to show that the early Carthusians belonged to any such 'school'. In any case, schools are always less revealing than individuals; and Adam is writing especially for the individual— the solitary. That is why so much of what he says will always be apposite for those who are in earnest about life in Christ.

8. STEPHEN OF SAWLEY

Hugh Farmer

STEPHEN OF SAWLEY is not a well-known medieval figure. About thirty years ago two of his *opuscula* were edited, under the apparently un-English name of Etienne de Sallai, by the late Dom Wilmart, to whom all students of the medieval religious outlook owe such an immense debt. More recently Stephen's directory to Cistercian novices was edited by Dom Mikkers, who is also preparing two other of his short works for the press. This sketch, based only on published material, must necessarily be provisional.[1]

Although so long forgotten, Stephen was an important man in his day. Born at Eston in Cleveland, Yorkshire, he became a monk at Fountains towards the end of the twelfth century. He was cellarer of this most important Cistercian abbey in the North for several years until he was elected abbot of Sawley in the West Riding about 1223. From there he became abbot of Newminster, Sawley's mother-house, in 1234. Yet a third time the choice of his brethren called him to high office: he became abbot of Fountains, the mother-house of Newminster and other abbeys, in 1247. His reign was a short one, for he died in 1252 while visiting the abbey of Vaudey in Lincolnshire. There he was buried and miracles were reported at his tomb.[2]

When he became abbot of Fountains, his house was at the height of its power. It had been founded in 1132 by thirteen monks of St. Mary's, York in search of a more austere life, under the protection of archbishop Thurstan. The beginnings were difficult. On a wild site in Skeldale they built huts under a spread-

---

1 A. Wilmart, "*Les méditations d'Etienne de Sallai,*" Revue d'Ascetique et de Mystique, X (1929, 368-415; "*Le Triple Exercise d'Etienne de Sallai,*" Ibid., XI (1930), 355-74; E. Mikkers, "*Le Speculum Novitii d'Etienne de Sallai,*" Analecta O.C.R., 1946, 3-32. There is no mention of Stephen in Dom David Knowles, *The Religious Orders in England.*

2 Cf. J. Macnulty, "Stephen of Eston, abbot of Sawley, Newminster and Fountains," *Yorks. Archaeological Journal,* XXXI (1934), 49-64 and *The Sawley Cartulary* (1936). See also J. Walbran, *Memorials of Fountains Abbey* (Surtees Society, 1863), especially the account of the abbots of the house.

ing elm-tree and cultivated a garden round it: conditions were poor and life hard. In time the community grew, attracting novices of wealth and standing and inevitably losing both the advantages and the disadvantages of the primitive, pioneering days. Very soon they became a power in the ecclesiastical politics of the North. They bitterly opposed, at St. Bernard's instigation, the election of St. William of York, and provided in their abbot Thurstan, appointed through St. Bernard's influence, an energetic and successful rival, who ruled the see of York from 1147 to 1153. But the experiment was not repeated. Fountains, in spite of being raided and burnt by St. William's supporters, went from strength to strength. Its wealth increased and so did its library, the monastic quarters were largely rebuilt, and, even more significant, the church was extended eastwards to form the beautiful Tau-shaped presbytery which was so soon to be copied and improved on in the even more spectacular Nine Altars transept at Durham. When Stephen became abbot of Fountains he succeeded John of Kent, who in a rule of twenty-eight years had built a cloister, infirmary and guesthouse besides making these additions to the church. Stephen's writings are indicative of the spirit which flourished in thirteenth-century Cistercian abbeys, and provide rare evidence of their outlook when the days of St. Aelred and Gilbert of Hoyland were over. His important offices enable us to regard him as a really authoritative spokesman.

His least known, but perhaps most interesting, work is the *Mirror for Novices*. Such an intimate guide to the novice's day, telling us how he thought, prayed and went to confession, is an extremely rare type of document, and therefore all the more precious.[1] It opens abruptly without a prologue:

> When you go to confession, use these words if you wish, adding to or subtracting from them according to your culpability. "My thoughts often wander through different places, especially during the Divine Office. I have thought too much about building the church, making books or arranging the house, and about the running of horses and similar things. Sometimes I take pleasure in impure thoughts, sometimes I consent to the desire for food, drink and sleep. Sometimes I judge others' words and work in my heart and even by

[1] The only comparable spiritual directory of medieval English *Black* Benedictines known to me occurs in MS Bodley 435, an Eynsham manuscript written c. 1300 containing a customary of that monastery, composed by Thomas of Woodeaton before 1230. Details about the novitiate may be found on ff. 3, 13, 19, 21-22, etc.

sign or word. Sometimes I murmur because of ill-health or supposed contempt. Or else at the fasting and vigils, the rough food and hard work, at corrections or injuries received, at permissions refused or disagreeable obediences imposed. I am exalted for my voice and beauty, my good family and fine way of speaking; I desire to be recognised as better than others. I like to think of myself as someone when I am nothing. Sometimes I speak in a worldly way or words of detraction or deceit. I have been angry and disobedient; I have indulged my selfwill, refusing to pray or hear Mass when I should. I waste much time in trivialities, torpor and tepidity. Sometimes I am full of resentment . . . I fear the eyes of men more than those of God. I come later to choir than to table. I obey unwillingly, exalting myself and despising others; I say the psalms and other prayers inattentively . . ." Here then is the mirror; when you see that you are wounded, go to confession.[1]

Immediately after confession the prayer *Ave sancta et gloriosa et perpetua virgo Maria* should be said three times with genuflexions. This version of the Hail Mary occurs elsewhere in Stephen's works and is one of their distinguishing marks.[2] After this, prayers of thanksgiving should be said, for Christ's mysteries and Redemption, for God's immense benefits such as deliverance from spiritual danger and the grace of a monastic vocation.

The abbot then takes the novice through the monastic day, teaching him especially to cultivate prayer, meditation and recollection at all times. When woken in the morning, he should immediately leap out of bed with a thought for Christ's Resurrection and a prayer of thanksgiving, with a *Requiem aeternam* for the dead.[3] In choir he should keep the guard of his eyes and heart, with the image of the suffering Christ always before him. At Matins he should consider the joys of the angels, at Lauds Christ taken prisoner, at Prime Christ before Pilate and scourged at the pillar, at Terce Our Lord on the cross or ascending into Heaven or else the coming of the Holy Spirit at Pentecost. At Sext he should embrace Christ's feet in spirit, using His nails as a pillow, at None think of His death and go with Him to Limbo; at Vespers return to Calvary and care for His body with Nico-

[1] *Speculum novitii*, c. 1.
[2] "*Ave, sancta et gloriosa et perpetua et pia Dei genitrix virgo semper Maria, gratia plena, Dominus tecum, benedicta tu in mulieribus et benedictus Dominus Iesus, dulcis fructus benedicti ventris tui. Amen.*" This use of the Hail Mary without the "Holy Mary" but with the genuflexions or prostrations which accompanied it was usual at this time; cf. H. Thurston, art. "Hail Mary" in *Catholic Encyclopedia* and "Ave Maria" in *Dictionnaire de Spiritualité*.
[3] *Speculum novitii*, c. 3.

demus and Joseph of Arimathea, and at Compline watch at Christ's tomb.[1]

His prayer is not over when he leaves choir. He should return saying, "Lord, I still have my private prayers of petition and praise to say to you apart from the others." At all times he should meditate, but especially, as St. Jerome says, in the early morning before the third hour. Twice a day he should pray privately in the church, twice a week go to confession.[2]

His habitual attitude should be one of thanksgiving. Remaining content with this and meditation will enable him to grow his spiritual feathers. He should remain in this state until he is told, "Friend, go up higher" to more lofty and subtle contemplation. He should appropriate verses of the psalms for adoration, praise and thanksgiving and form in his heart Christ walking in the monastic choir, followed by angels carrying twelve baskets of fragments, and He will say, "Open your mouth and I will fill it." Hence he will rejoice, realising that those who seek Him lack nothing and that even in temptation thanksgiving should be in the heart and on the lips.[3]

The subjects of meditation should be the mysteries of Our Lord's life, such as the Nativity, the Baptism, the Passion (in detail), the Resurrection and Ascension. But not all at once. The event in question should be called to mind by thinking of both the physical details and the spiritual significance of the scene. Thus the Annunciation should be evoked by considering Our Lady (following St. Aelred) reading the prophecy of Isaiah when the angel appeared and her feeling of unspeakable joy when she received the fullness of grace and realised how the salvation of the world awaited her *Fiat*.[4]

All during the day the novice should remain in the presence of God. When the bell goes for choir, he should give thanks that God has deigned to invite him to associate with the angels. When invited to hear private Masses, he should willingly accept. When he goes to the Chapter-House, he should practise meekness and patience, accepting "proclamation" like Christ before Pilate.[5]

---

[1] *Speculum novitii*, c. 23. St. Edmund also provided meditations on the mysteries of Our Lord's life for each of the canonical Hours, and on the Nativity for Matins; cf. W. A. Pantin, *The English Church in the Fourteenth Century*, pp. 222-4.

[2] *Speculum novitii*, cc. 7, 8, 18.   [3] *Ibid.*, c. 4.

[4] *Ibid.*, c. 6; cf. St. Aelred, *Sermo 8 in Annuntiatione B. Mariae*, P.L. 195, 254.

[5] *Speculum novitii*, cc. 9-10. Proclamation is the public accusation by monks of each other's breaches of the rule. The good monk does not excuse himself, but promises to amend.

When called to work, he should remember Adam's disobedience and rejection from Paradise together with the labour of Christ, especially in the Passion. While at manual work he should not lose his attention to God; if there is a rest there, he should not sit in a corner by himself, but join the others like Jesus among the doctors. In the refectory he should be neither the first nor the last to arrive. He must not go without food, but eat at least one of the cooked dishes, and both "if they are good." While he is growing he should eat at least three-quarters of a pound of bread each day and drink at least three-quarters of the wine or beer served to him. But above all, he should be content with what he is given, always blessing God and never murmuring.[1]

His reading is carefully planned. When he first comes to the monastery, he should read the Psalms, the Antiphoner and the *Consuetudines*, together with the *Vitae Patrum* and the Dialogues of St. Gregory. Afterwards, if he is able, he should take the more solid food of the Old and New Testaments, the Rule of St. Benedict, the Confessions of St. Augustine and his *Enarrationes in Psalmos*, especially on psalms 30-109 and 119-150. He should also read Cassian, selected letters of St. Jerome, the works of William of St. Thierry and St. Aelred. Gilbert of Hoyland on the Canticle is warmly recommended, but not, curiously enough, St. Bernard, although his famous passage on studying neither for curiosity nor vanity is cited by Stephen and made his own. Reading should pass easily into soliloquy: sometimes the novice should close his book and say, "How much dost thou owe the Lord, O my soul," etc. He should altogether avoid sophistical argument and contentious questions and whatever disturbs peace of soul.[2]

The principal moral qualities demanded of him are prompt obedience, a readiness to rejoice at others' virtue and fervour, assiduity without ostentation in serving them, and a detachment which enables him to receive easily the refusal of permission in habitual joy and thanksgiving.[3]

These are practised in the ordinary course of the monastic day, during the various exercises already mentioned. At the end of the day, when going to bed, he should think of the grave, commend himself to God and ask for protection from sin and danger.

[1] *Speculum novitii*, cc. 11-13.
[2] *Ibid.*, cc. 15-16.
[3] *Ibid.*, cc. 19. 22.

Again he should say *Ave, sancta et gloriosa et perpetua Virgo,* etc. If he goes to sleep, well and good; if not, he should say the Athanasian Creed seven times or else the seven penitential psalms. These will cure him of insomnia![1]

Temptation will certainly come. He will suffer from torpor and impurity and be tempted to impatience, disobedience and vainglory. When the monotony of monastic observance weighs upon him, he should remember that no labour is too hard, no time too long to acquire eternal glory: he is not yet perfect and never will be. If he is gripped by desire for travel, let him remember Dinah and Tamar and realise that the midday devil is responsible.[2] From the time of his entry into the monastery he must never receive or foster the suggestion that he would help himself and others more in a different religious order or a different state of life. If he does hearken to these suggestions, they will tear his soul apart, making it lose all wisdom and unction. Boredom, horror and despair will ensue. Instead he should consider the patience of Christ at the column and remember St. Jerome's words, "If the solitude of the desert annoys you, walk in spirit in Paradise; when you walk there, you are no longer in the cloister."[3]

Soon after this citation the *Mirror of Novices* ends almost as abruptly as it began. It is an interesting and authoritative spiritual guide to the Cistercian novitiate. Little of it has dated and most of its recommendations can still be followed. But one of the habitual weaknesses of medieval monasteries was the presence within them of unsuitable subjects. One may well think that teaching like Stephen's about temptation contributed to keep them there instead of weeding out the unsuitable. Although St. Bernard insisted against Cluny on the year's novitiate, it would probably be a mistake to think that he regarded his novices, still less his professed monks, as at any time spiritually free to leave the monastery: only long afterwards did the Church in her wisdom devise solutions such as exclaustration, and insist more clearly on the individual's freedom of choice. By experience it was learnt that it was not desirable to keep in the monasteries

---

[1] *Ibid.,* c. 20.

[2] This comparison is also found in Adam of Dryburgh, *De quadripertito exercitio cellae,* c. 10, P.L. 153, 817-9, developed perhaps from St. Gregory, *Regulae pastoralis liber,* c. 29, P.L. 77, 108.

[3] *Speculum novitii,* c. 24; St. Jerome, *Epistola ad Heliodorum monachum,* P.L. 22, 354.

monks whose hearts were no longer there. But within its limitations, written for novices rather than adult monks and reflecting
in some respects a point of view no longer shared by many, the
Mirror of Novices is an interesting and useful work. It shows that
Fountains of the thirteenth century was still fervent, and that
even if there is no record of a Fountains monk of this century,
like his predecessor of the twelfth, receiving an intellectual vision
of the Holy Trinity,[1] at least the novices were well formed at
the beginning of their monastic life in habits which might one
day dispose them for similar favours.

The *Triple Exercise* is a work of a different kind. Addressed,
like the *Speculum*, to monks, it deals not with monastic observance,
but with prayer. Its subject-matter for meditation is three-fold:
the grandeur and goodness of God, the privileges of Mary, and
the happiness of Heaven. Perhaps more interesting than the
presentation of these truths is the instruction on "technique,"
absolutely simple and direct:

> At whatever time of the day or night you begin, banish all bodily
> imaginings and raise your soul to the one supreme principle, the
> Creator of all, Father, Son and Holy Spirit, not as though we could
> comprehend Him, but praying in faith, let us give thanks to Him
> for all His benefits, both general and particular.[2]

But a certain elaboration follows. One should also recall the
happiness of Eden and consider the Fall, Baptism and one's own
sins. These should be confessed in general every day and the more
important ones in detail. We should beseech the Trinity to look
mercifully on our own trinity of a sluggish and sickly will, a
cloudy and erroneous intellect and a wavering and dissipated
memory. Following St. Augustine, we should ask each Divine
Person to fill and direct each of these three faculties. The medi-

---

[1] Ralph Haget, afterwards abbot of Fountains, once saw the Holy Trinity on a Sunday
at Lauds during two verses of psalm 117: "Nothing was there of form or figure, and yet
I saw in a blissful vision three Persons in Unity. I saw and knew the unbegotten Father,
the only-begotten Son and the Holy Spirit proceeding from both. . . . From that moment
no misfortune, no sadness has ever come to me which could not be mitigated by the
remembrance of that vision . . . and such confidence and hope was poured into my soul
by this showing that I could never after doubt of my salvation." Cited by Dom David
Knowles, *The Monastic Order in England*, pp. 357-8 from *Memorials of Fountains Abbey*,
pp. 121-2.

[2] *Triple Exercise*, p. 362. Mr. Eric Colledge, in *The Medieval Mystics of England*, pp. 43-4,
notes that this treatise is remarkable because it does not bother about external rules, but
goes straight to contemplation, and that in spite of its simplicity of intention and execution, it is a modern work. This was also the opinion of Dom Wilmart.

H

tation should conclude with the prayer of thanksgiving or one of praise like the *Gloria Patri* or *Te invocamus*.[1]

Stephen's teaching on Mary will be considered below: his meditation on Heaven is like a commentary on the feast of All Saints. Again he emphasises the need for simplicity and the absence of curiosity: the monk should above all trust in the intercession of those whom he invokes, whether patriarchs, prophets, apostles, martyrs, monks or virgins. Here are his words on the prophets, among whom St. John the Baptist is singled out for special praise:

> After these (the patriarchs), look upon the praiseworthy line of prophets, to whom God spoke and showed His secrets, so that, under the Holy Spirit's guidance, they might see in the present events like the birth of Christ from a Virgin, the Passion and Resurrection which were really far in the future. . . . Therefore commend yourself humbly to them and ask that as they were outstanding in knowledge of God and faith and assiduous in meditation and fervent devotion, so also they may obtain for you graces of illumination to despise temporal things and of love to desire eternal ones.[2]

He ends by contrasting the glory of heaven and our own unworthiness. We should make our own the prayer of the Prodigal Son and implore the prayers of all the saints that the devil may never harm us and that our prayers, through theirs, may reach the eternal temple of God.

Although inspired by the Liturgy, this meditation, like that *On the Joys of Mary*, is in some respects a modern work. The Cistercians for whom it was written did not confine themselves to "period" prayers or to an outlook which excluded all recent developments. Stephen is a witness to thirteenth-century Yorkshire monastic mariology, not as expressed in a learned treatise, but as lived and prayed in the cloister.

England had been remarkable for its Marian devotion. Before the Conquest, while others were disputing and discussing the doctrine, the feast of the Conception of Mary had been introduced. And where St. Anselm and St. Bernard had hesitated, the English Eadmer and other twelfth-century writers had

[1] Cf. St. Augustine, *De Trinitate*, 1, XIV, cc. 6-8, 12, P.L. 42, 1041-5, 1048, and *ibid.*, 1, XV, c. 51, P.L. 42, 1098. The *Te invocamus* is part of a responsory from the office of the Holy Trinity, based on an invocation of Alcuin added to his *De fide sanctae Trinitatis*. P.L., 101, 56.

[2] *Triple Exercise*, p. 369.

boldly defended it. Anselm, abbot of Bury, William of Malmesbury and Dominic of Evesham had been prominent in propagating the anecdotes about Our Lady's efficacious intercession which came to be known as the Miracles of the Virgin. But devotion to Mary was by no means confined to the learned. Church-dedications to her in medieval England numbered more than two thousand, or as many as twenty per cent of all dedications, about equal in number to those of All Saints and St. Peter put together. And in the thirteenth century Lady chapels were often added to the east end of important churches, while reforming bishops like Grosseteste, following the Synod of Durham in 1217, were insisting that the common people should know the Hail Mary. Popular shrines were numerous also, and surviving illuminations, roof-bosses and wall-paintings testify to belief not only in episodes like the Annunciation clearly in Scripture, but also in truths like the Assumption and the Coronation of Our Lady as queen of Heaven.

Stephen's meditations *On the Joys of Mary* are not a profoundly original work: they are to a large extent developments and glosses on the texts of the Liturgy. As in the *Triple Exercise*, the procedure is interesting, for it reflects an elaboration usually associated with writers of the Counter-Reformation and after. Each Joy is worked out in a uniform way. First comes a meditation on the subject and then an "elevation" of joy to Our Lady. Thirdly an appropriate petition is formed, and lastly comes the glossed version of the Hail Mary already mentioned. Each section is quite short. The fifteen joys do not altogether correspond to the mysteries of the rosary. They are: Our Lady's nativity, her vowed virginity, the Annunciation, the conception of Christ, the Visitation, the Nativity of Christ, the visit of the Magi, the Presentation in the Temple, the finding in the Temple, the marriage feast of Cana, the standing by the Cross, the Resurrection, the Ascension, Pentecost and the Assumption.

In a conventional introduction the author pleads his unworthiness:

> All my consolation, life, sweetness and hope depend after God on this most sweet Virgin, and as I am all the more conscious of my lack of merit, so do I trust in the help of this mother of mercy, in whose honour and praise I proclaim myself her unworthy servant. In my foolishness I will speak what little I know, aiming only at

edifying the simple, without prejudice to higher understanding and experience.[1]

Like his other works, it was written at the request of monks, and as in them, there is the same emphasis on simplicity and unpretentiousness. The first meditation begins thus:

> Consider in what misery the world was established when death reigned from Adam to Christ, when the sin of prevarication dominated the world and covered all with so much darkness, ignorance and despair that there was no holy, no innocent, no just man, not even the Baptist himself who did not go down to Limbo. For those who sat in the darkness and shadow of death the Virgin Mary arose like the dawn from the darkness, like the morning star in the midst of the cloud, and brought forth the hope of salvation . . .[2]

Then the elevation :

> Rejoice, glorious mother of God and holy Mary ever a virgin, who by your holy birth did proclaim joy to the whole world. You announced liberation to the souls in Limbo, salvation to men on earth, glory to the angels in Heaven and the rebuilding of the heavenly city.

The petition follows :

> Therefore, sweet lady, I ask you that in memory of the joy of your birth you enlighten my dark and wretched conscience with the light of spiritual desire so that I cast away the dark vanity of this world and by your help merit the joy of the light of truth, O clement, O loving, O sweet Mary.
>
> Hail, holy and glorious, ever-loving Mother of God, ever virgin Mary, full of grace, the Lord is with thee, blessed art thou among women and blessed is the sweet fruit of thy blessed womb, the Lord Jesus. Amen.

The other joys are treated in the same way, but after each group of five is a *pausatio* to resume the mysteries just considered. This must not be an excuse for idleness, but an occasion for diligently considering the excellence of Mary's motherhood. Noteworthy is the consideration of Mary by the cross as one of the joys. The sorrow of Mary is here described too, but the emphasis is on her joy at the redemption of the human race:

> Did you not remember in the straits of so much sorrow, lady, God's mercy in redeeming you and the whole world? Did you not

---

[1] *Les Meditations d'Etienne de Sallai*, p. 392.
[2] *Ibid.*, p. 393.

rejoice with incomparable joy when you knew in the immovable
certainty of faith that the whole world was being redeemed by
your son's precious blood, that hell was being stripped of its power,
the strong devil bound and the gate of heaven opened?[1]

This emphasis is notably different from that of two hundred
years later with the frequent pietas, the feast of Our Lady of Pity
and its taste for Lathbury's commentary on Lamentations with
its excessive preoccupation with the sufferings of Mary.[2] Stephen
of Sawley, for all his limitations, presented a more balanced
picture. His principal interest is as a witness to a tradition of
monastic spirituality that was still lively, meeting the needs of
the age and the spirit of the monastic founders. Like the Monk
of Farne a century later, Stephen was a figure of the second rank
who wrote for a very limited readership. Each in his way is
evidence of the monastic outlook at a time of few outstanding
monks in this country, and each should make us beware of con-
demning too hastily periods, monasteries or whole Orders which
did not produce the famous mystic or genius. At most periods
the monastic life is humdrum and uneventful: the slopes and the
valleys are part of the picture every bit as much as the lofty
mountain peaks.

[1] *Ibid.*, p. 406.
[2] For Lathbury, cf. B. Smalley, *English Friars and Antiquity*, pp. 223-7.

9. EDMUND OF ABINGDON

C. H. Lawrence

MONG THOSE writings on the spiritual life which helped to
form the religious sentiment of the later Middle Ages and
which the Reformation covered with long oblivion, an
important place must be assigned to the *Speculum Ecclesiae*, or
Mirror of Holy Church,[1] by St. Edmund of Abingdon. That it
was widely read, especially by Englishmen, in the thirteenth and
fourteenth centuries, is attested both by the large number of
manuscripts of the work scattered over the libraries of England
and the continent and by the many different versions, French and
English as well as Latin, that were in circulation. Its popularity
may be partly explained by the special boost that it gained from
the canonisation of the author. In 1244, four years after Edmund's
death, a papal process of inquiry was opened and on 16 December
1246, in a public consistory held in Lyons Cathedral, Pope
Innocent IV formally inscribed him in the catalogue of the saints.
The activities of the postulators and the gathering of evidence
aroused widespread interest in England. In the decades after
the canonisation many Englishmen made the journey to the shrine
at Pontigny Abbey, following in the steps of King Henry III.
Lives of the saint were written and were translated from Latin
into French and English for popular consumption. It is obvious
that the rapid spread of devotion to St. Edmund stimulated and
maintained interest in his work and that his canonisation gave
him a special title to be considered a magisterial guide to the
spiritual life.

[1] A version of the Latin text was published by M. de la Bigne in *Bibliotheca Patrum et
Veterum Auctorum Ecclesiasticorum*, 3rd. edit., vol. 5 (Paris 1610), cols. 983-1004. Unless
otherwise stated, my chapter references are to this edition. The French version, together
with a preliminary classification of the manuscripts of English provenance, was published
by H. W. Robbins, *La Merure de Seinte Eglise*, limited edition (Lewisburg 1925). Two
Middle English versions from the Thornton and Vernon manuscripts were printed by
C. Horstman, *Yorkshire Writers: Richard Rolle*, vol. I (1895), pp. 219-61. A modern
translation by F. M. Steele, *The Mirror of St. Edmund*, unfortunately reproduced a short
and defective version from which much of the most interesting matter is omitted. The
evidences for the life of St. Edmund will be found in the present writer's *St. Edmund of
Abingdon: a Study in Hagiography and History* (1960).

Apart from all this accidental publicity, reasons for the lasting success of the *Speculum* can be found in the character of the work itself. It offered in simple and direct language a comprehensive plan for the achievement of spiritual perfection. It led the aspirant through the lowlier stages of dogmatic instruction and meditation to a point where, in the concluding chapters, his feet were placed upon the traditional ladder of contemplative prayer. Moreover, in its final form, the treatise was adapted to the needs of many different sorts of people. Although it was originally designed for religious, the author reshaped it so that it served the needs of secular clergy also and of lay people. As compared with the exalted doctrine of Richard of St. Victor or the profound and subtle introspection of the *Cloud of Unknowing*, much of the *Speculum* appears to be pedestrian. But this was its strength. It was of its time. It met the needs of a rapidly widening public in a traditional but satisfying way.

Few devotional writers of the Middle Ages are so copiously documented as the author of the *Speculum*. The outlines of his life can be reconstructed in some detail. He was born at Abingdon, of relatively humble and obscure parents, in about the year 1175. According to one tradition, the father abandoned the family while the children were still young, in order to take the monastic habit. At all events, it is clear that the task of bringing up the family fell wholly on Edmund's mother and that she proved more than equal to the task. The influence of this devout and formidable woman is apparent at many points in his career. According to the Dominican theologian Robert Bacon, it was the appearance of her inexorable shade in his Oxford classroom that drove Edmund to fly from the frivolities of the quadrivium and embark on the theology course at Paris.

Edmund was sent to Oxford for his elementary schooling in grammar. Some of the best known of the hagiographical anecdotes cluster about these childhood days: the encounter with the Christ Child outside the town in the meadows, and the mystical betrothal to Our Lady. Edmund was still only a boy when he was sent off with his brother Robert to begin the Arts course at Paris. He incepted there as a Master and then returned to Oxford, where he taught in the Arts faculty for upwards of six years. Various fragments of evidence suggest that his regency in Arts extended from about 1195 to 1201, crucial and exciting years in the schools when the nascent university was formulating its constitution and the New Logic was penetrating the Oxford curriculum. At the end of this period Edmund went back to Paris to study theology. The following years are obscure. It is certain that he held at least one benefice during this time, but its whereabouts cannot be traced. Whether he incepted or taught in the theological faculty at Paris is uncertain. He returned home and, after a year's residence at the Augustinian priory of Merton, he incepted in theology at Oxford. There is good reason for placing this event in 1214, the year in which regular teaching was resumed at Oxford after the papal legate had made peace between the university and the civic authorities.

Edmund's distinction in the schools brought him to the notice of Bishop Richard le Poore, who in 1222 appointed him Treasurer of Salisbury Cathedral. He held this office, with the prebend of Calne in Wiltshire, until he was elected archbishop in 1233. His migration to Salisbury, while it probably removed him from the Oxford scene, did not end his teaching career. Richard le Poore had gathered about himself a learned and distinguished chapter and Salisbury had long had a vigorous cathedral school. A letter written by the bishop and chapter to postulate Edmund's canonisation contains references which suggest that, like several distinguished university masters of the thirteenth century, he continued to lecture in the less strenuous and competitive atmosphere of the cathedral precinct.

His election to the see of Canterbury in September 1233 brought Edmund on to the full stage of public events, where he remained until his death on 16 November 1240. The details of his stormy and litigious pontificate are not our concern. He was, it seems, a compromise candidate for the archbishopric whom the Pope nominated to the Canterbury chapter after three previous elections had been set aside. In some ways the choice was a curious one. A scholar by training and an ascetic by long acquired habit, Edmund was by instinct a recluse. His only apprenticeship to administrative and political responsibilities had been his years as a member of the chapter of Salisbury and those who knew him during this time testified that he found administrative business distasteful and that he could hardly be induced to examine the accounts or to attend to chapter business. He was happiest in his study, or quietly ministering to the wants of his rustic parishioners at Calne, or in retreat among his Cistercian friends at Stanley Abbey, where he often spent half the year. It is hard to avoid the impression that as an archbishop, Edmund was an occupational misfit.

Two distinct but converging traditions shaped Edmund's conception of the spiritual life. One was the traditional body of ascetical doctrine transmitted by monastic teachers and embodied in the twelfth century in the writings of the Cistercians and Victorines, the other was the teaching of the schools. Edmund throughout his career remained in close touch with the monastic life in its various forms and must have been well conversant with monastic spirituality. One of his university vacations was spent at Reading Abbey and before incepting as a theologian he stayed for a year at Merton, where he shared fully in the exacting liturgical life of the community. But the most lasting and significant association that he formed was with the Cistercians. It was his old Oxford pupil, Stephen of Lexington, who brought him into the Cistercian orbit. Stephen had quitted Edmund's theological school to take the Cistercian habit at Quarr and a few years later, when he had been made abbot of Stanley, he was able to offer his master a welcome refuge from the tiresome demands of chapter business. This attachment to the Cistercians remained throughout the rest of Edmund's life. During his last journey to Rome he stayed at Pontigny, where he sought, and was granted, confraternity. It was in accordance with his last wish that he was buried there. As will appear, the monastic tradition of ascetical theology is strongly represented in the *Speculum*. Indeed, in its first recension, it was designed for the use of religious. On the other hand, there is little trace of the new type of humanistic religious sentiment which was disseminated by the Franciscans. As archbishop, Edmund showed a sympathetic interest in the Mendicant Orders and gave them his patronage, but his formative years were passed in the pre-Franciscan age. He retired from university teaching two years before the arrival of the Friars Minor in Oxford.

Edmund was before all else a Schoolman and the Paris schools exercised a pervasive influence on his life and work. In the first half of the thirteenth century the theological faculty at Oxford was a tributary of the main stream which ran through the classrooms of Paris. If we look at the teachers who ruled the schools at Paris in the first decade of the century, when Edmund was studying there, we find a group of outstanding men who shared a common approach to theological problems and who were formulating a new kind of Biblical exegesis. The most distinguished of them was the Englishman, Stephen Langton, the future archbishop, who in 1206 was removed from the academic scene by his promotion to the cardinalate. The group also included Peter of Poitiers, now in his old age, and the Italian scholar Prevostin, both of them pupils of Peter Comestor, John of Abbeville, Robert Curzon, another Englishman who was elevated to the cardinalate, and, from the year 1206 onwards, Philip the Chancellor of Paris. The common factor in the approach of these men was the new attention that they gave to the literal sense of the Biblical text and to its historical context, and their concern with practical problems of moral and pastoral theology. "The discipline of Holy Scripture," writes Peter the Chanter, himself a teacher who helped to form the minds of this group, "consists of three things: lecturing (on the text), disputation, and preaching." The Parisian masters of this period, who administered this programme, were aware that they were doing more than propagating a race of scholars. They had the responsibility of training in their classrooms the future pastors and rulers of the Church.

Many of the Scriptural glosses of these early masters survive to show how they conceived of their task. When they expounded the "spiritual" sense of the text, they made it the basis for moral instruction, often using lively anecdotes to press home the point, as a good preacher would do. The academic lecture, in fact, shaded off into the sermon. At least one famous English preacher, Odo of Cheriton, drew much of his sermon material from Langton's university lectures on the Scriptural text. A by-product of this school were the Moralities, a series of homiletic comments on individual books of the Bible. Edmund's *Moralities on the Psalms* is one of these and is a typical work of its kind. It survives in only a single manuscript, written in the thirteenth century, now in the library of Worcester Cathedral. It is in fact the only known survivor of Edmund's academic works. The Psalter lent itself particularly well to this type of instruction and Moralities on the Psalms have been left by many of the Paris masters. Often they consist only of the homiletic matter which has been excerpted from the full commentary. This is so with the Moralities of St. Edmund. What we have is not a complete gloss, but only the excerpted moralisations, which give the work the character of a series of rather desultory *obiter dicta*. What is more, it lacks any of the vivid human illustrations or personal reminiscences which do so much to enliven the commentaries of some of the earlier masters.

The *Speculum* is not a product of the schools, but it shows in many ways the imprint of the ideas which were being inculcated at Paris in the early thirteenth century. It is an attempt by an academic theologian to provide spiritual and moral instruction for a wider public outside the classroom and, as such, it is an example of the way in which, in the lives of the great scholar bishops, such as Grosseteste and Richard le Poore and Edmund himself, the scientific learning of the schools illuminated and inspired pastoral activity. It reflects that awareness of new needs and urgent tasks which made the period an age of ecclesiastical reform. A leading part in this movement for reform was played by the papacy. Two great Lateran councils held in 1179 and 1215 outlined a far-reaching programme, a central point of which was the question of raising the intellectual and spiritual level of the parish clergy. The proliferation of schools in the twelfth century and the rise of three great European universities had, by creating a highly educated *corps d'élite*, in some ways accentuated the problem of the unlettered peasant priest living in a predominantly oral society. Something had to be done to remedy his deficiencies if the minimal requirements of annual confession and communion, laid down by the Lateran decrees, were to be enforced on the laity. English bishops wrestled with this problem in a variety of ways. They used the annual diocesan synod, which had been prescribed by the council, as an instrument for enforcing the conciliar decrees and training their clergy in the duties of their office. They licensed or, on occasion commanded, individual clergy to attend the schools. Sometimes these remedies were supplemented by the provision of manuals of instruction.

A considerable amount of didactic literature of this sort was produced in the thirteenth century, much of it of a quite humble and utilitarian kind. Works like the *Summa* on penance by Thomas of Chabham, himself a Paris theologian and sub-dean of Salisbury in the time of Richard le Poore, the *Templum Domini* by Robert

Grosseteste, and the anonymous *Manuel des Péchés* written in Anglo-Norman verse, were all designed to provide basic dogmatic and pastoral instruction for parish clergy whose educational equipment was small. In order to help the memory of their untutored readers the compilers of these works resort to elaborate schemes and diagrams which strike the more sophisticated eye with a certain quaintness. "In this table," writes Grosseteste, "is set out the whole duty of the pastoral care," and there follows a complete scheme of the Christian life reduced to a series of single words and carefully arranged in tabular form. The seven capital sins are to be memorised by attaching them to the days of the week: Friday (dies Veneris) for lust, Tuesday (dies Martis) for anger, and less comprehensibly Monday (dies Lunae) for envy, and so on. These treatises, with their elaborate pen diagrams and cumbrous mnemonic dodges, illustrate the early stages in the painful transition from an oral society to one in which the written word is accepted as a normal vehicle of communication.

There can be no doubt that in its original form the *Speculum* was a spiritual treatise written for religious. In some manuscripts it is in fact entitled "A Mirror of Religious" (*Speculum Religiosorum*). It opens by quoting *I Corinthians*, 1.26: *For ye see your calling brethren*, on which St. Edmund observes "These words of the apostle's concern (you) men of religion . . . and the apostle says this to rouse you to the pursuit of perfection . . . you, therefore, who live in religion or in a congregation, pursue the way of perfection and, if you desire salvation, leave all things that are in this world and all the concerns thereof and apply your might to perfect living." Edmund then goes on to explain the importance of detachment from natural affections. At several points the reader is reminded by a phrase or an illustration that the writer is addressing himself to monks or nuns. When he speaks of the corporal works of mercy, for example, he deals at length with the objection of a monk: "I am in religion. I have no power to give food or drink or clothing or shelter, since I have nothing with which I can do any of these things . . . " Then again, at a later stage a programme of meditations on the life and passion of Our Lord is suggested and these are to be made before each office of the night and day "which you sing in monastery or church." The probability is that the treatise originated as a series of conferences, what we should now call a "retreat," given by Edmund to one of the monastic communities where he was a frequent visitor.

Although the *Speculum* was first designed for religious, there are several passages in it which indicate that Edmund, or a later adaptor, reshaped it and added to it with the needs of a wider audience in mind. For instance the writer gives some practical but exacting advice on the observance of the commandment "See that thou keep holy the Sabbath Day" as follows:

> If you are well, rise from your bed in the morning and linger not on account of cold or sleep or comfort, for the harder it is for a man to do, the greater shall be his reward if he does it freely. Then should you go to church and devoutly say Matins or quietly hear Mass and all the Hours of the day without chattering. And afterwards, if there be any preacher at hand who means to give a sermon, you should quietly hear the word of God, commit it to your memory, and fulfil it in your works. And when you are at meat, give freely to the poor from the good things that God has provided for you and after dinner, give thanks to God for all his kindness. Afterwards you shall not go to the tavern to watch wrestling or to carollings or other foolish and vain games, for from such as these arise mishaps and mortal sins; but you should visit the sick and the hapless . . .

This advice is obviously not directed at a religious community, even a disorderly one. It might be applicable to a parish chaplain, not in priest's orders, who would be required to sing the offices in church. But it is impossible not to feel that the case best fits a lay person. After all, for the clergy the avoidance of taverns was a matter not of counsel, but of precept.

It is when Edmund comes to speak about the contemplation of God in Scripture, what he calls the second grade of contemplation, that the *Speculum* shows the most obvious signs of having been inflated with additional matter. Under this heading he sets out a complete catechetical scheme of doctrine, and it is this elementary doctrinal instruction that links the work with the other didactic literature of the period. Edmund expounds the seven deadly sins and the contrary virtues, the seven gifts of the Holy Ghost, the ten commandments, the twelve articles of the creed, the seven sacraments, the four cardinal virtues, the seven works of mercy, the seven petitions of the Lord's Prayer, the pains of hell and the joys of heaven. The scheme of classification has been taken, with slight adaptation, from a short treatise by Hugh of St. Victor entitled *De Quinque Septenis*. Edmund's treatment of these subjects is extremely simple and factual. The chapter on the sacraments, for example, include concrete instructions for the administration of Baptism and Penance: "If an infant be found and it is not known whether it is baptised or not, then the chaplain shall say to the child . . . . And let the priest take care that he does not immerse the child a second time . . ." It is clear that these instructions are intended for parish clergy. So too, most probably, are the frequent counsels about attentiveness during the recitation of the offices in choir. It should be remembered that in the thirteenth century public recitation of the office was an obligation resting upon the clergy serving a church. Private recitation was generally precluded by the character of the service books.

At the end of chapter 18 the writer actually refers to his purpose in inserting this elementary doctrinal matter into a treatise on the spiritual life:

> On the other hand, you have here matter for speaking to clerks, be they never so wise, and to lay people, be they never so untaught. When you speak to wiser people, take some of these matters and ask questions humbly. When you speak to persons simpler than yourself, teach them freely and gently. For here you have enough to think and speak of, in what manner you should rule your own life and amend the life of others.

In other words, the book up to this point will serve as a useful manual for a clerk, giving him personal guidance on his own spiritual life and pabulum for sermons or less formal instructions. The writer has in fact grafted a didactic treatise of a practical and pedestrian kind on to a more advanced work of spirituality which he had originally designed for religious. There is nothing surprising in this. Other works underwent a similar change in response to the changing needs of the thirteenth century. The *Ancren Riwle*, for example, was translated into Anglo-Norman and expanded to provide instruction on the sacrament of Penance to meet the requirements of a class of devout and French-speaking laity.

Were these changes in the original plan of the *Speculum* the work of St. Edmund himself, or were they the work of a later compiler? They suggest the kind of pastoral awareness that we should expect from a zealous bishop who had passed through the Paris schools at the beginning of the century and who had been a contemporary of Richard le Poore and Thomas of Chabham at Salisbury. But we can go further than this. The handling of these doctrinal themes in many ways reflects the stage which discussion had reached in the Paris schools at the beginning of the thirteenth century. This is especially noticeable in the way in which the virtues are classified and expounded. Edmund's brief synopsis follows the lines laid out by the earlier masters such as Langton and Prevostin. It seems rudimentary by comparison with the elaborate analysis of virtue and its relation to grace which we find in the work of William of Auxerre and the masters who followed him in the second half of the century.[1] It seems then that these accretions, which have been grafted into the *Speculum*, were indeed added by Edmund himself, for they bear the scholastic stamp of his generation.

The essential part of Edmund's treatise is a guide to the practice of contemplation, in the widest sense, for he understands by the term not only the infused contemplation of the authentic mystical experience, but also the more ordinary processes of meditation. After exhorting his disciple to embark on the life of perfection, to which his profession has committed him, he defines the essence of perfect living in a phrase of St. Bernard: "to live perfectly is to live in friendship, humility, and honour." Friendship is the proper relationship between a man and his neighbour. Humility is the proper attitude to self. Edmund passes rapidly over these and comes to honour, which he defines as the proper relationship between man and God, a relationship established by loving obedience to the divine will. But "this is the will of God, even your sanctification." This personal sanctification, to be gained by uniting the will with the will of God in contemplation, is Edmund's central theme.

Like all the masters of the spiritual life, Edmund teaches that the journey of the contemplative must start from the knowledge of self. At the outset, therefore, he proposes a series of points for meditation, which will lead to a deeper recognition of the

---

[1] The analysis of the virtues in the work of the Paris masters involves a number of technical questions which cannot be pursued here. The subject has received magisterial treatment from O. Lottin, *Psychologie et Morale aux xiie et xiiie siècles* vol. 3 (Louvain 1949), pp. 329-535.

soul's condition and of God's mercy in his dealings with it. He concludes this section by recommending two prayers for frequent use, one of thanks and the other of commendation. The first is inspired by the daily collect of Prime and the second borrows its phraseology from the most theologically perfect of all communion devotions, the prayer beginning *Domine Iesu Christe, fili Dei vivi*, which recalls the whole divine scheme of salvation. This prayer is now prescribed in the Roman Missal after the canon, but in the thirteenth century it was still only one among a variety of private devotions which were at the option of the celebrant.

After preparing his disciple to embark upon the way of perfection, Edmund sets out, in the sixth chapter, his conception of contemplation. There are, he says, three ways of contemplating God: the first in creation, the second in the Scriptures, the third in the divine nature itself. These ways are, in fact, three distinct grades or levels in the ascent of the soul to God. For Edmund, the contemplative life comprehends the life of meditation and study, which corresponds to the first two grades, as well as the mystical life properly so called, which is the third grade. In essentials, this pattern derives from St. Augustine, for whom contemplation is not an extraordinary phenomenon, but an integral part of his conception of the life of Christian perfection. It is not a special vocation, but part of God's universal invitation to which any man may respond. The fundamental sense of the Augustinian degrees is that the spiritual life is a progress which reaches its proper end in infused contemplation. This doctrine is reproduced by Hugh of St. Victor. When Edmund reaches the third grade, the contemplation of the divine nature in its essence, his debt to the first book of Hugh's great treatise *De Sacramentis* becomes apparent in his phraseology. But the Victorine influence is more subtle and pervasive than the occasional verbal borrowing would suggest. Edmund's whole treatment of the first grade of contemplation, the perception of God in his creation, is inspired by Hugh's vision of the created universe as a great book filled with signs which, like the words of a book, communicate to the attentive reader the ideas of the author.

Edmund's second grade is the contemplation of God in Scripture. It is here that he provides the catechetical scheme of doctrine, much of which bears no direct relation to the general plan of

his treatise. The relatively unlettered disciple for whom this was
designed would probably have found a direct study of the Bible
beyond his literary powers and would almost certainly have
found the acquisition of a complete text beyond his financial
means. In providing simple dogmatic instruction by way of a
substitute, Edmund does not lose sight of the central theme of the
book. Thus he expounds the *Pater Noster* so that each petition
becomes a basis for meditation. He speaks sharply of those who
neglect the Lord's Prayer for "multiple devotions," those "who
abandon and reject the prayer which God Himself made, and
accept the prayer of some simple saint or something that they
have found in a book." He insists upon the importance of reciting
it slowly and meditatively, a few words at a time. Frequent
repetition is unnecessary.

In the third grade the disciple is to contemplate God in Himself,
first in His humanity and then in His divinity. In order to help
the disciple to contemplate the Sacred Humanity Edmund
outlines a series of meditations on the life and passion of Our
Lord, linked to the divine office. For each of the canonical hours
he proposes two appropriate subjects for meditation, of which
one is a "mystery," or event, in the life of Christ and the other
is an incident of the passion. At Matins and Lauds, for example,
the disciple will meditate on the Nativity and the Betrayal,
before Prime on the Resurrection and the trial before Caiaphas,
and so on. The meditation in each case consists of a simple visual
reconstruction of the scene. There is little moralisation or introspection, but the scenes are described with vivid immediacy and
great tenderness of feeling. Thus for the Nativity, the disciple's
attention is directed to the crib, the ox and the ass, the cold of
mid-winter, the joy of Mary and Joseph:

> The time was in mid-winter, when it was most cold; the hour was
> at midnight, the hardest hour that is; the place was in mid-ward the
> street, in a house without walls. In clouts was he wound and as a
> child was he bound and in a crib before an ox and an ass that lovely
> lord was laid, for there was no other place empty. And here shalt
> thou think of the keeping of Mary and her child, and of her spouse
> Joseph—what joy Jesu sent them. Thou shalt think also of the
> shepherds that saw the showing of his birth, and thou shalt think of
> the sweet fellowship of angels, and raise up thy heart and sing with
> them *Gloria in excelsis Deo*.

This simple pictorial freshness of the New Testament story is something which is realised by the literal vision of the thirteenth century. We seem here to be very close to the genesis of the Rosary.

In many ways these meditations of St. Edmund's are a landmark in the history of medieval religious sentiment. An intense personal devotion to the humanity of Our Lord, a tender compassionate regard for the sufferings of the Saviour, mark a new orientation of Western piety which had its origins in the monastic spirituality of the eleventh and twelfth centuries. It was the writings of St. Bernard and the Cistercians which gave expression and impulse to this new kind of affective piety. Compassion, an imaginative identification, that is, with the sufferings of Jesus, was an important theme in Cistercian ascetical teaching. It was largely through the teaching of the Franciscans that in the thirteenth century it emerged from the cloister and became part of the religious experience of the ordinary Christian. St. Francis himself became the supreme example of compassion: he is the first ascetic known to have received the physical stigmata of the Crucified. This great change in men's intuitive and emotional response to the history of the redemption is vividly reflected in Western art during this period. In the century that separates St. Bernard from St. Bonaventure the static passionless figure of the triumphant Christ, crowned and reigning from the Cross, is gradually replaced by the sagging contorted figure of the Man of Sorrows which is characteristic of later medieval art.

In this path of development St. Edmund stands as a bridge between the monastic spirituality of the twelfth century and the popular piety of the Franciscan movement. The *Lives* tell us that he was an active propagator of devotion to the Passion. He frequently preached on the subject with a crucifix in his hand and aroused powerful emotions in his audience. The Pontigny writer tells us also that it was his practice to meditate daily upon the instruments of the Passion. The seven meditations on the Passion preserved for us in the *Speculum* are a series of brief word-pictures. When Edmund comes to the crucifixion and the grief of Mary, emotion breaks through into ejaculations of tenderness and compassion:

I know not what I should say here. For if all the sickness of this world and all the sorrow were in the body of one man, and that man

might keep as much hurt and anguish and sorrow in his body as all
the men of this world might think, it were full little or naught to
compare with the sorrow that he suffered for us in one hour of the
day ... Surely, there is not, nor ever was in this world, pain like to
thy pain, O most sweet Jesu. And also thou shalt think of our sweet
Lady saint Mary, what anguish she had when she stood at the right
side of her sweetest son and received the disciple for the Master and
the servant for the Lord, John Zebedee's son for Jesu, God's Son ...

These sharp tableaux, in which the reader is invited to make
himself a living participator, must have made an important
contribution to that devotion to the physical aspects of the
Passion which reached its height in the following hundred years.

An example of the sort of influence that Edmund's meditations
exerted on his contemporaries can be seen from the treatment
given to the fifth episode of the Passion which he recommends
for meditation before None. Here the disciple is asked to ponder
on the death of Christ and on the seven last words spoken from
the Cross. The Seven Last Words or utterances of Christ, conflated from the four Gospel narratives, became a popular theme
of devotion in the course of the thirteenth century. Before this
the history of the devotion is obscure. The earliest written
evidence of it comes from the work of Ernaud, a monk of Moyen-
moutier, who ended his days in 1156 as abbot of Bonneval.
He composed an elaborate treatise on the Seven Last Words,
but it cannot have reached a very wide audience. It was apparently
through St. Edmund's *Speculum* that the devotion was transmitted
to the Franciscans. In St. Bonaventure's tract on the Passion the
Seven Words—here arranged not in Ernaud's order, but in the
order that Edmund had given them—become the very foliage
of the wondrous vine that is Christ crucified by love. It became
a favourite theme for Franciscan preachers on the Passion.
Through these meditations Edmund helped to form the religious
experience of the thirteenth century which produced, as well as
the crib, the Office of the Passion and the *Stabat Mater*.

The meditations on the Passion and life of Our Lord are proposed as an introduction to the third stage of contemplation.
After they are completed, the disciple is told to make a brief
discursive meditation on the existence of God and the divine
attributes. Then, with rather startling abruptness, he is confronted
in the twenty-ninth chapter with the end and climax of his

spiritual journey. He is led by the traditional path to the summit of mystical contemplation. What Edmund has to say on this subject is of great interest because, although his account is derivative, he has inserted into it an unmistakable claim to have had mystical experience himself. The passage is worth quoting at length:

> Therefore, after you have established your heart in right faith, in steadfast hope, and perfect charity, lift up your heart to high contemplation of your creator. But often though your soul desires to see God in his own nature through contemplation, it cannot. And then it turns to itself and makes of itself degrees by which it can mount to divine contemplation, so that at the first it can see and search its own nature and afterwards, the nature that is above it . . . The first step of contemplation is that wherein the soul turns and recollects itself wholly within; the second step is that wherein the soul raises itself above itself . . . The soul must not pass on from self-knowledge until it has been taught to bridle all bodily and earthly images, and when it is touched in heart by any sweetness of sight, sound, taste, smell, or touch, then it must reject it and trample it down, so that it may see itself as though it were wholly without body.

Here Edmund is describing in classical terms the process of mental preparation which some modern writers on ascetical theology call recollection and "introversion."[1] The mind concentrates its powers and excludes all sensory images, shuts out the clamorous perceptions of the senses, and silences the activity of the intellect. Then, in introversion, it focuses its attention upon its own being. This exercise is, in a sense, the ultimate act of the contemplative. In the final stage of contemplation, St. Augustine's seventh degree, the soul is no longer master of its own faculties, but is possessed and directly fed by God.

The account which Edmund gives of this process is not, saving for a brief interjection, couched in his own words; it is drawn from St. Gregory's *Homilies on Ezechiel*. St. Gregory discusses the subject of contemplative prayer systematically in the second book of the *Homilies*, building up an elaborate allegory of the Temple which was seen in Ezechiel's vision. This passage became a classical source for ascetical writers. It is into St.

---

[1] *E.g.*, Cuthbert Butler, *Western Mysticism* (1922).

Gregory's account of the final stage of contemplation that Edmund has inserted his brief autobiographical statement:

> Expel from your heart all bodily imagining and allow your naked understanding (*nudum intellectum*) to fly, above all human reasoning, up to heaven, and there you shall find such sweetness and such secret things as no man knoweth save he who has proved it for himself. *And, although I, wretched man that I am, have myself proved it, nevertheless I could not describe it; for it is so secret that it passes all thought. Therefore it is meet and right that I should do this, and not teach it* . . .

His transcendental discovery has rendered the trained schoolman inarticulate. This inability of the contemplative to communicate his experience to others is, of course, axiomatic. The interesting thing is that in one version of the *Speculum*, a version which omits the elementary didactic matter and which therefore probably represents the earliest shape of the work, the author avoids making any such personal claim. In this version, after speaking of the sweetness of this experience, he writes:

> But if you desire to know this passing sweetness, there is none to teach you or explain it, and if I, a wretched sinner, had experienced it, I should not be able to tell such things . . . for these things are so profound and so secret that they cannot be told.

What are we to make of this revision? We cannot rule out the possibility that the passage has been doctored by a later copyist in order to place in the mouth of St. Edmund a claim that he never himself made. On the other hand, we have seen that the *Speculum* was later revised and adapted for a wider audience and that the revision was probably the work of St. Edmund himself. Perhaps it is not stretching the evidence too far to suggest that at some point between compiling the original conferences and reshaping them for wider use, Edmund had himself penetrated the third heaven of the contemplatives and heard "the secret words which it is not given to man to utter."

It is significant that in order to describe the ultimate goal of infused contemplation Edmund has borrowed his language from a classical patristic source. It is hardly thinkable that he was not acquainted with the mystical doctrine of the pseudo-Dionysius, which in the twelfth century was just entering upon its remarkable career in the West for, through the writings of the Victorines, such ideas must have been in the air of Paris in the time of St. Edmund. On the other hand, he displays no direct acquaintance with the Dionysian writings or with the elaborate map of contemplation provided by Richard of St. Victor in the two Benjamin treatises. He attempts no detailed analysis of the different "states" of the contemplative life. For Edmund the unitive experience is not the subject of a separate and autonomous science as it was to become in the hands of the Rhenish mystics and their later English disciples. For him it is the looked-for consummation of the devout life of spiritual reading and meditation, the upper reaches of the stream of prayer which the monk entered when he made his profession. This was the traditional ascetical doctrine of monastic teachers from Cassian to St. Bernard, and here, as elsewhere, Edmund shows himself to be a pupil of the traditional monastic spirituality.

10. PIERS PLOWMAN

Edmund Colledge and W. O. Evans

No ACCOUNT of medieval English spiritual writing can ignore *Piers Plowman*, but it is extremely difficult to relate it to any other religious writings of its time. It is a wholly original work, it was written by a man of perplexing and enigmatic personality, and very often it is difficult to know what it is that he is trying to say. The account of the poem which follows must of necessity be in part an appraisal of some of the controversies between the critics: there can be no greater tribute to the vitality of this poem than the fact that it has, through the centuries, provoked and baffled those who have tried to solve its riddles.

We know that it enjoyed great contemporary popularity, that it was read and owned in every class of society, and quoted and imitated by writers of sympathies very unlike those of its author. He tells us that he made many enemies, and we may guess that he found friends where he did not want to be praised, notably among the Lollards, enemies of the unity and power of the Church whom he revered as his mother, holy, despite all the imperfections of her sons. And so in each succeeding age men have been able to find in *Piers Plowman* what they have looked for, by ignoring or misinterpreting what was unwelcome or incomprehensible.

In the last hundred years, since scholars first began the still unfinished work of making reliable editions from the plethora of surviving manuscripts, much time has been spent on the discussion of two topics which can be dealt with here very briefly, because today their insignificance is obvious. The first concerns the author's identity. For the sake of convenience he will here be called 'William Langland', and he may well háve been the son, possibly base-born, of Eustace Rokayle, a West Midland squire; but we cannot be certain of any of this, and what the poet, so careful to preserve his anonymity, tells us about himself is far more important. From a hint here, a few lines of overt reminiscence there, we can construct a life history which accords with the whole temper of the work and does much to clarify it: it is the story of a poor but gifted boy with a family at first willing to help him, who reads theology, though at neither university, and who receives the Church's minor orders with the manifest intention of advancing to the secular priesthood. But on the way something (we are never told what) goes wrong, and by the time that his poem has reached its final form he is an ageing man, living in penury in Cornhill, supporting himself and a wife and daughter on the odd jobs which were the best that the Church could allow in an age grown less tolerant towards her married clerks: he could copy legal documents, he could recite the offices of the dead for his patrons, he could eat the bread of charity, and all the while he could watch around him the frantic pursuit of riches and honours. It is far from flippant to say that *Piers Plowman* is the earliest English commentary on life's rat-race; and it has all the irony and disillusion and embitterment of that genre.

This, then, is what we know about the poet's life, and it is far more significant than a mere name. But the second controversy which has been pursued for long is of greater importance. The poem has come down to us in three versions, and there have been many critics who attempted to prove that the two revisions, one of the 1370's, one of the 1390's, were not written by the author of the 'A Text', which internal evidence shows to have been composed about the year 1370, when the Holy See was severing its ties with Avignon. But today the theory of multiple authorship has fewer supporters. There is no serious incongruity of teaching, social or theological, between the three versions; and it is hard to accept that B and C could have been written by mere pupils or heirs of the great master whose poetic genius can stir us as readily in the later versions as it does in A. This second debate is doubtless not yet closed; all that we can say here is that we vote with the majority who believe that A, B and C are the work of one man.

Had he lived long enough, he might well have written a fourth, a D text. The end of C shows him still grappling with problems, intellectual and artistic, to which he has not yet found the answer; and in its earliest form we can see that the poem is a fusion, not very skilfully contrived, between his original plan and a grander design which presented itself to him whilst he wrote.

In several of the earliest and best manuscripts of the A text, the fusion is indicated by a rubric such as that in the Chaderton MS, *explicit visio willelmi de petro le plouzman*; *eciam incipit vita de dowel, dobet et dobest*, occurring at the end of Passus Eight. The prologue to the poem and these following eight sections contain, it seems, what the author first intended to publish, and this is known by the name given to it in such early rubrics, the *Visio*. It is indeed a great vision of life and of the world. A dreamer falls asleep, and dreams that he sees a microcosm in which every walk of life is represented. Though this is never clearly stated, there seems at the beginning of the poem to be a struggle to win the human soul between the two women who appear before the dreamer. One of them explicitly reveals herself as Holy Church, but it is only through her scornful directions that the poet and we see the other woman, the Lady Mede; she seems at first to be the antithesis of Holy Church, a kind of Antichrist, the personification of the riches, the excess profit, the worldly honours for which most men would be happy to barter their immortal souls. With the appearance of Lady Mede, the poet states the first of the problems which he is trying to solve: how much money is it right for men to make? He is well schooled in canon law, and he knows all the classical answers, which forbid passive investment and usury. But he can see that these principles have little application to the times of industrial revolution in which he is living; and although he himself despises wealth, he is uncertain that gain is in itself so evil as the canonists teach. This is skilfully conveyed to us, during the debate between Lady Mede and her unwilling suitor Conscience. Conscience seems to speak for the poet, as well as for the traditional evangelical teachings of the Church, when he shows how Mede corrupts men's souls; but it is Mede herself who argues that even if men shall not live by bread alone, still, if they are to live, they must eat.

This debate is never resolved, and it has been observed that it seems in the end to fade away, that the Lady Mede disappears from the story because no one regards her as any longer important. The poet's last word, though it is far from conclusive, is when he tells us how his company of pilgrims, the whole human race, wandering and questing for the shrine of 'St. Truth', find in the end a leader and guide who is neither a cleric—their directions are vague and misleading—nor the *ex professo* palmer who has visited every place of devotion in Christendom but who has never heard of a saint called Truth. They are to be led by a simple, unlettered tiller of the soil, Piers the Ploughman; and Piers, not by roaming far and wide but by staying at home and doing his proper work, gains an indulgence for mankind in which the mercantile classes, though originally they received no mention, are added 'in the margin', with the provision that they use their wealth to promote God's work, and, specifically, to relieve the distress of the poor.

It is this concern with the alleviation of human distress, providing a constantly recurring theme, which makes the poem in its age so remarkable. It is because he knows and feels for the afflictions of the starving, suffering peasants that his great allegory of the pilgrimage, the nexus of the *Visio*, develops as it does. In the celebrated scene of the preaching mission, humanity, personified for us by the Seven Deadly Sins who come up in turn to declare their heavy burden of evil doing, is bidden to seek indulgence at Truth's shrine. Piers is then brought forward, late in the day, as the central character, the repository of all the poet's hopes for the human race, the idealised honest labourer who knows what has been hidden from scholars and prelates, where Truth is to be found.

So Piers sets out, with all this sorry rabble following him; and we may guess that what the poet intended hereafter would have been something like what Bunyan, who learned from him, was to write three centuries later. But this design was never completed. Instead, we have some perfunctory lines in which we are told that when Truth heard that Piers intended to travel to his shrine, he sent him a message to stay at home and conveyed in it the indulgence which he would have gained. The poet is at great pains at this point to make it plain that he is not questioning the power of the Church to grant indulgence: all that he is doing is to deplore the human credulity which places more reliance upon written guarantees of indulgence *a poena et a culpa* than it will upon the works through which such indulgence can be gained:

At the dreadful day of judgment, when the dead shall arise,
And all come before Christ to render their accounts,
How you led your life on earth, and how you kept his law,
What you did day by day your doom will relate.
A pocketful of pardons then, and letters from provincial priors,
And grants of confraternity from the four orders of friars
And twofold indulgence will do you no good unless Do Well
    help you.

This message is brought home to us in the mysterious scene
which winds up the *Visio*, when Piers reads the indulgence
which he has been granted, and finds that all that Truth tells him
is that 'those who do well will go into everlasting life, those
who do ill into everlasting fire'. With one of those jibes at the
Church's slick professionalism which he can seldom resist, the
poet makes a priest read the indulgence over Piers' shoulder and
say that it is no indulgence at all; and then Piers tears it into
shreds 'in sheer anger', and says that henceforth he will devote
himself less to manual labour and more to the work of the
salvation of his soul. At this point in the poem (in the A Text,
Passus Eight) we encounter a whole complex of textual obscuri-
ties; but still we emerge from these knowing that Piers, instead
of seeking the shrine of Truth, must find out for himself what
are the three lives of Do Well, Do Better and Do Best.

These three lives are the theme of the second part of the poem,
a theme which plainly was not in the poet's mind when first he
began to write; and it is his struggles to say, for his own instruction as well as ours, what is the nature of these three lives, which
account for most of the complexities of text and the opacities
of sense which we find in the three versions of the poem.

It would be well at this point briefly to describe certain recent
attempts to resolve these difficulties which, though they have
been made by most eminent scholars, have not succeeded.

One such theory would see in William Langland an English
Dante; but though the personal histories and the minds of the
two poets have much in common, it is manifestly absurd to
claim for *Piers Plowman* the order, balance, comprehensiveness
and authority of the *Divine Comedy*. More ingeniously, another
critic, over-persuaded by the claims made for the *Divine Comedy*
as a work of mystical theology expounding a *via affirmativa*, has
attempted to equate the 'three lives' with the classical descriptions

of the soul's advance to union with God through the purgative, illuminative and unitive ways; and this has recently produced several attempts to establish vital relations between *Piers Plowman* and contemporary English mystical writers, especially Walter Hilton and particularly his *Mixed Life*. Yet another school of criticism has sought to throw light upon the many dark places in the poem by applying to them the technique of Scriptural interpretation practised in the late Middle Ages; but it cannot be said that this has eased or deepened our understanding of what the poet is trying to say. All these essays in critical appreciation have from the outset defeated themselves by trying to prove that *Piers Plowman* is something which it is not—a treatise in mystical theology, or a Scriptural key—and ignoring what it is, a wholly poetic account of the intellectual struggles, never fully resolved, of a man who was not looking either to the great mystics or to the schoolmen for the solution of his unending problem of how he can best save his soul.

He knows exactly where to look for help, to the Scriptures, to the Church's dogma and to the classical writers upon grace and redemption; but he cannot see anywhere one perfect and sufficient answer to his questions. Though he is of a speculative disposition, he is in no way drawn to the contemplative life; and though he is very sure that salvation is found in the Church, he has few marks of devotion to her sacraments, and he detests her corrupt ministers. When he seeks for signs which will assure him that creation is indeed formed in the image of its divine maker, he finds them rather in the natural order which man alone seems to him to disturb; and constantly he reverts to his main problem, the reconciliation of man's fallen state and the orthodox belief about hell and damnation, with his hopes that all men may yet be saved.

The tone of the second part of the poem is markedly less sure and didactic than the *Visio*, and the poet is telling us that at different times he thinks differently about his problems, and that he is confused and bewildered by the multiplicity of answers which other men give him. The *Visio* seems to set out on the high road to the new Jerusalem; but Do Well, Do Better and Do Best are a sorrowful commentary upon the poet's wanderings in a maze. We cannot here follow all his false starts and wrong turnings: we can only examine a few of the main themes which he discovers as he progresses.

In all three versions, the dreamer encounters a succession of characters who give him different and often contradictory definitions of Do Well, Do Better and Do Best. One difficulty is to know how authoritative these answers are meant to be. The first to whom he applies are two Franciscan masters of theology; and here, as often elsewhere, the poet ventilates his dislike of the mendicant orders, whom he finds for the most part avaricious, self-complacent, and wholly concerned with an academic expertise which has little relation to true learning and piety. All this is reflected in his encounter with these friars, who promptly tell him that Do Well lives with them; but towards the end of their desultory argument, it is one of the friars who first suggests the topic which comes presently wholly to occupy the poet's mind, that Do Well is Charity. We cannot tell why he puts this answer into the mouths of friars, of whom usually he has no good to say. Still less can we understand what principles determine the allocation of the many succeeding definitions among such personifications as Thought, Intelligence, Learning and Imagination. The allegorical method which had served him well in the *Visio* seems now to have gone beyond his control, and as topic after topic comes tumbling out, we feel that he does not know how to organise what he wants to say, that we have here a highly emotional account of the stages of thought and feeling encountered by a Christian striving to live as best he can. Part of the confusion, then, is unavoidable; it is the confusion of life, and it is life which is the poet's material.

> I could muse upon man and on his mate together;
> Poverty and plenty, both peace and war,
> Joy and sorrow I saw at the same time;
> And how men grubbed for money and scorned mercy.

The pattern is of the life of a man who strives to do the best he can in all circumstances, and just as there is necessarily progress in such a life, so there is progress in the poem. It is difficult at any particular point in either to look back and be fully aware of a coherent and significant pattern, and difficult too to see clearly where one is going, especially when previous paths seem to have led nowhere. Yet in both the progress is sure—progress towards maturity; in this apparently haphazard plan each successive incident and situation is charged with greater significance because of what has gone before, the man is more 'whole', judgment is less crass. Study and Learning, for example, will travel more easily with Good Sense and, above all, Charity. The progress seems slow, but the man who tries to do well always does better; and if he spends his life in this way, directs himself strenuously in the direction of Right Conscience, searches for Piers, he does in fact do best, even though this is not apparent to him. 'Do Well and Do Better are two infinites leading to Do Best', and none is easily apprehensible.

We have already said that the Dreamer's progress is towards greater charity, and *Piers Plowman* is a manifestation of the broadening horizons of Christian charity during the medieval period. It is the first major work in English really to reflect this change in emphasis, this insistence upon the essential brotherhood of man; its spirit pervades the book and at times it is made explicit:

> It was on Calvary that Christendom sprang from the blood of
> Christ,
> And there we became blood brothers, born from the one Body
> As *quasi modo geniti*, each of us of gentle birth:
> None of us beggars or base except only by sin.

By Christ's death we were all made members of His family (*gentil*—originally of the *same* family), the Mystical Body, and therefore everyone is our brother and our neighbour and we are as bound to him in charity as we are to our closest friend or relation. This is the great shift of thought which is being made in the fourteenth century among the more practical thinkers— practical in the sense of being concerned with the difficulties of living a Christian life in the world, as distinct from the School-men and their theoretical distinctions.

The attention of the poet is directed not only to the charity of man for man but to the extent of God's love, too, in its application to mankind; his emphasis is on the greatness and far-reaching nature of God's love. It is very doubtful, one feels, that he would have subscribed to the literal interpretation of the words 'no salvation outside the Church' held by most contemporary and earlier theologians, and very doubtful too that he would easily accept what was thought to be St. Augustine's teaching, that

unbaptised infants suffered physical torture in hell. His attitude
to Saracen and Jew, for instance, is remarkably mild and tolerant
compared with what we are used to in contemporary and earlier
English writing. Take the following passage:

> If our priests were perfect the people would mend their ways
> Who break Christ's law and hold Christendom in contempt;
> For all Saracens pray and have perfect faith
> In one God who is holy and mighty, and they ask for his grace,
> And they entreat Mahomet to intercede for them.
> So they live in faith, but their mediator is false.

This is not an attempt to prove the poet's lack of orthodoxy; he
believes that the Kingdom of Christ is the only true one, but
the inescapable suggestion in his mind is that these people are not
necessarily damned, any more than Aristotle and other worthy
pagan teachers are damned. Here, for all his other similarities
with Dante, he lacks the latter's stringent traditional insistence,
and one wonders if the disagreement might have been less if
Dante had written at the end of the fourteenth century rather
than the thirteenth. Basically the distinction in viewpoint is one
of interpretation of Baptism of Desire. Is it possible to receive
the sacrament in this way if one has not even heard of Christ?
The whole tenor of *Piers Plowman* would suggest that searching
for Do Best was, in fact, searching for Christ, and that this in
itself would be tantamount to baptism; and although this may
be a very common view in later times, it was certainly not
prevalent in the Middle Ages.

An accumulation of detail could be cited in support of this
impression. Christ's dying prayer to His Father for the forgiveness of His persecutors, for example, had obviously always
been known to Christians, but it had seldom received emphasis
from writers on the Passion. In works like *The Dream of the Rood*
the tone is one clear battle between good and evil: those who
crucify Christ are enemies and there is not the slightest consideration of their possible salvation. The Cross can save those
who believe in it and fear it; all others are complete outsiders.
And this, in varying degrees, is the general attitude of subsequent
writers, but Langland sees fit to point to Christ's dying intercession for His persecutors:

> Meekly he spoke and Mercy he entreated
> To have pity on the people who tormented and killed him.

But the clearest indication of the poet's trust that God's mercy extends to all mankind is in the Harrowing of Hell, so similar to the York Mystery in many respects, but in this particular so unlike. Although he is concerned elsewhere to warn men of eternal damnation, here he seems to suggest that at the Last Day God's infinite mercy will extend to all mankind, and that no one will be left in Hell. Christ here is addressing Satan.

> Then I shall come as a King, crowned among the angels,
> And I shall bring out of hell all men's souls.
> All devils, great and small, shall stand before me
> And be at my command wherever I please.
> And my nature will then require me to be merciful to man,
> For we are blood-brothers, though not all in baptism.
> But all who are wholly my brothers by blood and by baptism
> Shall not be condemned to everlasting death.

The whole of this speech (in B, Passus 18, in C, Passus 21) deserves close attention. Our Lord goes on to compare Himself with an earthly king who, coming upon the scene of an abortive execution, has it in his lawful power to grant the felon pardon. So 'my mercy will be shown to many of my brethren' (this is Skeat's reading in B, his C text reads 'to many of my half-brothers', but in either case the application to the unbaptised is clear, although 'many' suggests a prudent reservation). And the passage ends with a significant quotation from St. Paul: 'And I heard secret words which it is not granted to man to utter.'

It will be seen that the *Visio* and the quest for the three lives, so unlike in form, and directed in quite separate directions, are none the less unified by the poet's constant concern, widening and deepening as the poem goes on, to bring all men into his scheme of salvation. What in the end he has to tell us is far from new, but it is unique for the passionate insistence with which it is said. When finally Piers Plowman reappears on the scene, it is Holy Week, and he is all stained with blood and carrying a cross to Calvary, and the poet is told that this is Christ, who has put on Piers Plowman's armour, our humanity, in which to joust against Death. We have earlier been prepared for this identification. Anima has told the dreamer that if he truly longs for redeeming Charity, only Piers can help him find it, 'Peter, that is Christ'; and in this conflated allusion to *Tu es Petrus*

(Anima has just said that the Church, so evil and corrupt in its members, can still be the source of all good) and *Petra erat Christus*, the poet seems to be reaching out to his conclusion. The three lives, it seems, are in the end all degrees of love, of Charity; they can be perfectly lived by simple layfolk, and penitence and good works can bring even such sinners as Haukyn the Active Man back to Charity through grace. Haukyn and the poet and every human being are brothers in Christ, and it is this kinship which calls them to be perfectly formed in Christ, which calls Christ to show to all men His perfect charity, never more perfectly exemplified than when the dreamer sees Him and cannot tell Him from Piers for all His sufferings and sorrow.

But it would have been false to the entire temper of the work if it had ended on any note of triumph, if it had brought any sense of doubts resolved. Instead, it seems to drift back into the darkness in which it has moved for so long. Age overtakes the poet, Antichrist appears and threatens to conquer an enfeebled clergy, and Conscience sets off on yet another pilgrimage, this time to seek for Piers to help him to restore the Church. That Piers, *id est Christus*, can do these things we do not doubt; but the poem ends, as it began, with a departure, for man's true pardon has not yet been gained. In this, surely, we have one of the poet's deepest observations of the life of the soul: that our pilgrimage never ends, and that we never shall know fully what we search for, on this side of the grave.

K

II. RICHARD ROLLE OF HAMPOLE

E. J. Arnould

THE FOURTEENTH CENTURY was the heyday of English mysticism and is also famous for its hermits and anchorites. Richard Rolle, whose life-span covers the first half of the century, has a marked place among both hermits and mystics.[1] Professor R. W. Chambers has observed that "in English or in Latin Rolle was, during the latter half of the fourteenth century and the whole of the fifteenth, probably the most widely read in England of all English writers." His works came to be regarded by later generations as standards of orthodoxy—a fact attested not only by the numerous copies that found their way into the libraries of many religious houses on the Continent as well as in England, but also by the spurious ascription to him of popular books of common doctrine (such as the *Pricke of Conscience*, of which over one hundred copies have survived to this day); and, above all, by tributes paid to him well into the times of the Counter-Reformation, when he was still acclaimed as *Strenuus ac divinus catholicae fidei athleta Ricardus*, the valiant and godly champion of the catholic faith.

That Richard Rolle died in the odour of sanctity is attested by a Latin *Office* written in anticipation of his beatification, complete with the miraculous cures worked on his tomb in the precincts of Hampole monastery in Yorkshire. This *Office* is our main source of information on Richard's life. It depicts for us a young man of fiery temperament, who, after a few years at

---

[1] The most convenient comprehensive account of the man, his times, and his works (in spite of a number of outdated passages) is still Miss Frances M. M. Comper's *The Life of Richard Rolle, together with an Edition of his Lyrics* (Dent, London, 1928).

The canon of Richard Rolle's works has been established by Miss Hope Emily Allen in *Writings ascribed to Richard Rolle of Hampole and Materials for his Biography* (P.M.L.A., New York, 1927).

Oxford and at home, one day resolutely turned away from what he called his sinful youth, ruthlessly cut himself off from his worldly environment and thenceforth strove, amidst difficulties and temptations, towards union with God in solitary contemplation.

Such a summary portrait is amply confirmed and completed by Rolle's own writings—providing these are read in full and without bias. These two conditions, unfortunately, have not always been fulfilled even by competent and sympathetic scholars. As a result, a very inaccurate picture of Rolle has, until recent times, been offered to us. He came to be described, on the one hand, as a Doctor of Theology and a student of the Sorbonne, even a priest, and, on the other, as a rebel against Church authorities and a declared enemy of some religious houses. Fortunately, these inaccuracies and distortions have now been rectified, thanks to the careful editing of Rolle's main works. He appears to us in a truer light, as a dedicated young man with a sound theological training, steeped in the reading of the Bible, bent on achieving the perfection of union with God and, not unnaturally, anxious to draw disciples to his own way of life both by his example and his writings. No evidence can be found for suggesting that Rolle ever swerved from his allegiance to the Church. Throughout his life his motto remained: *I bow in alle thynge till the lare of Haly-kirke*, "I submit in everything to the teaching of Holy Church." Nor did his charity exclude even his detractors: "I have loved those who despised me. I did not call perdition upon those who derided or slandered me. I have always loved those who opposed me and denounced me as worthy of contempt." His exultation over God's gifts to him emanated not from pride but from the gratitude of a candid mind, the true mark of humility: *Non sic lingua nostra appetat humilitatem ut veritatem relinquat*, "let not our tongue thirst for humility to the extent of forsaking the truth."

Rolle was a prolific writer, and his works are far from presenting a uniform pattern. If we omit the delightful *Canticum Amoris*, a youthful outpouring of his love for the Mother of God[1] and fragments of doubtful authenticity, they may be

---

[1] A. Wilmart, "Le Cantique d'Amour de Richard Rolle," *Revue d'Ascétique et de Mystique*, xxi (1940), pp. 143 sq.

The Oxford Book of Medieval Latin Verse, ed. by F. J. R. Raby (Clarendon Press (1959), p. 442).

classified into three groups, each of which corresponds to a particular stage or aspect of Rolle's spiritual career.

First we have the didactic writings, which belong to the traditional type of medieval devotional literature. They are nearly always commentaries of some Scriptural text or texts, and essentially compilations from previous authorities. Such are Rolle's Latin commentaries on the *Magnificat* or on *Psalm XX*, or on the first chapters of the *Apocalypse*, and two complete commentaries of the *Psalms*, one in Latin, one in English. These works, particularly the English Psalter (which is not, as has been asserted, a mere replica of Rolle's Latin Psalter), bear the stamp of our hermit's mind, and offer a good deal of corroborative evidence on his views and experiences.

Far more original and representative is a small group of treatises, which though they have the traditional ring, nevertheless contain many passages displaying the exclusive characteristics of his very personal style. The most important of these are the *Judica me Deus* (which takes its title from the 42nd Psalm), the *De Emendatione Vitae*, and the *Form of Living*.

The first part of the *Judica* reveals a youthful Rolle, the apprentice-hermit (*si heremita dicerer, cuius nomine indigne vocor*, "if I were called hermit, a name which I bear unworthily"), endeavouring to help a young priest-friend by compiling for him a manual of the chief duties of a parish priest, including a model sermon on the Last Judgment. The compilation is rather amateurish, and mainly derived from an almost contemporary Latin work known as *Pars Oculi* or *Oculus Sacerdotis*.

The *De Emendatione Vitae*[1] is of greater interest. Written for every Christian who aspires to a life of total dedication, it reflects Rolle's circumstances at this stage of his own spiritual progress. He describes his first steps in the way, from the contempt and renunciation of the world, through the practice of a regular and devout life and especially the meditation of Our Lord's Passion, up to the higher regions of love and contemplation. *Noli tardare*, "do not delay your conversion," begins Rolle. He describes conversion as "turning our minds towards Jesus and ceaselessly medi-

---

[1] The best edition of the *De Emendatione Vitae* is by Léopold Denis, S.J., *Du Péché à l'amour Divin ou l'Amendement du Pécheur*, Editions de la Vie Spirituelle, Paris, Desclée et Cie, 1926. There is also an English translation by Frances M. M. Comper, *The Fire of Love and Mending of Life* (Methuen, 1914).

tating on his counsels and commandments, with the resolve to follow and obey them." The obstacles (wealth, feminine charms, the grace and beauty of youth, that "threefold cord that is not easily broken") must be overcome through persistence. Contempt of worldly possessions is equally essential, for "attachment to worldly goods and the love of God are incompatible: the couch is so narrow that one of the bed-fellows must fall off." As a logical sequel, poverty becomes a necessary condition—poverty not only in fact, but in spirit, that is without regret, afterthought, or envy of others—humility of mind and heart.

> Learn from me, says Jesus, for I am meek and humble in heart. He does not say: Learn from me because I am poor. Poverty is not a virtue in itself, it is misery. It is not worthy of praise in itself, but only a means of perfection: it helps us to gain Heaven and spares us many occasions of sin. . . .

When these first obstacles have been removed, it is necessary to devise a rule of life for oneself. One must first eliminate what pollutes the soul, sins of thought, speech, and deed; next, seek what purifies it, contrition, confession, satisfaction, fasting, prayer, almsgiving; thirdly, safeguard the soul's purity—purity of thought by constant meditation, control of the senses, honest occupation such as reading, pious conversation, writing or other useful work; purity of speech, by reflecting before speaking, by avoiding idle talk, and showing a horror of untruth; purity of deed by temperance, avoidance of corrupting company, and meditation on death; fourthly, one must try to make one's will conform to the will of God, mainly by seeing His image in His creatures, by trying to live in familiarity with Him through prayer and meditation, and by thinking of the happiness of heaven. This happiness can be partially enjoyed in contemplation.

In this state of spiritual well-being, however, new obstacles must be expected and overcome—the tribulations which tempt us to look back towards worldly comforts. The remedy for this is the virtue of patience sustained by the thought of the rewards that await perseverance, and of the alternative facing us: material happiness in this world and eternal suffering in the next, or patient suffering on this earth and eternal bliss thereafter. In this serenity and firmness of purpose the soul is free to labour towards its goal: union with God. Prayer is the essential and consistent activity, one enriched by the reading of the Scriptures, one that grows easier by practice, until every action is itself a form of prayer. Its most important form is meditation—on the great mysteries of God's love, on the vanity of the world (a clear echo, this, of Pope Innocent III's classic work *De contemptu mundi*), and the mysteries of faith.

Finally, the soul reaches that "purity of heart that makes one see God and is accompanied by such joy and happiness that one feels these can never again be lost." Continuous enjoyment of this love is ensured by contemplation, the essential occupation of the soul dedicated to God. "The sweetness of contemplation is only acquired at the cost of immense efforts," but these efforts (later unnecessary, as Rolle himself emphasises in his later works) are soon munificently rewarded: "For, what is *grace*, if not the beginning of *glory*? And what is the perfection of glory, if not the consummation of grace, which holds in reserve for us a glorious eternity and an eternal glory?" Thus ends the *De Emendatione Vitae*.

The *Form of Perfect Living* is an adaptation of the *De Emendatione Vitae*. A classic of the Middle English devotional literature, it was written for a recluse named Margaret, probably the lady Margaret of whom the *Office* states that "Richard loved her with the perfect affection of Charity." Far from omitting the advice given to beginners in the *De Emendatione*, Rolle insists, here, too, on the main obstacles to conversion and the main snares of the Devil. He proclaims the greatness of the solitary life, but warns of its dangers (various temptations, excessive fondness of material ease, dreams and other illusions or delusions). He defines holiness: "Those alone are holy, whatever their status or position, who desire no earthly thing beyond their bare needs, who burn with the love of Jesus, and are bent on enjoying heavenly bliss." But he speaks at greater length than in the *De Emendatione* on the love of God, that same "insuperable, inseparable, singular" love, centred on the devotion to the Holy Name, one of Rolle's own favourite devotions in his youth. At some greater length, Rolle again defines this love: "a burning yearning for God, accompanied by a wonderful pleasure and sweetness, that makes us one with God." And, while clearly stating that "no man on earth can with certainty or without a special grace know whether he is in the state of perfect charity or not," Rolle enumerates seven signs by which one may feel confident of living in union with God.

Inevitably, the *Form of Perfect Living* ends with a chapter on the active and the contemplative modes of life, which is a concise summary of Rolle's views on the subject. Rolle is clearly biased in favour of the solitary life. We know that he was, at one time, engaged in a heated controversy on this question with partisans of the "regular" life in some order or community. But his views are well supported by authorities such as St. Bernard and St. Thomas Aquinas. He also distinguishes at least two grades in the contemplative life: one, the more common, is essentially a life of prayer and meditation, the other is the mystic stage more akin to rapture or even ecstasy. The latter, Rolle points out, is a "gratuitous gift," and the indescribable joy it affords finds its expression in "inexpressible praise of God"—a remark aptly illustrated by his later and larger works, the *Incendium Amoris*[1] and the *Melos Amoris*.[2] These two works are his masterpieces. They reflect Rolle's maturity in the contemplative life. Both are eminently personal.

The *Incendium Amoris* remains the more accessible. Since it contains a comprehensive account of Rolle's mystical career, apart from its final stages, a brief summary of its scope and contents will not be amiss:

> The *Incendium Amoris* [writes Miss Deanesly] is a rambling biography, an explanation of "how Richard Hampole came to the Fire of Love". . . . The purpose of the book is described in the Prologue: "I have wondered more than I can tell," Rolle says, "when first I felt my heart grow warm and glow with no imaginary but with a real and, as it were, sensible flame. For I had not reckoned that such a warmth could happen to any man in this exile. . . . Therefore I offer this book to the sight, not of philosophers and wise men of this world, nor of great theologians wrapped in endless questionings, but of the simple and untaught, those who seek to love God rather than to know many things. For not by disputing, but by doing, is He known, and by loving. . . . Wherefore, because here I incite all to love, and I shall seek to explain the burning and supernatural feeling of love, let this book be allotted the title of Fire of Love."

[1] Cf. Margaret Deanesly, *The Incendium Amoris of Richard Rolle of Hampole* (Manchester U.P., 1915). French annotated edition: Dom N. Noetinger, *Le Feu de l'Amour, le Modèle de la Vie Parfaite, le Pater*, par *Richard Rolle de Hampole* (Tours, 1928).

[2] E. J. Arnould, *The Melos Amoris of Richard Rolle of Hampole* (Blackwell, Oxford, 1957).

The book itself takes forty-two chapters to accomplish this end. In the Prologue, Rolle states his own desire to prove to others the joy of the life he has himself chosen. The next eleven chapters are devoted to considerations preliminary to the understanding of such a life; then come two chapters [XII and XV] where he passes from advice to autobiography and which contain most of the passages quoted in the *Office*. The remaining chapters are mainly a series of discourses strung together with no particular plan, on the various difficulties of the contemplative life, interspersed with prayers and meditations which are the Latin counterpart of Rolle's better known Middle English work. . . . The main idea of the book is simply: that the solitary finds Him whom he loves with a rapture and completeness no other life can afford. . . .

The *Melos Amoris* (wrongly called *Melum Contemplativorum* by Horstman and others after him) has been edited from all extant manuscripts: these are only ten in number, and, when we compare it with the ninety or so manuscripts of the *Incendium Amoris*, this number is significant. For the *Melos* is written in a curious kind of medieval Latin which accounts not only for the small number of manuscripts extant, but for the long-felt want of a complete printed text, as also for the absence of a translation. It is indeed doubtful whether such an extraordinary book can ever be satisfactorily translated. Certainly, no translation could hope to render the unique effect of the most lyrical and most alliterative Latin prose ever written. This style, highly artificial in appearance, yet quite spontaneous, has a charm of its own and is an instrument perfectly attuned for the expression of mystical experiences.

The *Melos* takes up where the *Incendium* left off: it carries us one stage further, and the emphasis is now on the climax of Rolle's mysticism: the melody. Having reached full enjoyment of union with God, Rolle is now less inclined to refer to the past or to preach a message. Although he still describes his endeavours, and the favours he has received, in order to encourage others, he is mostly concerned with the expression of joy and gratitude. Whatever the precise chronology of Rolle's works, there is no doubt that his *Melos Amoris* marks the climax in the spiritual elevation of the hermit. The apotheosis of Love which he describes there is, to him, a foretaste of the joys of heaven.

The last few pages of the book, on "the glory of the saints" as promulgated at the Last Judgment, are the fitting culmination of the many chapters he has devoted to "the perfection of the saints," as exemplified in his own spiritual pilgrimage. His conclusion is a farewell: "I now proceed towards a happy end—for I have nearly completed my arduous progress—in order that, trampling corruption under foot, I may find consummation in song." Either Rolle foresees the end of his earthly pilgrimage, or, more probably, having achieved the aim he had set himself, he now prepares to enjoy this highest gift, the *melos*, to the full.

From all these works of Rolle there emerges a fairly clear picture of his activities, of his experiences, and even of his temperament. For none of them, however traditional in character, is totally devoid of some autobiographical element. One gets the impression of a man with a sound university training—witness his expert handling of the Latin language both in verse and prose—particularly familiar with the Old and New Testaments, but bent on his own purpose (*singulare propositum*) and, in spite of his dependence on the traditional and Patristic literature, largely independent in the elaboration of his views on spiritual matters. This independence, however, entails no breach either of orthodoxy or charity. And it must be noted that on the few points of dogma to which he has occasion to refer, such as the question of predestination, the authority of the Scriptures, or the infallibility of the Church, his orthodoxy is unimpeachable. Again, when describing his own mystical experiences, he acknowledges these not as rewards for his endeavours, but as free gifts from God's bounty: nor does he claim credit for them, except, perhaps, in so far as he has striven to prepare for them. Even so, he does not present them as purely arbitrary privileges. It follows that his own case is not presented merely as an object of wonder and envy, but as an example containing a practical lesson even for beginners in the way of spiritual perfection.

Rolle's spiritual pilgrimage began with his "conversion." The *Office* gives a lively and somewhat melodramatic picture of a young man, freshly returned from Oxford, running away from home and friends, making for himself a crude hermit's outfit with one of his sister's dresses; and, a little later, boldly standing up in church, marching up to the pulpit—admittedly with the approval of the parish priest—and delivering an extempore sermon which those present declared to be the finest they had ever heard. Whatever the facts behind these highly-coloured scenes, Richard clearly came to a sudden resolve to flee the world of his youth and to devote his life to the pursuit of perfection. His first endeavours on that path show nothing exceptional. He meditates on the Passion of our Lord, one of the mysteries of divine love that had particularly struck him and contributed to his conversion. Then he turns to the worship of the name of Jesus, and, at the same time, his devotion to the holy Mother of God provides an outlet for the highly sensitive soul of the young hermit: a beautiful expression of this devotion is found in Rolle's *Canticum Amoris.*[1] He remained faithful to these devotions of his youth, but allusions to them are naturally less common in his later works, since they were eclipsed by the great mystical gifts on which the later works concentrate.

The young man's progress was not, however, without difficulties. Some of these were due largely to his impulsive, intransigent, and even eccentric temperament. He clashed with some of his patrons, like John Dalton, a friend of his father; he objected to interference from former gay companions; he had to face temptations of a sentimental, if not sensual, nature; loneliness sometimes seemed to him hardly bearable; and he suffered from temporary frustration in his yearning for perfect quiet, and in his desire to preach the ways of salvation to others. Hence his wanderings, "like Cain in flight after his crime," in search of the ideal hermitage; wanderings that were denounced by unfriendly tongues as a sign of restlessness—although Richard Rolle was certainly never the type of "Robert renne-aboute" pilloried by *Piers Plowman.* At last, he was able to settle down, probably in the vicinity of Hampole nunnery. In the solitude ultimately found, he continued to read and meditate, mostly the Sacred Books. Among these he recommends the Prophets, the Gospels and the canonical Epistles, and he quotes freely from the *Apocalypse.* But his favourite seems to have been *The Song of Songs.* It is from this that he borrowed the phrase which recurs as a leit-motiv in most of his works: "Amore langueo." Characteristic of this time of reading and meditation are his "postils" or brief commentaries. He described himself as *"probatus postillator,* experienced writer of postils." Reading and meditation were his preparation for contemplation—*labor, sed dulcis,*

[1] A. Wilmart, "Le Cantique d'Amour de Richard Rolle," *Revue d'Ascétique et de Mystique,* xxi (1940), pp. 143 sq.

desiderabilis et suavis . . . bonus labor. As usual Rolle speaks from experience, and it is from experience also that he describes the joy that rewards earlier efforts. It was surely in order to alleviate these efforts, and to ensure greater freedom from material conditions, that he came to adopt the sitting position at prayer, and insisted on this apparently trifling detail with a curious obstinacy in his English as well as his Latin works.

Gradually, almost imperceptibly, one can watch him pass from these early stages to higher spheres. Eventually the "door of heaven" opens before him, and he begins to be prepared for what would now be called the transforming union. He repeatedly describes these experiences, which are summed up in the three words: "*dulcor, calor, canor*" (later *melos*). Of these, only the last two are mystical gifts in the strict sense. "Sweetness" was felt by him as soon as the difficulties previously encountered had been overcome: it no doubt represents the sensation of relief and moral well-being normally experienced by a soul freshly detached from worldly bonds.

As for the "heat"—a phenomenon curiously parallel with Blaise Pascal's famous ecstasy—Rolle has given us an account of it with unusual precision, in the *Incendium Amoris*:

> Eventually I made great progress in spiritual joy. From the beginning of my change of life and the transformation of my soul, three years, less three or four months, elapsed until the heavenly door opened before me, when the eye of my heart was able to behold the denizens of heaven and to discover the way to my Beloved and how I could go on sighing for Him. Since then, the heavenly door remaining open, barely one year passed until the time when I felt the heat of eternal love within my heart: I was sitting in a chapel and, enjoying the sweetness of prayer and meditation, I suddenly felt in myself an unusual and pleasant warmth. At first I wondered where this came from, but after a prolonged experience of it, I realised that it emanated not from a creature but from the Creator, for it became ever more ardent and more pleasant. This material and inexpressibly sweet warmth remained with me nine months and a few weeks, until the time when I received from above the gift of hearing the celestial melody. . . .

There is, however, a noticeable difference in his description of his experiences in the *Melos Amoris*. In the *Incendium Amoris*, Rolle says that the fire was succeeded by the "gift of hearing the celestial song." He is speaking here merely of "internal, or spiritual song" as opposed to the external and material, having been rebuked, so he tells us, for not taking part in public singing in church and having replied to this accusation at length. In the *Melos Amoris* the song becomes "melody," the main theme of the book, Rolle's last work. He describes it as the highest grade in the love of God; it drives away care, grief, and fear; spiritual joy turns to rapture when this supra-material harmony is heard. But only the soul in close union with the Beloved, and especially the solitary, can enjoy it fully. For the *melos* is incompatible not only with earthly songs, even those of the liturgy, but also with worldly contact of any kind. It is a foretaste of heavenly joys and, as such, defies accurate description.

Although these three gifts, *dulcor*, *calor*, *canor* (or *melos*), are the special reward of solitaries and contemplatives, they can be experienced by anybody, in any milieu. Even the *melos* can be enjoyed in the midst of various occupations, as was the case with Rolle. But one cannot expect to receive them as of right; and, admirable and desirable as they are, these exceptional gifts are not the sole or necessary signs of mystical union. What is more, they do not constitute the essence of perfection; and Rolle never refrains from giving more commonplace advice to beginners. He insists on remote preparation, on purity of mind and body, and on the other Christian virtues, humility, patience, self-denial—all necessary preliminaries before love can reign in the soul and transform it.

This way of preparation, too, is exemplified by Rolle's personal experience. And once he has reached the summit, he finds himself in a state of steadfastness, serenity, and confidence, which, in its highly lyrical expression, might easily, especially when taken out of context, be mistaken for overweening pride: God himself has been his teacher, and to God he appeals against all contradictors. Nothing will ever deprive him of the joy he derives from his permanent union with the Beloved or of his conviction that his salvation is assured. Such confidence is, of course, the logical result of his profound conviction and his trust in God. It gives expression to feelings that cannot accurately be described, still less adequately explained. Intransigence is here a form of refusal to compromise with error or sin. Exhilaration in the description of God's gifts is a form of tribute to God's munificence. But Rolle's intransigence and his accents of triumph never degenerate into rebellion or vainglory. Indeed, in contrast to the eccentricities of his "conversion" as related in the *Office*, and despite the fierce tone he occasionally adopts in discussion, despite also the extravagance of his style, Rolle was never inclined to excess or violence. Just as his submission to the Church on any point of official doctrine was absolute at all times, so his attitude in practical matters of asceticism was always governed by common sense and reason. This may well explain his peculiar insistence on the advantages of the sitting position during prolonged contemplation. It also explains how he had occasion to refute malicious accusations of mixing with sinners (an accusation which, as he rightly pointed out, had been levelled at Jesus by the Pharisees) or of not practising severe fasting and maceration (to which he replied that mortification of the flesh should not be carried to the point of rendering mind and body unfit for prayer and meditation).

Again, no extraordinary supra-natural phenomenon marked Rolle's mysticism. He himself never claimed any special power over natural forces, even though the *Office* tells us that, through contact with him, Margaret, a recluse and his disciple, recovered her lost speech and her health. On the whole, Rolle remains profoundly human and, apart from the frequent lyrical outbursts found in his works, every one of these works contains useful advice. Unlike, for instance, Walter Hilton or the anonymous author of the *Cloud of Unknowing*, Rolle does not set out to teach. With the exception of the short works addressed to individuals— probably, in such cases, on request—he does not write treatises of the usual kind. Rather than a teacher, Rolle is a witness. His example, as he had hoped, presents a concrete case of man's elevation, through the normal stages of purgation and illumination, to constant union with God, and of the joy resulting from this intimate union. St. Teresa defined mysticism as "that which no skill or effort of ours, however much we labour, can attain to, though we should prepare ourselves for it, and that preparation must be of great service." This definition applies to Rolle perfectly and would have won his approval. Even the beginner can derive much benefit from following the holy hermit on his pilgrimage. To all, at one stage or another, Rolle is a guide as well as an example.

It is true that the average reader may sometimes find Rolle's style abstract or even abstruse. It is true also that a fair knowledge of Latin is required for a full appreciation of the verbal fireworks in the *Melos Amoris*, since, as we have already observed, a translation could hardly be more than a necessary evil. But Rolle's style is always appropriate to his mood of the moment; and, in several works of his, Latin or English, especially the latter, the thought is conveyed with great simplicity and clarity, while bearing always the personal mark of its author. The quality of Rolle's English writings can be judged from the fact that Rolle was selected by Professor R. W. Chambers as a master link in the continuous development from the Old English of King Alfred to the Elizabethan English prose of St. Thomas More and his school. Richard Rolle's style, like his message, has lost nothing of its freshness or its vigour. Both have won for him a permanent place of honour in the pageant of great English religious writers.

12. THE MONK OF FARNE

Hugh Farmer

THE FARNE MEDITATIONS,[1] written in Latin, are the work of a Benedictine monk of Durham, who became a hermit on the island of the Inner Farne off the Northumberland coast about the middle of the fourteenth century. From the convergence of various scraps of evidence in the Durham and Farne Account Rolls, it seems that he should be identified with John Whiterig who became a monk of Durham *c.* 1350, was Novice-Master for several years from 1356, settled at Farne in 1363 and died there in 1371, probably at the age of less than fifty. These meditations are his only surviving writings, and they tell us most of the little we know of his life and personality.

In his youth he had studied at Oxford and narrowly escaped death by drowning in the River Cherwell. Perhaps it was then that by his own account he shared to excess the current taste for "fables." A further reference to the Black Death, more probably the epidemics of 1361–2 or 1368–9 than the more famous one of 1349, and an allusion to his being the inhabitant of an island while he was writing, all but complete the scanty biographical data we know of him.

He lived during an eventful period of history. The Church was ruled by the popes of Avignon, England (for most of his life) by Edward III. Relations between Church and state were difficult, but in practice a *modus vivendi* was found. Ecclesiastical

[1] The single extant manuscript of these meditations, in a good hand of the later fourteenth century, is in the Durham Cathedral Library. The meditations were first described by J. Raine, *North Durham*, 1843, pp. 343 ff., and more recently by W. A. Pantin, "The Monk Solitary of Farne," *English Historical Review*, May 1944, pp. 162–86. The Latin text was published in full by the present writer in *Analecta Monastica*, Studia Anselmiana, Rome, *IV* (1955), pp. 141–245; and an English translation by the Benedictines of Stanbrook Abbey was published in 1962 by Messrs. Darton, Longman and Todd. The present article, which includes material from the Introduction to this book, is published with their kind permission.

controversies were numerous: at Oxford seculars and mendicants disputed about the legitimacy of ecclesiastical ownership, the basis of jurisdiction, and the nature of dominion and grace, until all united against Wyclif's heretical teaching on the Eucharist. At Durham itself in 1346, the year of Crecy, a Scottish invading army had been heavily defeated at Neville's Cross, just outside the town, and the Black Rood of Scotland captured and placed in the cathedral, where it remained until the Reformation. Spasmodic border warfare by land and sea continued, however, for the greater part of Whiterig's life.

The fourteenth century was not in all respects an age of decadence and strife: the mystical writings produced during it both in England and on the Continent surpassed in quantity and quality those of any other medieval century. It was the age of Tauler and Suso, Hilton and Rolle, Juliana of Norwich and the author of the *Cloud*. Although Whiterig had certain affinities with some of these writers, his outlook was rather different from theirs, for he represented, in the main, the traditional way of the Black Benedictine of the cloister, and his thought was based very closely on Scripture, the Liturgy and the Fathers.

Durham cathedral priory in the fourteenth century was perhaps at the highest peak of success. It recovered quickly from the Black Death and had a learned and able prior in John Fossor, and a theologian of national importance in Uthred of Boldon. The splendid tomb and throne of Bishop Hatfield is symbolic of the magnificence and generosity of one who considerably enlarged Durham Castle and endowed Durham College at Oxford for the monks. The cathedral itself was enriched with large new windows and the Neville screen, while new monastic buildings were also erected, the most famous of them, the monks' dormitory, being begun soon after Whiterig's death. The Durham community, with several dependent cells in the North, numbering perhaps a hundred monks in all, occupied a high social position in the land, and the Northern magnates sent their sons to be educated in the Prior's household.

It was perhaps partly in reaction against this splendour that Whiterig retired as a solitary to the austere and bleak Inner Farne, following in the footsteps of St. Aidan and St. Cuthbert in the seventh century and St. Bartholomew of Farne in the twelfth. In so doing he was also following a slender but persistent tradition in Benedictine monasteries, of which such famous abbeys as Cluny, St. Albans and Westminster provided examples. But the urge to the eremitical life did not only belong to the past. In the fourteenth century English Carthusian monasteries increased from two to seven in number, while a number of other religious, notably Dominicans in the North, are known to have lived as solitaries. Traces of at least seven hermits, laymen or priests, have been found in Northumberland at this date, and another seven in Durham, to whom the priors used to give alms. But the total number of hermits and anchorites there was probably very much greater.

Farne itself had long been used as a hermitage by Durham monks. Geoffrey of Coldingham's life of St. Bartholomew of Farne described it as "formerly the fortress of devils but now a cloister and a school for saints. It is a kind of Purgatory on earth, suitably established for healing souls and bodies. It always contains, indeed it actually forms, men of virtue, for when someone is led by the Spirit into the desert he must expect to be tempted by the devil. As a consequence he either cultivates sanctity or else leaves this holy place."

Its material conditions, especially in winter, were such as to ensure the survival only of the physically and spiritually fittest, but in summer, perhaps Whiterig would write his meditations on the cliff-tops, with the birds and the sea for company, in the intervals between his duties of prayer and work. The latter included cutting wood, presumably washed up by the sea, and the records mention boats belonging to the Farne Monks who fished from them with both net and line. They supplemented their rather meagre endowments with the sale of seals, porpoises and other fish as well as eider-duck eggs.

Seven in number and of unequal length and quality, the Farne meditations form a coherent whole which reveals their author as one whose outlook was completely centred on the Person of Christ and who, while being a sturdy traditionalist, was also sensitive to the more affective piety of his own day. His very choice of meditations as his literary form is significant. These had been popularised by writers of the twelfth century like St. Anselm and John of Fécamp and can be contrasted with the later and more elaborate productions favoured by St. Edmund of Canterbury, John Mirk and others. Also typical of his deep

L

roots in the past are his very frequent use of the Bible and texts from the Fathers and the Liturgy, which are woven together with great skill somewhat in the style of St. Bernard, who indeed was probably the greatest non-Scriptural influence upon him. His affinity with other writers of his age may be seen especially in his tender devotion to the Crucified Christ, which is nevertheless restrained and far from the sentimentality of certain other writers of the later Middle Ages. These features, together with his emphasis on doctrine rather than on sentiment, tend to give to his writings a timeless rather than a "period" flavour and should be attractive to readers of our own day.

The first of the seven meditations, addressed to Christ Crucified, is nearly twice as long as all the others put together, and is also the most important. A miniature treatise on the spiritual life, its principal theme is God's love for men, revealed especially by Christ's death on the Cross, which requires man's total love in return as the only attitude befitting a redeemed creature. This meditation is also the key to the others which work out the author's thought about Our Lady, the Angels and his favourite saints, all of whom have already been mentioned at some length in the first one. It seems likely that it was written first.

This meditation falls naturally into three main parts. After an introductory chapter, the author addresses Christ under a series of Old Testament types, including Adam, Abel, Noah, Isaac, Joseph, Samson and David. Here especially biblical citations abound, perhaps excessively. The most important chapter of the section presents God's Son speaking to the Father on our behalf and expressing His readiness to undergo the Incarnation in order to fight and conquer the devil, a patristic rather than an Anselmian presentation. Then follows the first of several verse passages, presumably by the author, which form an unusual feature of these writings.

The second part of this meditation is a direct consideration of the crucified Christ from several different points of view. His sufferings of varied torments for our sake are listed with deep sympathy and reverence. In return Christ asks for man's heart and his love, and this response should be complete.

I know well, Lord, that thou desirest my whole self when thou askest for my heart, and I seek thy whole self when I beg for thee. I know too, Lord, that thou wishest to possess me entirely in order that thou mayest be entirely possessed thyself, and this thou dost for my sake, not for thine own.

The devout soul is visited by Christ with extraordinary sweetness and joy; such experiences gave surpassing strength to the martyrs and saints of old. These examples of the triumph of divine grace lead on to a brief consideration of predestination and the danger of blindness of heart and ingratitude, shown especially by lack of charity and preferring creatures to the Creator. Nevertheless none should despair of God's mercy. The sacraments of baptism and penance were instituted to enable us to return to God. Christ has given us a sign of hope. That sign is Himself, with arms extended on the Cross to embrace man and draw him to union with Himself. In comparison with knowing this sign of Christ crucified, other knowledge is rather ignorance.

The meaning of the sign of Christ crucified is then explained according to the allegorical, the moral and the anagogical senses. Allegorically the outstretched arms represent the Law and the Prophets or the two Testaments. Morally we are led into the heart of Christ to be united with Him who by a word created the universe. Anagogically the right hand signifies eternity, the left hand riches and glory in this present world, through which the Church passes to enjoy the embrace of her bridegroom in heaven.

Then the author exhorts the reader to draw near in spite of his unworthiness and learn to read the open book of the Saviour's body on the Cross. The letters of this book are His wounds; the words are His actions and sufferings. Knowledge of this book is necessary for salvation, a deep knowledge of assimilation obtained by metaphorical eating and digesting, which will lead us by penance to complete what is lacking in the sufferings of Christ.

In the two following chapters occur the culminating points of this section of the meditation. The author sees the events of his past life as the expression of God's merciful love on his behalf:

Thou, sweet Jesus, art all my good: thou art my ability in work and eloquence in conversation, my proficiency in study and achievement in enterprise, my consolation in adversity and caution in prosperity. Whichever way I turn, thy grace and mercy go before me, and often when it seemed that all was over with me, thou didst suddenly deliver me. Thou didst bring me back when I went astray and instruct me in my ignorance; thou didst correct me in my sin, console me in my sorrow and comfort me in my despair.

During a crisis caused by this despair the author experienced a vision of Christ Himself, who consoled him.

O Lord of hosts, Jesus most lovable, what caused thee to be so solicitous in my regard that thou hast not only willed that the heart of thy servant should experience that delightful, hidden presence, which overflows with fullness of joy and avails for love's close embraces, not only chosen to give me that hope which thou givest to other sons of the Church through patience and the consolation of the Scriptures? That wouldst not suffice thee, but over and above it all thou must needs teach me, not through Thy beloved evangelist John who proffered my petition to thee, but with thine own mouth, how I could be saved on the day of Judgment; for that was my petition. Merrily and with mild countenance thou didst call out in reply : "Love, and thou shalt be saved."

The section concludes with a prayer of confidence that as Christ has given this pledge to the writer, so He will deign to lead him further towards the heights: "Perfect, good Jesus, what thou hast wrought in me . . . what I ask for is exceedingly great and sublime, and can only be reached by degrees."

The mention of the degrees of love leads on to the third part of the meditation which is a description of the spiritual life seen as the progressive ascending of these various degrees by the faithful soul. Although the author nowhere says, "Love is repaid by love alone," this saying of the best-known modern saint does sum up the thought of the monk of Farne. And like St. Bernard, whose influence in this section is both obvious and dominant, Whiterig saw the development of the spiritual life in terms of the progress of charity. "St. Bernard," wrote one of his modern disciples, "wrote no treatise on mysticism; for him mysticism is quite simply the last rung on the ladder of charity. . . . St. Bernard's mysticism is not a function of mental prayer, it is simply a perfect participation in the love which God has for himself: *sic affici deificari est.*" The Monk of Farne cited and made his own many of the fundamental texts of St. Bernard's mystical teaching, and the same principles of interpretation should be applied to each. It may be remarked that nowhere does the monk of Farne make a division of the spiritual life into two sections, "ordinary," and "extraordinary" or "mystical," but clearly sees the unfolding of the life of grace and charity as one single process with the highest degree of charity (including mystical experience) at the end. Of his own experience he says little beyond the passage already cited. But he envisaged the highest degree of charity as something within range of his practical aspirations as well as of his speculative thought.

The progress of the soul towards God is traced through the early stages of what St. Bernard called carnal love of Christ by means of hearing of Christ and mortification. There follow the stages of a more rational love: study of Christ, joy and unworldliness reached through trying always to do what pleases Christ, whatever the consequences and in all circumstances. To these stages correspond the precept to love God *toto corde* and *tota anima;* to love *tota virtute* corresponds a third stage of unitive love, characterised by extreme ardour combined with liberty, by distaste for the present life and finally by a certain loss of the use of the senses, and even by death through charity rather than through any particular disease. This phenomenon was also described by St. John of the Cross.

As he could not witness to such an event from his own experience, Whiterig made use of the evidence of other writers. First of all he cites the relevant stanzas of the long lyrical poem *Philomena* by Archbishop Pecham, which describes the death of the nightingale as a figure of the death of a spiritual person from the love of God. Another example is given in a delightful story of a medieval solitary, told in a revelation that a certain girl in a distant province was predestined to the same degree of glory as himself. When he went to visit her he found that she appeared to do nothing extraordinary either in her devotions or in her austerities, but that she was a virgin who had dedicated herself to the love of God in great and continual joy. During the hermit's visit she died from no other apparent cause. Further descriptions of this highest degree of divine love are cited from standard authors, especially from Hugh of St. Victor. Our Lady and St. John are evoked as examples of saints who were spared the martyrdom of the sword so that they could die as martyrs of divine love. The author then expresses the wish that he might be guided in the spiritual life by one who had experienced its highest degrees, and sees in the lives of such souls the vindication of the Incarnation and Passion of Christ.

I know, Lord, and I know it well and truly that from all eternity thou didst foresee such as would be wounded by the darts of thy love, and so thou didst take flesh. To redeem them thou didst choose to die, not that they had merited thine incarnation and death, as though anyone had first given to thee and afterwards thou hadst repaid him, but it was rather by virtue of thy death that they were able to do what thou didst from all eternity foresee they would do. Thus thy death . . . was itself the cause and origin of every meritorious act whatsoever.

The meditation ends with a prayer in prose and verse for present needs and final perseverance.

In this, the longest of the meditations, the chief characteristics of the author's spirituality and style are to be found. His personal devotion to Christ and his frequent representations of the wisdom of the past as expressed in Scripture, the Liturgy and the Fathers have already been noted. He relies on the soundest teachers rather than on his own experience, and this is not surprising in view of his comparative youth and limited knowledge. His doctrinal emphasis and his disciplined restraint, together with his taste for traditional spiritual wisdom, are almost certainly characteristic of the monastery which formed him.

We may also note his special prayer for the Durham community to which he still belonged, and it is perhaps significant that there is no specifically eremitical tendency expressed in his writings. Nor is there even a description of his own surroundings or a passage in praise of solitude. He tells us nothing of his abandonment of the amenities of Durham for the bleak austerity of Farne, and only as *obiter dicta* does he let fall a few scraps of information about his former life. Like many other monks before and since, he was more concerned with Christ than with spiritual autobiography, with sound doctrine than the description of his experiences.

In contrast to the author of the *Cloud of Unknowing*, he shows no trace of the negative or so-called Dionysian approach to contemplation. His experience of prayer appeared to be through the formulae of the Liturgy, fed by assiduous meditation on the text of Holy Scripture. In contrast to Margery Kempe and even to Methley there seems to have been nothing unbalanced or overwrought about him. In contrast to Rolle, he considered the Passion not in terms of the bursting out from Christ's limbs of the Precious Blood, but instead he compares the honour shown to the sacred Head by angels with the insults and sufferings inflicted on it by men on Calvary. Here he was perhaps nearer to St. Thomas and St. Bonaventure than to some of his contemporaries.

But by his treatment of the Sacred Heart the author deserves a small place among the spiritual writers from St. Gertrude to St. Margaret Mary Alacoque who propagated this devotion, sometimes wrongly regarded as a product of Counter-Reformation spirituality. Whiterig wrote of the Sacred Heart as a refuge of sinners:

> Precisely because I am a sinner, I have fled to thee, since there is nowhere I can flee from thee save to thee . . . I will run to my Lord as he beckons me to come and by touching him, I shall be cleaned from all impurity of body and soul . . . I will enter into thee and not stay without, for outside thee there is no salvation . . . Kind, humble heart, allow me to hide with thee from the face of the Lord's anger, for he is coming to judge the world. If thou choosest the left side, then let me remain on the right: Christ's body is not so strait that it cannot hold us both at once. So let us make here two tabernacles, one for thee and one for me, and there will still be room for Abraham, Isaac and Jacob to take their places, together with all those who follow their way of life. And the heart of Jesus answers me: "If thou didst not desire to dwell with me, I would not have allowed thee to enter here. But now, since it is my delight to dwell with the sons of men, I will not cast out him that cometh to me. Where I am, there let him be whom I love and by whom I am loved."

Whiterig gives the impression of a sane, holy and well-adjusted person. One point which illustrates this is his admirable balance between compunction and joy. He had neither the gloom of the Puritan nor the neglect of repentance, so common in our own day. Other passages already cited are sufficient evidence for his compunction; the following shows his thought on joy:

> Cheerfulness adds just as much to our actions as action adds to a right intention, for cheerfulness in the doer is at once both a sign and an effect of a loving heart, and if we have not got that, all that we do goes awry.

Lastly it may be asked whether the monk of Farne was anti-intellectual: in some passages he attacks those who prefer knowledge to piety, in others he exalts the kind of knowledge which cannot come from books. But parallels to these passages can be found *mutatis mutandis* in the Fathers, and even St. Thomas

Aquinas praised the old woman who knew more about the immortality of the soul than the philosophers. In fact the theme is almost perennial, and can be traced back to St. Paul's teaching on the wisdom of this world contrasted with that of Christ crucified. St. Bernard too had written in similar vein; each was representative of monastic spirituality on the relation between learning and charity.

Both would have agreed that reading and meditation, especially of Holy Scripture, are a preparation for contemplation; if they are to be fruitful, continual effort at penetration and memorising must be made. But in moments of contemplation all images are suspended, and the soul adheres to the Mystery of God without being able to explain it. Whiterig cites St. Gregory's aphorism, that love is itself a kind of knowledge, and the words of Ambrose Autpert: "If we seek to understand thee, we do not discover thee as thou art; it is by love alone that thou art attained." William of St. Thierry, among others, taught the same. In so doing, he and others were representative of monastic spiritual writers, who combined a just appreciation of the primacy of charity in contemplation, with a proportionate emphasis on the importance of the preparatory intellectual element of *lectio divina*. St. Bernard did not want his monks to be foolish, and every page of the Farne meditations is witness to our author's assiduity in sacred reading. Neither would have supported a cult of ignorance or encouraged the suppression of intellectual activity in spiritual matters, but both recommend the simplification of intellectual activity in harmony with an asceticism which should lead to perfect union of God by charity. But meditation on the truths of faith through *lectio divina* is its normally indispensable preliminary.

The meditations to the saints share the same general outlook as that to Christ crucified, of which indeed they may be considered the completion. In that work warnings were given against the undue exaltation of any creature:

> Therefore do not by your love make for yourself a god of any one save him alone who loved us so greatly when we did not as yet exist. I do not forbid the love of the saints, but I do desire that right order should be kept in loving them.

This admirable recommendation was doubtless kept by the

author; but there is one passage in the meditation to Our Lady which seems to contradict it. Misled by a text attributed to St. Augustine, Whiterig, whose intentions were perfectly orthodox, fell into inaccuracies of language. Taken out of its context the sentence "The flesh of Mary is God and may be adored without blame" would be condemned as heretical. But when we look into the context of such an astonishing statement we find that the phrase "the flesh of Mary" is used of the humanity of Christ, not of the flesh of Mary's own body. It means, as the author says, "the flesh which thou dost possess in thy son, for it will never cease to be thine own flesh since he will never cease to be thine own son." Such an explanation exonerates him from any evil or erroneous intention, but his choice of language was, to say the least, unfortunate. In the same meditation he described the sanctification of Mary at the Annunciation by the Holy Spirit as including the elimination of "every trace of original sin in thee." At the time when the author wrote this the Immaculate Conception was not a dogma, but a matter of theological opinion. Scotists insisted on the unique privileges accorded to the Mother of God, while Thomists insisted rather on the need of every creature, Mary included, for the grace of Redemption, accomplished through the death of her Son on the Cross. Each side had one aspect of the truth, and what was good in each was included in the definitive settlement of the controversy by the Bull *Ineffabilis Deus* of Pius IX in 1854.

On the subject of the angels the author's personal affective outlook is again very much in evidence, and his meditation forms a notable addition to the series of medieval prayers to the angels collected by Dom Wilmart. It is also closely connected with an English prayer to the Guardian Angel preserved in another Durham manuscript book of meditations:

> Myn angel that art to me ysend
> Fro God to be my Governour,
> Fro all yvyl thu me defend
> In every dyssese be my succour.

This meditation, which contains most of his meagre autobiographical data, is also one in which the author recalls the theological teaching he had received years ago, and shows sufficient interest in disputed points to opt for the opinion of Peter the

Lombard and St. Thomas on the angels' spirituality and for that of St. Gregory and St. Bernard on the role of the Seraphim and other higher angels.

The meditation on David and Abraham is more unusual in its subject-matter, and is written evidence for the devotion to the patriarchs and prophets so often shown in medieval sculpture, stained glass and miniature painting. In the early chapters of the meditation to Christ Crucified the patriarchs were seen as types of Christ and David as a type of the Church, but now, they are studied rather as models respectively of repentance and obedience. Both are invoked in face of the "misery and pestilence by which we are afflicted." Also worthy of note is the author's supposition that Adam had lived for only six hours before the Fall, an opinion much nearer St. Irenaeus' "child Adam" than St. Thomas' picture of a perfect adult man. On a less serious level we may also notice, apropos of a jocular use of words of the Psalter in an accommodated sense:

> Any comedian, out to raise a laugh in his audience, would find passages from the psalms, did he but know them and care to make use of them to enhance his performance; though to debase such sacred mystic words to such profanities would be no slight sin.

The final meditation on St. Cuthbert is unfortunately incomplete. It might have told us more both about Durham and about hermit life on Farne. But it is perhaps most reasonable to suppose that death overtook John Whiterig before he could complete it, that, worn out by the austerity of the Farne hermitage, he passed while still young to that perfect love of God whose earlier stages he had already described in the meditation to Christ Crucified.

To the contemporary reader the timeless elements of the Farne meditations will appeal, even if the mode of expression, which would have pleased the presumably monastic readers he wrote for, is occasionally unfamiliar or wearisome. The cult of Christ crucified and devotion to the saints who modelled their lives on His are as necessary and desirable today as in the fourteenth century. The degrees of the love of God have not changed since then, nor are the sacrifices necessary to attain its heights any less taxing: the exigencies of the Gospel do not change from one age to another. His strongly Scriptural interests will appeal to the present age of the revival of Biblical studies, the balanced outlook manifest in his writings throws fresh light on the mentality of the late medieval cloistered monk. But most appealing of all are the many expressions of his personal relationship with God: "Give me thy self," he says, "and the rest take for thyself. Whatever there is besides thee does not satisfy me without thee, nor hast thou any gift to bestow which I desire so much as thee."

Remember, sweet Jesus, whom I seek to please, that it is Thee I desire to love above all. Make me joyfully to fufil thy commands so that I may see thy face for ever, and deal with me so mercifully before I die that I may know that I love nothing so much as God. May I be protected by thy hand from all present evils, and find firm support in the sign of victory! Ward off famine, foe and plague, grant us all-pervading peace, and for the sake of tranquillity cause brethren to be of one mind. Put an end to wars, keep far from us the deadly injury of sin; and lest souls rush headlong to perdition, be thou to us a tower of strength!

13. WILLIAM FLETE

Benedict Hackett

ST. THOMAS MORE in his *Dialogue of Comfort against Tribulation*, written probably not long after his imprisonment on 17 April 1534, devotes a chapter to what he calls the daughter of pusillanimity, namely scrupulosity. The ex-Lord Chancellor puts his finger on this baneful problem of the spiritual life when he writes:[1]

> the scrupulous person . . . of that which is no sin, maketh venial; and that that is venial imagineth to be deadly . . . and then he feareth that he be never full confessid, nor never full contrite, and then that his sins be never full forgiven him; and then he confesseth, and confesseth again.
>
> Moreover, he (the devil) maketh him to take for sin some thing that is none, and for deadly, some such as are but venial, to the intent that, when he shall fall in them, he shall by reason of his scruple sin.

These passages, however, do not represent an original contribution to the theology of scrupulosity. Whether or not St. Thomas was aware of it, they are in fact derived from a treatise written not later than the summer of 1359 by William Flete, an English Austin friar.

Flete, if we can trust a contemporary writer who knew him personally in Italy, was born about 1310. There is reason for thinking that he was a native of Fleet in Lincolnshire and entered the Augustinian Order *c.* 1325. He appears to have studied theology at the concursory school attached to the Lincoln friary, and was later sent to Cambridge to qualify for the degree of master of theology. The earliest certain date in his career is 29 February 1352, when he was licensed for the diocese of Ely. Very probably he had been designated by the provincial chapter of 1351 to read for the degree of master of theology at Cambridge, which accounts for his residence there early in the following

[1] *A Dialogue of Comfort against Tribulation*, Book II, xiv (ed. London 1847?), pp. 123-4.

year. At this period the English Austin friars experienced an awkward and at times acerbated situation over promotions to higher studies. An influx of foreign students added to the difficulty, though there can be no doubt that the extraordinary turn which Flete's vocation took was decisively influenced by his contacts with Italian *confrères* at Cambridge. In 1353 he appears to have entered upon the statutory year of opponency and was admitted to lecture on the Sentences at the beginning of the academic year 1354-5. Having duly completed the required course of lectures he proceeded to lecture on the Bible and to prepare for the final exercises leading to his inception as master. This was due to take place when the university resumed on 10 October 1358, but some time before 17 June he made it known that he was not taking his degree. Flete's movements during the twelve months that followed his renunciation of the coveted *magisterium* are uncertain. We do not know even if before leaving Cambridge he had set his heart on going out to Italy, or whether this resolve took shape and hardened some time later. At all events he left England with two companions on 17 July 1359, fully determined never to come back, no matter what the cost might be in terms of human feeling. His destination was the celebrated monastery of his Order at Lecceto outside Siena.

At Lecceto or *Selva del Lago* Flete from the day he was formally assigned the status of a conventual (8 September 1359) until his death some thirty years later lived the life of a true Hermit of St. Augustine. A Florentine writer has recorded the following notice of him fifteen years after his entry to Lecceto:

In Selva del Lago four miles from Siena there is a place of the friars hermits of St. Augustine in which there lives an English friar who is called the Bachelor of Selva del Lago, and has been there for more than twelve years. This is a man of great learning, a venerable man, of great sanctity and solitude. He lives mostly in the said wood in his cells which he himself has made in dark and rough places; and there he brings with him his books in order to escape the conversation of people. And to this place he goes, and comes from the church to the wood and from the wood to the church. This is a man of mature counsel, a friend of God, and a man of great example; and he speaks little except when necessity obliges him.

The accuracy of this sketch is vouched for by another contemporary, Ser Cristofano di Gano Guidini, who says perhaps
all that need be said of Flete's reputation when he describes him
as *un spiritualissimo religioso.*

Though Flete had to do violence to nature in order to with-
stand the pull of homeland and old friends, at Lecceto he had
the compensation of winning the friendship of the three outstanding personalities of late *Trecento* Italian spirituality: St.
Catherine of Siena, Blessed Giovanni Colombini, founder of
the *Gesuati,* and Blessed Giovanni dalle Celle, the great penitent
of Vallombrosa. It is arguable that Catherine's theological
formation during the crucial years 1362–74 was mainly the work
of William Flete. The predominant Augustinian character of her
thought has been noted by Professor Dupré Theseider, and it is
significant that Flete was the only authoritative theologian and
spiritual master to whom Catherine could turn for guidance
before Raimondo da Capua became her confessor and director
in June 1374. Already, the Virgin of Fontebranda had written
at least twenty-one letters which contain almost all the funda-
mentals of her spiritual doctrine.

Flete's last years were clouded by the painful memory of his
estrangement from St. Catherine in 1379 when he refused to
come to Rome to give direct moral support to Pope Urban VI.
It must have been some consolation, however, that she not only
forgave but fully reaffirmed her confidence in him before her
death on 29 April 1380. In Siena his reputation as a man of sound
judgment and exceptional holiness remained unshaken, and when
he died *c.* 1390 the city regarded him as a saint.

Despite his limitations he was unquestionably one of the most
remarkable figures in the history of late medieval English
spirituality. He enjoys the distinction of being the only direct
contact between the so-called English school of mystics and the
Italian. Whether he himself was strictly speaking a mystic is open
to question; certainly his extant writings afford little or no reason
for believing that he was. It must be remembered, however, that
none of his letters to St. Catherine have survived, while two to
Giovanni dalle Celle and one each to the *Signorie* of Siena and
Florence have likewise disappeared. Altogether five letters, a
legend of St. Catherine's life set in the form of a lengthy sermon,
an excellent summary of her spiritual teaching known as the

Documento spirituale (7 January 1377) and a treatise on the remedies against temptations constitute the sum total of his available literary work. The most valuable are three letters addressed to his English brethren and the opuscule, *De remediis contra temptaciones*.

The setting and contents of the three letters which Flete addressed to the friars of his native province early in May 1380 have been discussed elsewhere[1]; it is not proposed to do more here than summarise the main points, except where the author should be allowed to speak for himself. His intention was not to plot a map of the religious life but to impress on the English Augustinians the necessity of reform and to show the direction it should take. The emphasis throughout is on the eremitical character of the order as exemplified in its official title, Hermits of St. Augustine. Flete insists that the friars should be "lovers of holy and solitary religion," and this line of thought which lies behind his own vocation to Lecceto and the peculiar mode of life he practised there show clearly that the English spiritual tradition fully harmonised with his view of things.

For Flete the precise sources and standards of Augustinian life are the Rule of St. Augustine and the constitutions of the Order. What he sets down as the principles of religious life are directly related to the opening chapters of the rule or rather to some of its significant passages. Augustine's maxim, "love God before all things" demands first and fundamentally that we keep the commandments. Love of one's neighbour, the second cardinal point, rules out at every level—provincial, community and personal—any species of discord. Union of spirit and oneness of soul, as prescribed by the rule, mean, says Flete, that the friars should preserve complete and lasting concord and that all without exception, as far as possible, say the divine office together in church with all diligence, distinctly, exactly, slowly and devoutly. These and the observance of the common life "are the principles of holy religion; they foster charity and edify the neighbour." His attitude to mendicant poverty is strict without being extreme; but he castigates those who would make their friaries stepping-stones to masters' degrees, honours, authority and easy living. Students need proper training in right values, and

---

[1] B. Hackett, O.S.A., "The Spiritual Life of the English Austin friars of the fourteenth century" in *Sanctus Augustinus vitae spiritualis magister*, ii (Rome, 1959) 482-92.

Flete admonishes the masters of theology to teach them not to lose the substance for the accident:

> You ought to assist the priors so that all, both students and others, humbly obey them, and instruct the students not to lose the substance for the accident; as they advance in learning, let them more strictly uphold the Order and its observances. They should be more instant in divine things in so far as place and time allow, and make corresponding progress in morals. Otherwise, perhaps, their study will be to them a torment. Those who neglect observance for study waste their time and study, and in the end find themselves deluded and deceived. They should principally study not for a degree but out of obedience. Such an intention as studying for a degree is a corrupt intention. *Every corruptible work fails in the end.*

The masters themselves must be models of virtue. Some of them, for example Richard Brotherton, had been fellow-students with Flete; and it would be interesting to know how they reacted to this piece of pleading:

> You more than all others are bound to be removed from worldly pomps, conditions and conversations, and to observe common poverty and the common life with the rest, just as the blessed Augustine did; and as place and time allow, stay in your rooms as in a hermitage, in solitary cells, and there apply yourselves to study, contemplation, devotion and prayer. There, when God inspires it, do your penances in secret so that henceforth a master's room be not like a tavern to the confusion of souls and the destruction of the Order, but for the edification of souls. Let it be a place of solitude and contemplation; otherwise you do not deserve to be reputed masters of the Order of St. Augustine, but worldly masters.

Flete considered nothing more disastrous for religious Orders than members who must always be out. If charity or necessity or obedience compels one to go somewhere and mix with people this may be tolerated; but, he writes, too many for no good reason spend the whole day away from their convents. Often there are more outside than inside the monastery: *aliquando plures sunt in foro quam in loco, pauci in choro.*

There is much other material in Flete's letters which might be cited for its wisdom and sound psychology, such as the formation of novices and occupational interests. Nothing, however, gives us a surer insight into his own mentality than his teaching on charity. He begs the English provincial, Henry Teesdale apparently, to get the friars to preach charity:

> Many religious are deceived, because they observe the husks of religion, namely silence and such-like external trappings, when going to chapter, to the refectory, etc., and lack charity. They envy others, discredit them, they murmur, blacken the reputation of others. They form parties or set one Order against another, or brother against brother because of a degree or state. Monks keep silence; they speak with their fingers but they don't observe charity by receiving our brethren or the Carmelites at the guest-house. They say that it is not their custom. A bad custom should be abolished. Let them beware lest Christ say to them: *I was a stranger and you did not take me in; go you cursed into everlasting fire.* Religious perfection does not consist in these external things: it is principally founded on works of charity and hospitality and such-like. The apostle says: *Be hospitable to each other without murmur.* Love hospitality. Religion is also based on obedience, patience, humility, meekness and the other interior—not exterior—virtues.

This spirited assessment of religious values is all the more impressive because it comes from one who himself led a life of dedicated asceticism. Flete appreciated fully the place which silence and bodily mortification hold in the Christian scheme, but he makes it quite clear that they are not the principal thing. The interior virtues, particularly obedience, patience, humility, meekness, and, above all, charity, are what matter. Ascetical practices and customs which clash with the claims of charity and lack interior balance he considers "vain and presumptuous." When he speaks of charity he means charity which is active, sincere and unselective; it is what St. Augustine calls *amor socialis*. Flete's hidden life at Lecceto and indeed each of his three letters to England prove beyond a shadow of doubt that he upheld the primacy of the contemplative life. He also held that the perfection of contemplation is achieved by works of charity such as hospitality.

The treatise on the remedies against temptations must have been written before Flete's departure from England on 17 July 1359. This short essay, on a subject which Abbot Vonier once complained still awaits a thorough theological study, became one of the popular spiritual manuals of the later Middle Ages in England. Thirty-seven Latin and English manuscripts survive,

M

and at least five more are unaccounted for. In fact the work must have had a much wider circulation, and so far we have identified not less than four recensions of the Latin and three of the English texts. Hilton appears to have studied it though in an interpolated text. St. Thomas More, as we saw above, was influenced by it; and Fr. Augustine Baker inserted a late Middle English recension of the text into his *Anchor of the spirit* (1628–9). Direct or indirect quotations appear in the *Discerning of spirits* and *Speculum christiani*, both of the fourteenth century, and in the *Of the direction of a man's life, Fervor amoris* or *Contemplations of the dread and love of God, Speculum spiritualium* and *Donatus devotionis* —all fifteenth-century compilations. At least one spiritual director *c.* 1400 drew heavily on it for a letter of counsel to a client, and complete texts of the treatise were acquired by priests, religious and laity.

The *De remediis* opens with a discussion on temptations against faith, "the foundation stone of the Church and origin of all virtues." We are shown how the devil attempts to undermine faith, and if unsuccessful will try to set up a state of continual doubt in the soul. His wiles are to be warily and spiritually resisted, and in attacks against faith and morals

> a man should not wonder or dwell on them or stick at them or analyse or investigate much their causes, since the more one insists on analysing what is erroneous or false, the more he plunges himself into error. A man should not anger himself on account of such objects or blame himself or impute them to his own fault, because a temptation of faith or hope is most painful and grievous, the pain is hardest, the fault is least. To one who is faithful it is altogether involuntary and displeasing, and therefore painful and no sin. For every sin is voluntary and if not voluntary there is no sin according to Augustine.

None the less, a soul under stress of temptation may think itself alienated from God. On the contrary, as Isidore teaches, he thinks more of the soul because it praises him while suffering. Though the devil cannot tempt beyond the limits set by God, the just man is never free from his attentions, and under the stress of diabolical infestations of the mind and heart he may be brought to the point of despair. If, however, he continues to love and fear God, his sufferings in fact deepen his virtue.

Temptation sometimes takes the form of diffidence or hesitation about matters of faith. This condition is the result of fear instilled by the devil, causing the soul to think it has committed grave sin when such is not the case:

hesitation in the faith in order to be sinful must be wilful and complacent or at least feigned ignorance, which tends more to error than truth. And therefore, since faith is a habit of the will, the will to believe is faith, the will to hope is hope and the will not to waver is firmness. *With the heart one believes unto justice.* For merit and demerit reside in the will which alone cannot be forced.

It may happen that the mind becomes so overclouded that a man cannot see what his will is. This should not upset him, since good works are a proof of goodwill, and they are always to be presumed good until the opposite is reasonably certain. If the temptation becomes really fierce, then we may on rare occasions declare our belief. But nobody should be deceived by the devil who is a liar; and in any case "the enemy is weak who only conquers the willing and this with a will which is deliberate, agreeable and fixed."

Flete offers a further explanation of mental obscuration in terms of natural philosophy. The Evil One explores each person's complexion or disposition and vexes in a spiritual way those who are prone to melancholy. Natural philosophers—Flete has Constantinus Africanus in mind—describe how the light of reason is obscured by a dark smoke rising to the brain which prevents the mind from seeing clearly. People so afflicted are sad and timid, pusillanimous and arid because of their complexion. They believe what is false to be true. And so, the devil assesses each man's weakness and tempts him accordingly. By agitating his complexion and instilling fear he succeeds in causing such despondency that life itself is regarded as a torture and death a release. At this point Flete assembles a cluster of apposite quotations from the scriptures and shows that trials and temptations are used by God to purify the soul. In the words of the *Ancrene Riwle*, one needs spiritual fortitude to bear like Job this bitterness patiently and humbly. Did not Christ himself suffer desolation? It is little indeed that we suffer in this moment of time in comparison with the eternal reward which we may hope to receive from God's mercy.

Spiritual people are singularly tried; but as long as goodwill remains they cannot lose faith or hope; rather they are confirmed in every virtue:

> This kind of temptation and the remedy is hinted at by the Saviour when he said to his disciples: *Behold Satan has sought to sift you like wheat.* A man is sifted when he is intimately and perfectly examined. On the other hand he is strengthened and perfected when confirmed in good through the virtue of patience and prayer and the wise counsel of his neighbour.

Flete also recommends prayer, recitation of the psalms, scripture reading, particularly the prophets and the gospels.

St. Catherine once criticised him on the grounds that he made too much of spiritual consolations. The charge does not seem to be quite just. In his *De remediis* Flete expressly teaches that the withdrawal or absence of sensible devotion makes for great progress in prayer. St. Bernard says that when we seek God He hides Himself in order that we may seek Him with more earnestness, and Augustine explains that the Lord does not deny His gifts but sometimes delays to give. By obliging us to ask, seek and demand He increases our capacity and turns our desires to greater things. At the beginning of their conversion certain souls experience a state of sensible sweetness, and then when they are solidly established in the love of God He withdraws this grace so that they may increase in merit and thus win a higher reward. Virtue, according to Aristotle, has to do with what is difficult; hence that which is acquired with greater difficulty is more virtuous. Developing this point, Flete introduces the Pauline distinction between the milk and solid food of Christ's doctrine:

> At first God feeds some with the milk of sweetness and devotion and then He builds them up with the food of attrition and tribulation. It is indeed sweet and delightful to follow God when one is happy at heart and enjoys unruffled tranquillity of mind; but it is arduous and most perfect to follow God with entire desolation of heart and continual assaults against faith or mind. It was sweet and easy for Peter to be with Christ in His joyous transfiguration when he said: *It is good for us to be here;* but it was truly hard and frightening for Peter to be with Christ in His cruel persecution when he said: *I know not the man.* And yet he who was terrified by the voice of a servant-girl, when later fortified by the Holy Ghost, confessed Christ without hesitation unto death before the council of the leaders.

Once again Flete turns to the relationship between man's complexion or temperament and the passion of fear. He advises the sufferer not to withdraw into himself or search too deeply into things; it is best to open the mind to the right person, a man of discretion, and abide by his counsel. Sadness and pusillanimity are to be counteracted by the joy and *élan* which strength of soul and virtue produce; and in fits of depression and fear we should rouse ourselves with bursts of gladness and fun.

Some practical problems arise from the devil's ability to transform himself into an angel of light by suggesting vice under the guise of virtue and error under the cloak of truth. For example, he brings up thoughts of past sins when one is reading his breviary and urges on him the necessity of examining his conscience. The aim is simply to distract the reader. In this matter and at all times during prayer the one great remedy for getting rid of fantastic flights of imagination and spiritual temptations is to pay them no attention. At other times it is suggested that certain sins have not been forgiven or at least only doubtfully. The suggestion must be subtly declined even though an erroneous conscience may urge otherwise, since the devil's intention is not purity of conscience but turbulence in the soul: "though confession of sin is useful and necessary when demanded by true remorse and saving compunction, nevertheless it is of no use and unadvisable when suggested by a false and doubtful opinion." We must use discretion and follow the example of Christ who refused to cast Himself down from the pinnacle of the temple, choosing instead to walk down by the steps of discretion. Another artifice on the part of the devil is to perplex the mind by painting something as sinful and wrong which in reality is either good or indifferent, and as mortal something which is only venial. The idea is to unhinge the soul through repeated confessions and paralyse it from doing good by inducing a false conscience. It may happen that the devil will impel one to obey an erroneous conscience rather than submit to the judgment of a prudent man. Discretion is absolutely necessary; it is the hand which guides all the virtues and saves us from being deceived under the pretence of good.

As Augustine points out, it is often difficult to decide whether one is moved by a good or evil spirit. A good spirit inspires good, whereas an evil spirit deceives; it deceives even in things that are manifestly good so as to win credence and then seduce the soul. We may regard, for instance, some thought or concept as our own when actually it is the devil's work. Here again it is essential not to insist on one's own opinion but regulate it by obedience to truth and discretion. Failing in his attempt to lead the soul astray, the Evil One turns to harass it with false fears and to instil the poison of his wickedness. We must manfully resist these deceptive suggestions and accept patiently and humbly the pain of mental anguish.

If he fails to bring a person to commit sin while awake, the devil has recourse to nocturnal visitations, oppressing the soul with various kinds of illusions and terrors in the form of dreams. God, as St. Gregory comments, allows the elect to undergo these trials so that even in their sleep they may have the reward of suffering. "Oh in what wondrous and varied ways," exclaims Flete, "is the soul of a God-fearing man driven and buffeted!" And he adds:

> how pious and useful it is, how charitable and salutary to comfort and strengthen one so troubled and afflicted, who is passing, more-over, through the fire of trial and the water of tribulation, and to lead him forth into the refreshment of quiet and consolation, which quiet and consolation so desired in spirit even if the one thus troubled may not immediately obtain it or must certainly go without it for a long time, let him firmly hope that he must finally have it, *because many are the tribulations of the just and from all these the Lord will deliver them.*

By way of postscript and as an expression of the underlying spirit of his study, Flete recites in full the sixth and most moving chapter of the *Stimulus amoris*, which sounds the depths of God's mercy in allowing men to be tempted, and where those who are afraid to go to Christ because of their wickedness are recommended to place themselves in the hands of Our Lady who will grant them their request.

The value of Flete's treatise on temptation can best be judged by comparing it with those of other medieval writers on the subject. The treatment is sober, restrained, sympathetic and grounded on sound theological and psychological principles. The style is straightforward and devoid of the imagery and anecdotage that mar the otherwise useful and indeed valuable works of medieval writers on the vices and virtues. Flete's deficiencies, however, are obvious enough; apart from faults of loose construction and repetition, he completely overlooks the steadying and energising influence of the sacraments of penance and holy eucharist on the soul under trial. Here as elsewhere he reflects the spiritual attitude of his time. Yet one must regret that he did not set down in writing his views on the wider aspects of the spiritual life, for he was exceptionally well qualified by theological training and personal experience of the secret and deep movements of the soul. His real significance lies no doubt in the peculiar story of his vocation to Lecceto. Newman had perhaps more reason than he realised for assigning William Flete a place in his projected lives of the English saints.[1]

[1] Cf. "Lives of the English Saints" in J. H. Cardinal Newman, *Apologia pro vita sua* (ed. London, 1890), p. 338, Note D, where opposite the year 1400 Fr (Car) Austin occurs.

14. THE CLOUD OF UNKNOWING

James Walsh

W HEN Richard Methley, a professed monk of the Charterhouse at Mount Grace in Yorkshire, made his Latin
translation of the *Cloud of Unknowing* towards the end
of the fifteenth century,[1] he complained that books on contemplation are understood only with great difficulty "in modern
times" because the Charity of God has grown cold. But almost
immediately after he had written his famous book on contemplation, the late fourteenth-century anonymous author appears
to have found himself under heavy fire from contemporary
theologians. So he told the disciple to whom he had addressed
the *Cloud*, in *A Letter of Private Direction*: ". . . some folk say
(and I am not speaking of illiterate men and women but of very
learned theologians) that what I write to you and to others is so
difficult and so profound, so subtle and unfamiliar that it can
scarcely be understood by the subtlest theologian or most intelligent man or woman alive." "Whereas," the author claims for the
method of contemplative prayer which is the thesis of the *Cloud*,
"if we look at it properly, we find it to be a simple and easy
lesson given by an illiterate."[2] Some students of comparative
religion have purported to see as the foundation of this book of
contemplation a basic 'natural' mysticism common to Christians
and non-Christians alike; whilst certain modern philosophers,
who favour a refined agnosticism, have asserted that the God of
the *Cloud* is not the triune God of revelation, but one whom
theists of every creed may worship. Though several Catholic
scholars in recent years have clearly demonstrated the perfect
orthodoxy of the author and the traditional nature of the *Cloud*'s
spirituality,[3] most Christians are inclined to regard it as a *disciplina*

[1] Methley was professed a Carthusian in 1476. The Pembroke College (Cambridge)
Ms. of the *Caligo Ignorancie*, which bears Methley's name, is dated 1491.

[2] The modernisations of the Middle English of all the works of the author of the *Cloud*
cited here are my own.

[3] Cf. Eric Colledge, *The Medieval Mystics of England* (London, 1962). David Knowles,
O.S.B., *The English Mystical Tradition* (London, 1961). Conrad Pepler, O.P., *The English
Religious Heritage* (London, 1958).

arcana, a new kind of gnosticism or, at the least, as teaching an esoteric doctrine meant only for an *élite*. After all, the author himself warns us at the outset — and he repeats his admonition at the end of the book — that he is not writing for everyone, but only for those who have been called to the contemplative life.

Yet we must notice one important qualification which has perhaps today more significance than it had in fourteenth-century England:

> I must, however, make an exception for those who are 'actives' in their outward form of living, yet because of their inward striving after the hidden spirit of God are disposed by an abundance of grace to share in the work of contemplation at the highest level; not of course permanently, as is proper to true contemplatives, but every now and then. If men such as these read this book, it should, by God's grace, be a great source of strength for them.[1]

There are many in the Church today, layfolk as well as religious, who fall into this category, potentially at least. These pages are written primarily for them.

At the same time, it is essential to remember that the *Cloud*, like most of the author's other extant works, was written with one person in mind: a young man, the direction of whose soul the author has recently undertaken. He is one who was first called out of the world to the religious life, but who has subsequently received a further call "to the third degree and manner of living, which is called singular . . . a solitary form and manner of living."[2] This second call appears to have taken place after the author had undertaken the direction of the disciple. In a previous letter to him, *On discerning spiritual impulses*, our author had warned him against following his impulse for the solitary life until he should arrive at "the clear and true knowledge of himself and of all his inward dispositions." We have no means of knowing the external circumstances of this "singular" vocation. There is no evidence to show that the disciple withdrew from a more apostolic form of religious life to the solitary life, as did Hugh of Lincoln or Adam of Dryburgh; we cannot even conclude from the phrase describing his first vocation, "he kindled your desire with an abundance of grace, and led you by it to a more

[1] *Cloud*, Prologue.
[2] *Cloud*, c.I.

special state and form of living, to be a servant of his special servants," that he was a laybrother in the Carthusian or any other order. In any case, the author of the *Cloud* is not concerned with the variety of outward circumstances of contemplative living. This is the reason for his slightly unusual division of the active and contemplative lives. For him, there are two aspects of the active life: the exterior works of mercy and charity, and the interior exercises proper to this life — "good spiritual meditations on man's fallen state, on the passion of Christ and the joys of heaven."[1] This second aspect of the active life is also the first stage of the contemplative life. It is the stage to which all religious indifferently, and, indeed, the type of layman to whom Walter Hilton addresses his letter on *Mixed Life*, are called.

The second stage, the way of contemplative perfection, requires a special call to a solitude of mind and heart. A fairly long apprenticeship in the first stage is normally required before this special grace is given, though the author never tires of repeating that the call is in no way merited by fidelity and fervour in the life of the first stage; it is entirely gratuitous. The call is also highly individual, completely independent of circumstances of time or place; and a high degree of discernment is required in order to judge whether the call has or has not been received.

It is with this way of contemplative perfection, and the preparation for it in the first stage, that the author of the *Cloud* concerns himself in all his works. What appears to be his earliest extant writing, *A study of the pursuit of Wisdom, entitled Benjamin*, is an exposition of the virtues of reason and will proper to the lower stage of the contemplative life — *qua* contemplative — which culminate in discretion, that knowledge of self which is an absolute prerequisite for the contemplative knowledge of God. This work is a highly skilful précis and simplification of the *Benjamin minor* of Richard of St. Victor, which uncovers, after the manner of the medieval exegete, in the Bible story of Jacob and his wives and children, the progressive purification and reform of the soul in the divine image to the point "when it is purified and aflame and you steadfastly behold it, a certain brightness of God's light begins to shine in your soul, and a kind of spiritual sunbeam becomes visible to your spiritual sight. By means of this the eye

[1] *Cloud*, ch. 21.

of your soul is opened to behold God and Godly things, heaven and heavenly things."

For a right understanding of the *Cloud's* spirituality, we need at least an elementary knowledge of the traditional psychology which the author adopted, ultimately from St. Augustine. This is the reason for his discursus in the *Cloud* on the five powers of the soul, three principal, Mind (which is a general power comprehending all the others, "properly speaking, it does not work itself," but the other powers work "in it," and it works by them), Reason and Will or Affection, and two secondary: Imagination and Sensuality.[1] "The sensuality is a power whose sphere of activity is in the bodily senses; through it we have knowledge and experience of all bodily creatures, whether they please us or not. It has two functions: one through which it looks to our physical needs, the other through which it ministers to the pleasures of our senses." Before the fall, the sensuality was the true servant of the will, "but now it is not so; for unless it is ruled by grace in the will, so that it can accept the pains of original sin, which it experiences in the absence of things pleasant demanded by the body, and in the presence of unpleasant things beneficial to the spirit . . . all our living becomes beastly and carnal, instead of being human and spiritual."[2] The imagination is similarly affected by the fall:

> This disobedience of the imagination can clearly be seen in those who are recently converted from the world to a life of devotion, in the time of their prayer. For until the imagination is in great measure controlled by the light of grace in the reason, as it is in continual meditation on spiritual things . . . they cannot get rid of the elaborate variety of thoughts, fancies and images which are served up and imprinted on their minds by the light and curiosity of the imagination.[3]

Preparation for the contemplative way consists first of all in that co-operation with grace to acquire the virtues described in *A Study of Wisdom* whereby sensuality and imagination are brought under the control of will and reason.

The ultimate purpose of the special call to contemplation is

---

[1] *Cloud*, chs. 62–66. It has been suggested that these chapters have the appearance of an addition, perhaps for polemical purposes. But it clear from ch. 67 that the author considered this brief psychological explanation as essential for an understanding of "spiritual words and works ".

[2] *Cloud*, ch. 66.

[3] *Cloud*, ch. 65.

"to be carried up in your affections and beyond your understanding," to "experience Him directly, as He is in Himself, in
the supreme point of your spirit, by being made one with His
love," the highest degree of union with God which is possible
in this life. The psychology of the author of the *Cloud* received
its final shape through the influence of the Dionysian school of
spirituality.[1] The starting-point of all the medieval Dionysians
was the *Mystical Theology* of the Pseudo-Dionysius. They believed
that the writer of this short treatise was Denis the Areopagite,
the Athenian disciple of St. Paul, who is mentioned in the Acts
of the Apostles.[2] Paul had said that he was concerned to teach
wisdom amongst the perfect, a wisdom hidden in mystery which
his converts were not spiritually mature enough to understand.[3]
The medieval students of Denis considered that he had been
commissioned by Paul to proclaim this hidden wisdom amongst
the perfect, such as Timothy and Titus; and that the core of this
teaching was contained in the *Mystical Theology* and in another
work, *On the Divine Names*. The author of the *Cloud* is one of the
most eminent exponents of this medieval Dionysian school. "If
anyone will examine the works of Denis," he says at the end of
the *Cloud*, "he will find that his words give obvious support to
all that I have said . . . from the beginning of this treatise to the
end." And he himself has left us an English version of the *Mystical
Theology* under the title *Denis's Hidden Theology*. The medieval
Dionysians all accepted the comprehensive dichotomy of the
powers of the soul into reason and affection or intellect and will.
The author of the *Cloud*, following closely the master of the
school, Thomas of St. Victor (whom he mentions in the prologue
to *Hidden Theology*), expresses it thus:

> All rational creatures, angels and men alike, have in them one princi-
> pal working power which is called a knowing power, and another
> principal working power, which is called a loving power. To the
> first of these two powers, the knowing power, God, who made
> them both, is eternally incomprehensible. But to the second, the
> loving power, he is completely and fully comprehensible—though
> in a different way in every soul; so much so that one loving soul
> alone, by the power of love, can comprehend in itself him who is
> enough and more than enough to fill all the souls and angels that

[1] Cf. *Dictionnaire de Spiritualité*, art. *Contemplation*, tome II, cols. 1973-8.
[2] Acts 17, 33.
[3] I Cor 2, 4-7; 3, 1.

THE CLOUD OF UNKNOWING

could ever be.[1]

It has been suggested that the psychology of the author of the
Cloud differs in one important respect from that of Thomas of
St. Victor and his followers. The Victorine "teaches that the
supreme mystical apprehension of God is achieved by a special
faculty of the soul which he calls *principalis affectio* . . . The author
of the *Cloud* gives quite a conventional account of the faculties
of the soul."[2] Thomas's doctrine is that in the ascent to God, a
point is reached when both intellect and will are drawn upwards
by special contemplative graces and transformed, in preparation
for union. The name given to intellect and will when their full
powers are thus energised is *apex intellectus* and *apex affectus* (or
principalis affectio); these powers are, at the moment of the transforming union, in some way separated from the mind which
contains them. The term used by the author of the *Cloud* for this
full extension of intellect and will in unitive contemplation is "the
supreme point of the spirit". "When you are in this state", he
says, "your love is both chaste and perfect; now it is that you
see your God and your love of him both together; and you
also experience him directly, as he is in himself, in the highest
point of your spirit, by being made spiritually one with his
love".[3]

But in the actual comprehension of God, the final consummation of the union when "a marriage is made between God and
the soul",[4] the power of the intellect, even supported as it is by
special graces, special illuminations, fails, and it is in the affection
alone that union is experienced. The most vivid description
given by the author of the *Cloud* of this moment of union is
worded thus: "And therefore give heed to this exercise and its
marvellous working in your soul. For rightly understood it is a
sudden and unheralded stirring speedily springing up to God
like a spark from the coal".[5] The Latin name given to intellect
and will as they work together in the way of contemplation is
synderesis, the natural impulse by virtue of which the soul is

---

[1] *Cloud*, ch. 4.
[2] Phyllis Hodgson, *The Cloud of Unknowing and the Book of Privy Counselling*, Early
English Text Society (London 1944), p. lxvii. Miss Hodgson repeats the suggestion in
her edition of the other treatises attributed to the author of the *Cloud*: cf. *Deonise Hid
Divinite* (London 1955), p. 121.
[3] *A letter of Private Direction*. Cf. also *Cloud* ch. 37.
[4] A Letter on Prayer.
[5] *Cloud* ch. 4.

the image of the Sovereign Good, and naturally adheres to it. This impulse, when perfectly purified by the love of God, is called the *scintilla synderesis*, for it flies above the soul like the spark above the fire. "Here you are above yourself . . . made one with God, in spirit and in love and in union of wills . . . You or anyone else who experiences the perfection of this exercise may truly be called, by reason of that union, a God, as scripture testifies."[1]

Substantially, the *Cloud* is hardly more than a detailed explanation, diffuse in texture and highly personal, of what the author believes to be the method of contemplative prayer taught to Timothy by Denis, the disciple of St. Paul:

> My friend Timothy: whenever you apply yourself, by the impulse of grace, to the practical exercise of your dark contemplation, be intent on abandoning with an intense, intelligent and loving contrition both your bodily senses . . . and your spiritual faculties also— those which are called your intellectual operations, and all those things outside yourself which can be known by any of your five bodily senses, and all those things within you which can be known by your spiritual faculties . . . and in so far as it is possible (for me to speak of this and for you to understand), be intent on ascending with me under the impulse of this grace, in a way that you can never comprehend, to be made one with him who is above every substance and every kind of knowledge. For it is by passing beyond yourself and all other things, and so purifying yourself of all worldly, carnal and natural love in your affection, and of everything that can be known according to its own proper form in your intellect, it is in this way, when all things are done away with, that you shall be carried up in your affection and above your understanding to the substance beyond all substances, the radiance of the divine darkness.[2]

The references to contrition, grace, love and affection are, we know, grafted on to the speculative 'negative' theology of the neo-Platonist, which owes more to Greek philosophy than to Christian revelation, by the medieval spiritual tradition. In his *Letter on Prayer*, the author of the *Cloud* gives a practical account of the method in terms which are scarcely recognisable as Dionysian. He begins in a manner which calls to mind the first stanza of the *Spiritual Canticle* of St. John of the Cross.[3]

[1] *Cloud* ch. 67.
[2] *Denis's Hidden Theology* ch. 1.
[3] Cf E. Allison Peers, *The Complete Works of St. John of the Cross* (London 1953), Vol. II. pp 186-7.

"At the very beginning of your prayer . . . bring it home to yourself, and this without any play-acting, that you are going to die at the end of your prayer . . ."[1] For if you do, you will see that to consider in general your sinfulness and in particular the shortness of time left for amendment will bring into your heart a truly effective fear" — the fear which is beginning of wisdom. A short prayer made in these terms, after sacramental confession and amendment, assures us of God's love and mercy; so that fear is joined by hope. Supported by these two virtues "you can safely climb the high mountain of perfection, that is, the perfect love of God. For the graces God gives to strengthen this special awareness of his mercy and goodness in realising that he accepts this little and short service to make up for such long neglect", bring "a great surge of love for Him who is so good and merciful towards you". Fear, hope and love combine in a single spiritual experience, which the author calls reverent affection — true devotion, according to the definitions of St. Thomas Aquinas and St. Bernard. The rest of the letter is a eulogy of this spiritual experience; it is far more meritorious than all other ascetical exercises and austerities; it is a *sine qua non* of salvation; when we offer it to God "you shall be called God's own child, loving him with a pure love, for himself and not for his gifts"; in the perfection of this reverent affection, the soul's reason "is illumined by the clear beam of everlasting light which is God, so as to see and experience the loveliness of God as he is in himself"; and during the time and moment of the experience, "the soul has lost all consciousness of any good deed and kindness that God did for it in this life . . . it neither sees nor appreciates any reason for loving God except God himself"; with this reverent affection, the soul does not ask to be freed from pain nor for the sweetness of love in this life: "you do not care nor take account of whether you are in pain or bliss, as long as you have him whom you love".

No method of prayer could be, it would seem, more simple or more orthodox and traditional than this. For, as we see from his language, it is the pure prayer of love, the *castissima oratio* of the contemplative. It is, in fact, the author's own explanation of the substance of the exercise of dark contemplation, "the

---

[1] It is worth noting that Pope John XXIII insisted with himself on a similar attitude. Cf. THE MONTH (New Series, Vol. 30, no. 3), Sept. 1963, p. 166.

simple intention of the mind reaching out to God".[1] "I call it a simple intention, because in this work the perfect apprentice does not ask to be freed from pain, or for a higher reward . . . neither cares nor takes any account of pain or bliss, but only that the will of Him whom he loves should be done".[2] "This same exercise is the reverent affection . . . it is the Cloud of Unknowing; it is the hidden love established in purity of spirit; it is the Ark of the Testament. It is the Mystical Theology of Denis." The contemplative is called to love God as perfectly as possible in the way in which God reveals himself as loving us: "he has made himself equal to us by adapting his Godhead to our soul."[3] The perfection of this loving condescension is revealed in the incarnate and crucified Christ; so that contemplation is Christ's own sacrificial work in and for his Church. "For Christ is our head and we are his limbs, as long as we are in his love. And whoever wishes to be a disciple of our Lord must lift up his spirit in this spiritual exercise for the salvation of all his brothers and sisters of human kind, as our Lord lifted up his body on the Cross".[4] The same principle of condescension operates in the moment of transforming union, "which is in fact the high wisdom of the Godhead descending through grace into man's soul, knitting it and uniting it to himself in spiritual wisdom and discernment." The allusion to the book of Wisdom and its use in the Christmas liturgy is not lost on us.[5] Like Christ himself on the eve of his passion, the contemplative knows that he has come from God, and that his love and worship of God is the constant movement and effort to go to God[6] in the spirit of Christ's love.

The contemplative exercise is the striving to walk in that love which Christ showed to us when he gave himself up as a sacrifice on our behalf. This is why the exercise is couched for the most part in terms of negation and reparation. The response to the call is to leave all things and offer oneself for purification that the unitive will of God might be accomplished. In the Christian terms of the author of the *Cloud*, the Dionysian ascesis begins

---

[1] *A Letter of Private Direction*. The idea has a scriptural root, traditional in medieval spiritual writing. Cf. Phil 3, 12.
[2] *Cloud* ch. 24.
[3] *Cloud* ch. 4.
[4] *Cloud* ch. 25.
[5] Cf. The introit antiphon for the Sunday after Christmas.
[6] Jn 13,3.

with sacramental contrition (though the Pseudo-Denis never dreamed of giving it any such meaning) and amendment — the renunciation of those creatures which effectively hold back the soul from God. This contrition sums up for the contemplative the knowledge of himself and the effective separation from the world and from all the creatures towards which he is drawn in his affection: a knowledge and separation granted to him in the first stage of the contemplative life, by means of his meditations on his sins and the passion of Christ — "the earthly activity of himself and of God, mourning over what is sorrowful and rejoicing over what is joyful". So he is brought to Christ, the door keeper and the door itself of the inner life; and then he is called to enter in, "to contemplate the love and goodness of the Godhead".

The negative way, then, of this *mystique* of darkness is far from being an abstract quasi-philosophical exercise. It presumes, first of all, that "passing beyond oneself" which is "purifying yourself of all worldly, carnal and natural love in your affection": that is, as near a likeness to the Christ revealed in his earthly life as is possible for man to achieve with the help of grace. Then he must stand at the door, "until, in the judgment of his directors and his own conscience, the greater part of the heavy rust of his coarse earthiness is scrubbed away; and most important of all, until he is summoned to advance further in by the instruction of the Spirit of God."[1] But there is a further sacrifice, another, deeper, self-forsaking:

If any man love me . . . let him divest himself of himself if he truly wishes to be clothed in me who am the rich garment of everlasting love that shall never have an end.

And here is the essence of the contemplative exercise, which is the abandonment of "the spiritual faculties . . . of everything that can be known according to its own proper form in the intellect."

Commentators have not been slow to recognise that this exercise of dark contemplation has much in common with what John of the Cross was later to call the prayer of loving attention. But it can fairly be argued that the teaching of the author of the *Cloud* is in some respects more precise and less complicated, particularly with regard to the positive and sacrificial aspects of

[1] *A Letter of Private Direction.*

the exercise, and the 'signs' which assure the disciple that he is called to the perfection of the contemplative life and prayer. We have said that the author insists again and again on the special call. The exercise is first of all a *response* to a special impulse of grace. This touch is not always felt interiorly, particularly when the soul first enters on the way of contemplation. But it can be known in faith, and it manifests itself by external signs — those sweet desires and longings which are usually called the consolations of prayer. It is possible that these external graces are intended merely to "encourage us to work in the realm of ordinary graces," as will be the case if the desire and the spiritual sight are intimately connected with one's regular devotional and meditative exercises. Similarly, the intense attraction for union may merely be the spontaneous gladness any true Christian should feel when he reads or hears about the divine perfections. But if the outward attraction and inward desire are constant and increasing, and particularly if the desire "forces itself between the soul and its usual spiritual exercises," then these are signs of the authentic call to contemplation.

When the author speaks of the effect of the exercise, he says that "your spiritual affection shall be filled to overflowing with love and powerful faith in God." The reference here to faith should not be overlooked. Though it is constantly asserted that ordinary knowledge of every kind is useless and even harmful in contemplative prayer, this does not mean that the "knowing power" has no part to play in contemplation. The intellect, too, has its "supreme point," which is energised in two ways: first through faith, when in the initial stages of the exercise, under the impulse of grace, the soul labours to concentrate its attention on the simplicity of its own being as assimilated to God who is "its all"; secondly, in the spiritual sight — the luminous faith — which always accompanies the comprehension in love, from its first manifestations when the desire is awakened. It is true that the loving power always sets the pace; but sometimes the divine response to love as it strives to penetrate the darkness is the illumination of the intelligence: "Sometimes God wills to send out a ray of spiritual light, piercing the cloud of unknowing which is between you and him, and to show you some of his secrets." It is true that the mind's activity is almost entirely in the will: the effort to extend, submit and dilate itself to the action and invitation of the Holy Spirit; but there are also times when the intellect must labour: not merely in the negative way of keeping the attention focused, in faith, on the ground of one's being, but also in responding actively to the illuminative graces which are given as proximate preparation for union.

For the author of the *Cloud*, the perfection of the contemplative life is the ultimate of spiritual poverty, the state in which all creatures — and at the summit, man's highest gifts — are rejected in order to have God, the all-in-all: *nihil habentes sed omnia possidentes*. All that remains is that love of God which is poured out in our hearts by the Spirit of God. The exercise of dark contemplation is simply the recognition in daily living, that, with this gift, God gives himself directly.

15. WALTER HILTON[1]

Joy Russell-Smith

"ALSO THESE WORDS that I write to thee, they long not all to a man which hath active life, but to thee or any other which hath the state of life contemplative."[2] Such a conclusion seems to suggest that Walter Hilton, like many of his contemporaries, sees contemplation as the function of a particular state of life. Contemplation he defines as the ghostly feeling and knowing of God. And though his definition reminds us of Ephesians 3, 17–18, where St. Paul prays that *all* his Christians might come to know the length and breadth, the height and depth of God's love, yet for Hilton this knowing is "the occupation of a contemplative man."[3] So he will say, in his *Epistola de Utilitate et Prerogativis Religionis*,

> in the body of Christ, the Church, not all the members have the same work, for one sees in contemplation, another hears in obedience, another eagerly tastes the sweetness of devotion, another touches through the bodily performance of the commandments of God.[4]

The allusion to the famous Pauline text on the Mystical Body shows that he writes in the context of the traditional division between the two "lives" of action and contemplation. Other passages, too, suggest that Hilton wishes to restrict his teaching

---

[1] Nothing certain is known of Hilton's life, except the brief information given in various Ms. colophons, that he was a canon regular of Thurgarton Priory, Nottinghamshire, and that he died there on the Vigil of the Annunciation, 1395.

[2] *Scale I*, Ch. 93, p 223. Quotations of the *Scale of Perfection* are from Evelyn Underhill's edition (Watkins, London, 1948); of *Mixed Life*, from D. Jones, *Minor Works of Walter Hilton* (Burns Oates, London, 1929). Minor modernisations have occasionally been introduced, and all italics are my own.

[3] *Scale I*, Ch. 13, p. 27.

[4] MS. Bod. Lat. th. e 26, fol. 130.

on the ideal of contemplation to those dedicated to the "life" of contemplation—solitaries and some religious.

Yet there are aspects of his teaching which stand in contrast to the accepted division. Not only is he amongst the foremost spiritual directors of his age in his concern for the spiritual needs of *all* men, and his desire to lead them to the fullest love of God; but he is also unusual amongst fourteenth-century contemplative writers in the consideration which he gives to the relationship between outward works of charity and the life of contemplation. Naturally, one cannot speak of oral and personal advice, or of the hidden grace of God in individual lives: I am concerned with the aims of written teaching only.

Hilton obviously shows himself aware that a full turning of the mind and heart to God, a total offering of the self, is not restricted to the vowed offering:

> Certainly God has his own, whether beginning, proficient or perfect, outside regular religion as well as in. For, just as those in religion who fulfil their profession as fully as the great frailty of our modern times permits can attain the perfection of Charity by God's gift through exercising the virtues of obedience, chastity and voluntary poverty, so outside regular religion, if any person *for the love of Christ turns from love of the world and all its concerns and preoccupations* (*at least in the whole direction of his mind*) and chooses poverty, steady prayer and continual meditation, and devotes himself to the other virtues as whole-heartedly as human frailty allows, certainly he may aspire to the same fullness of Charity and spiritual gifts through the grace of Christ as he might if he had entered religion.[1]

And in the first treatise in the *Scale* he reminds the enclosed woman solitary in her contemplative "state" that it may happen that "some worldly man or woman, as a lord or a lady, knight or squire, merchant or plowman, or what degree he be in, man or woman, shall have more meed than some priest, or friar, monk or canon or anker enclosed . . . for he loveth more God in charity of his gift."[2]

Yet the manifold distractions and responsibilities of everyday life in an active state do present special difficulties, and Hilton

[1] *Epistola ad quemdam seculo renunciare volentem*, MS. British Museum, Royal 6 E III, fol. 119 r.a.
[2] *Scale I*, Ch. 61, p. 147.

faces some of them in *Mixed Life*. It is a remarkable work in its period. In it Hilton considers the growth of holiness in the life of someone subject to all the "interruptive" circumstances of a parent and landowner, seeing to his finances, keeping his servants up to the mark, disturbed by his children; someone who also had public responsibilities which in this instance meant attention to his feudal dependants, and the administration of justice.

The core of Hilton's teaching on the contemplative "life" in these outward circumstances is set out in the first chapter, and is based on the text, *ordinavit in me caritatem:*

> Thou shalt not utterly follow thy desire to leave occupation and business of the world (which are needful to use in ruling of thyself and of all others that are under thy keeping) and give thee wholly to ghostly occupations of prayers and meditations, as it were a friar, or a monk, or another man that were not bounden to the world by children and servants as thou art; for it falleth not to thee, and if thou do so *thou keepest not the order of charity*. Also if thou wouldest leave utterly ghostly occupation—especially now after the grace that God hath given unto thee—and set thee wholly to the business of the world in fulfilling works of active life, as fully as another man that never felt devotion, *thou leavest the order of charity*.[1]

As this quotation shows, much of the teaching and emphasis of *Mixed Life* is directed against allowing a deep and exclusive longing for God to turn to self-indulgence in spiritual matters. The layman is urged to perform the secular duties of his state *gladly*, and not be loath sometimes to leave ghostly occupation and intermeddle with worldly business. I doubt whether this slightly negative emphasis was *generally* needed at that time, or is to-day, yet it does not detract from Hilton's positive attitude in reaching out to give help to any man in similar outward circumstances who had been brought to special graces in prayer.

Probably the most remarkable instance of this positive attitude is found in Hilton's adaptation of traditional teaching on the Pastoral life, for here he discusses, in the context of this teaching, the problems of a person with a vocation to carry the responsibilities of secular life. The phrase "active life" with Hilton, as with others, has several meanings. But in the context of the relationship between the two "lives" it means either the life of charity

[1] *Mixed Life*, p. 9.

shewed outwardly, the corporal and spiritual works of mercy,
or those acts of penance, purgative works, which prepare a man
for the contemplative life.[1]

Traditional teaching had little or nothing to say of the interior
life of contemplation in relation to active works of charity,
except with regard to Prelates and Preachers; Hilton's contemporaries spoke of the "mixed life," the blending of action and
contemplation, only in the Pastoral context. But Hilton signifi-
cantly adds:

> also it belongeth generally to some temporal men, which have
> sovereignty with much wealth of worldly goods, and also as it
> were lordship over other men to govern and sustain them—as a
> father hath over his children, a master over his servants and a lord
> over his tenants—*the which men have also received of our Lord gifts
> of grace and devotion, and in part savour of ghostly occupation.*[2]

Usually, no doubt, these "temporal men" would be classified in
the simple active category as they are in *Scale I*, Chapter 2, but
the traditional descriptions of active men do not include all that
Hilton has in his mind when he thinks of such men as receiving
the grace of contemplation. Active secular men are thus encouraged to live a deeper life of prayer by analogy with the state
of prelates, whose outward works ought to be directed and informed by their life of contemplation. I have always been impressed
by Hilton's thinking here: it seems an indication of the force and
insight of his direction that he saw the analogy and applied it.

In this way Hilton gives profound, clear-sighted teaching to
people who have not been called by God to a state of contemplative retirement, or who have never had the intensive spiritual
training of a religious noviciate. He is mindful of the somewhat
haphazard way in which holiness must grow in the shifting
currents of secular life, in obedience to the oddest assortment of
external circumstances in family and professional life. His
teaching stresses not only how there should be time set apart
(on awakening from sleep) for prayer and meditation, but how
even in the most trivial of daily occupations, and also in the
most exacting, the attention of the mind may rest on God. To
the question whether desire for God may be had continually,
he answers:

[1] *Scale I*, Ch. 2, pp. 3–4.   [2] *Mixed Life*, p. 16.

This desire may be had as to virtue and profit of it in habit continually, but not in working or in using, as by this example: if thou were sick and thou should have, as each man hath, a natural desire for bodily health continually in thine heart, whatever thou did, whether thou sleep or thou wake, but not aye alike; for if thou sleep, or else wake and think on some worldly thing, then thou hast this desire in habit only and not in working, but when thou thinkest on thy sickness and of thy bodily health, then thou hast it in using . . . and therefore when thou doest a good deed, or prayest, or thinkest on God, think not in thine heart, doubting whether thou desirest or not; for *thy deed showeth thy desire.*[1]

Nevertheless, with his usual careful discrimination Hilton adds:

though it be so that all thy good deeds bodily and ghostly are a showing of thy desire to God, yet there is a diversity between ghostly and bodily deeds. For deeds of contemplative life are properly and naturally the working of this desire; but outward deeds are not so. And, therefore, when thou prayest or thinkest on God, thy desire to God is more whole, more fervent, and more ghostly, than when thou doest other outward good deeds unto thy even-Christian.[2]

The conclusion and crown of the early chapters is an exhortation to the imitation of the "mixed" life of Christ. It is, again, an application of the traditional teaching on the Pastoral life to the life of the contemplative layman:

One time he communed with men and mixed with men, showing to them his deeds of mercy; for he taught the uncouth and uncunning by his preaching, he visited the sick and healed them of their sores, he fed the hungry and he comforted the sorrowful. And another time he left the conversation of all worldly men and of his disciples and went into the desert upon the hills, and continued all the night in prayers alone as the Gospel saith. This mixed life showed Our Lord to ensample of all others that have taken the charge of this mixed life . . . and, soothly, for such a man that is in spiritual sovereignty, as prelacy in cure, government of others (as prelates and curates be), or in temporal sovereignty (as worldly lords and masters are) I hold this life meddled best and most behoveful to them as long as they are bounden thereto.[3]

As I have said already, Hilton is sometimes at one with those who see contemplation as the prerogative of the contemplative

[1] *Mixed Life*, pp. 48, 50.   [2] *Ibid.*, p. 51.   [3] *Ibid.*, pp. 19, 22.

state. Hence, before turning from *Mixed Life* to the second treatise in the *Scale*, there is a need to consider further his opinions on contemplation in the active state of life. In the classifying chapters of *Scale I*, Hilton's second part of contemplation "lieth principally in affection, *without light of understanding in ghostly things*,"[1] and it is characterised by fervour and devotion during prayer and meditation. Hilton observes that men who are active may have this "when they are visited by our Lord as mightily and as fervently as they that give them wholly to the contemplative life, and who have this gift." Later, when he speaks of his third part of contemplation, "the illumination of the understanding in delights of loving," he says, "though a man which is active have the gift of it by a special grace, nevertheless the full use of it may no man have but he be solitary and in life contemplative."[2] And it is not only when Hilton is in the realm of theory that he accepts a restriction on contemplative life placed by a man's outwardly active state. The same restriction seems implicit throughout the extremely helpful teaching of *Mixed Life*, for one may notice there that he speaks mostly of the middle stage of "devotion." Thus he writes, "If thou by thy prayer get devotion," and again, "if devotion of prayer bring into thine heart a ghostly thought of the manhood of Our Lord." When he uses the term "contemplation" in this work, Hilton usually turns it to mean this one part alone: "Rachel . . . betokeneth life contemplative"; "When he weened to have Rachel (that is rest in *devotion*) . . . Rachel that is grace of *devotion* and rest in conscience."[3] Only at the end of the work is there a discreet mention of his third part of contemplation:

> It is enough to thee and to me to have a desire and a longing to Our Lord. And, if he will of his free grace, over this desire, send us of his ghostly light and open our ghostly eyes *to see and know more of him than we have had before by common travail*, thank we him thereof.[4]

Some people would not use the term contemplation for this stage of "devotion" to which Hilton and the author of the *Cloud* are ready to welcome all generous and devout "active" men; and although Hilton does treat devotion as the result of God's free and special grace, the "sight" or illumination is

[1] Ch. 5, p. 9.   [2] *Scale I*, Ch. 9, p. 18.   [3] *Mixed Life*, p. 33.   [4] *Ibid.*, p. 74.

excluded by the term. Hilton sometimes reserves the term "contemplation" for his third stage alone. For instance, in chapter 75 of the first treatise, he remarks that although "devotion" may even be increased by bodily pain, whether of sickness or penance, "soothly I expect that it letteth the fervour of love in contemplation, which may not be had nor felt soberly, but in great rest of body and of soul."[1] It may well be that Hilton's conclusion to *Mixed Life* shows that he recognised that the man to whom he addresses the epistle is included among those to whom the term "by special grace" applied; but the epistle was evidently intended for the reading of others too, and the general trend of his teaching in this book bears out the opinion expressed in *Scale I*, that the height of contemplation is not usually for a man in an active "state."

The classifying chapters are perhaps not so much Hilton's opinion of what *ought* to happen as his observation of what usually *does* happen.

Nevertheless it seems that he was later perhaps less ready to lay much stress on the outward state of life. The second treatise in the *Scale* seems to me of great importance in illustrating Hilton's later thought on such questions as why so few persons come to the full experience of contemplation; how it is that many worldly-minded Christians impede themselves by simply not caring; that even those who do desire it often impede themselves. The second treatise is markedly different in character from the first, and not only in its main subject, the more advanced stages of contemplation.[2]

The two works appear separately in a number of manuscripts, and, when they do occur together, they do not always carry the title *Scale of Perfection*. To-day both are usually treated as a unity, and there are some signs that Hilton meant them to be so regarded.[3] But the audience of the second treatise appears to be

---

[1] *Scale I*, p. 186.

[2] The separateness, and some of the differences, have been stressed by Miss H. Gardner in *Medium Aevum* V (1936), pp. 14–15, and by Dom Gerard Sitwell in *Downside Review* (1949), p. 277. In his Orchard Series edition, however, Dom Gerard Sitwell treats the second treatise as designed for an anchoress (p. 196).

[3] In the opening paragraph the reference to "an image the which I have before this time in part described to thee" seems an evident link with the last chapters of the first treatise (rather than the *De Imagine Peccati*); also the reference in chapter 20 to the "first party of this writing" probably refers to chapters 64, 71, etc., of the first work, rather than chapter 14 of the second.

conceived differently from the audience of the first (the anchoress and "any other which hath state and the purpose of life contemplative.")[1] The kind of reader an author has expected to serve, or perhaps, less consciously, has felt, can sometimes be discerned in his manner, or in the selection and treatment of material. Sometimes it is made explicit in a preface or by some other means, as in the prologue and concluding chapters of the *Cloud*: the twenty-four year old disciple of Chapter 4 stands for others called to the "sovereignest point of contemplative living possible in this life." The *Epistle of Privy Counsel* is emphatically addressed to one man only. Several of Hilton's writings too were written for a person in some particular outward circumstances or state of life. After indicating what these circumstances were he sometimes adds a general reference to other people.[2] His favourite method seems to be to write to one person with the idea that certain others might listen or read if they wish. In the second treatise of the *Scale* there are no limiting indications of audience at all. We learn nothing of the "thou" because the manner of address is generalised:

> What work that it be that thou should do, after the degree and the state that thou standest in, bodily or ghostly, if it help this gracious desire that thou hast to love Jesus, and make it more whole, more easy, and more mighty to all virtues, and to all goodness, that work hold I best.[3]

Certain groups *are* addressed or mentioned, but these are not religious, contemplative or secular, but souls in various stages of the spiritual life, or souls who are experiencing particular trials: "Souls beginning and profiting have not this love . . . nevertheless unto *such souls* that cannot think of the Godhead ghostly . . . *other souls* that are not subtle in kind nor are not yet made ghostly through grace, it is good to them that they keep their own working in imagination with manly affection."[4] There are many such discriminating passages, and I think they are important as indications of what is in some ways a new type of spiritual writing.

[1] *Scale I*, p. 36.
[2] E.g., "to thee or any other man hath the manner of working in custom" (*Mixed Life*, p. 73), "*te et alios*" "*an tibi vel alii congruant nescio*" in two of his Latin epistles.
[3] *Scale II*, Ch. 21, p. 308.   [4] *Ibid.*, Ch. 30, pp. 359, 361, 363.

Secondly, a great difference in Hilton's manner and bearing is also noticeable, particularly in the absence of those protestations of unworthiness and inexperience which are fairly numerous in the first treatise: "I am full far from that knowing and further from the working";[1] "I feel me so wretched, so frail, and so fleshly, and so far in true feeling from that I speak and have spoken";[2] "Not that I have it in feeling and in working as I have it in saying."[3] Such expressions are entirely lacking in the magisterial manner of the second treatise, even when the very greatest graces of contemplation are discussed. The one remotely similar passage serves only to point to the different orientation of the work. Of the "opening of the ghostly eye . . . principally by grace of the Holy Ghost," he says:

> I dread mickle to speak aught of it, for me thinketh I cannot; it passeth mine assay, and my lips are unclean. Nevertheless, for I expect love asketh and love biddeth, therefore I shall say a little more of it as I think love teacheth.[4]

Hilton never states that he has not experienced what he describes in the second treatise, nor is there any suggestion that he writes there "for my profit as well as thine" or that "I would by these words, such as they are, first stir my own negligence to do better than I have done."[5] The greater security in utterance goes, I think, with the firmer organisation and greater clarity and precision of statement so often characteristic of the second treatise.

Thirdly, the content of the second treatise is much more theological than that of the first. It appears to be a considered formulation of Hilton's doctrine of contemplation in relation to theology. It proceeds from the fallen state of man to the Redemption, and the transmission of supernatural life through the sacraments of Baptism and Penance. Both these sacraments are studied as the means of the "first" reforming of the soul, which yet leaves it apt to sin, and therefore in need of another conversion or "reforming":

> Thou shalt understand that the sacrament of Baptism or of Penance is not of that virtue to let and destroy utterly all the stirrings of fleshly lusts and painful passions, that a man's soul felt no manner of rising nor stirring of them no time.[6]

[1] *Scale I*, Ch. 30, p. 177.   [2] *Ibid.*, p. 34.   [3] *Ibid.*, p. 222.
[4] *Scale II*, Ch. 40, p. 416. [5] *Scale I*, Ch. 93, p. 222. [6] *Scale II*, Ch. 8, p. 251.

This early account of the first seed of grace is retained in the background until Hilton comes to discuss the perfection of the life of sanctifying grace, the grace of infused contemplation:

> This grace is not another grace than a chosen soul feeleth in beginning of his conversion; but it is the same and the self grace, but it is otherwise felt and showed to a soul. For grace waxeth with the soul and the soul waxeth with grace, and the more clean that the soul is, far departed from love of the world, the more mighty is the grace, more inward and more ghostly showing the presence of our Lord Jesus. *So that the same grace that turneth first them from sin and maketh them beginning and profiting by gifts of virtues and exercise of good works, maketh them also perfect.*[1]

The whole treatise is a coherent, comprehensive account of the supernatural life at all its stages, including the greatest experience of contemplation, with a very careful study of grace and its absence and increase.

This exposition of the supernatural life, in its entirety and multiplicity, is a reason why the summary of the second treatise in the Orchard Series 1952 edition of the *Scale* might be a little misleading, where it describes Chapters 1–20 as "a comparison between the state of ordinary Christians and of contemplatives."[2] It might obscure a little the architecture of Hilton's book, and the whole point of his long section on the early stages of the life of grace. It is, of course, an accurate summary in so far as Hilton does speak in these early chapters of the majority of Christians who have "reforming that is only in Faith,"[3] but the conclusion to Chapter 18 brings out the point that this section is by way of preparation rather than comparison:

> And soothly it is wonder to me, that since grace is so good and so profitable, why a man when he hath but a little thereof, yea! so little that he might no less have, that he will say "Ho! I will no more of this, for I have enough. . . ." Mickle more then should a chosen soul covet ghostly good, that is aye lasting and maketh a soul blessed; and he never should cease of his coveting if he did well, get what he get might. For he that most coveteth, most shall have; and soothly if he did thus, he should profit and wax in grace greatly.[4]

[1] *Scale II*, Ch. 40, p. 423. Cf. Dom Gerard Sitwell in *Downside Review* (1950), pp. 22–5, and the introduction to his edition of the *Scale* (Orchard Series 1952), p. xi.
[2] p. xix. [3] *Scale II*, Ch. 10, p. 255. [4] *Ibid.*, Ch. 18, p. 292.

The importance of the "reforming in Faith" as the ground and source of the spiritual life is underlined by Hilton's insistence elsewhere (most particularly in one of his Latin epistles) on the theological virtue of Faith:

> You have conceived Christ in your heart through Faith, but perhaps he is not yet brought to life in you through the light of understanding nor formed in the sweetness of charity . . . Truth (Christ) says in the Gospel "If you have Faith but as the grain of mustard and say to this mountain 'Go into the sea' it shall happen." A mustard seed is hot and burns the mouth. Therefore although at first your Faith may be cold and as if without life, nevertheless afterwards it will begin to warm and burn . . . and if your Faith burns so that Christ is formed and brought to life in you through Charity, if you say to the spiritual mountain, the mountain of the evil one, "Go into the sea" it will happen.[1]

This consciousness of the presence and importance of Faith throughout the spiritual life is perhaps one reason for the sharpness of Hilton's tone when he speaks of heresy, which he regards as a malignant disease in the Christian body, or a wound impeding the capacity of the individual to grow in the love of God.

It is not easy to be alert to the significance of these and many other characteristic features of the second treatise. Some of them may suggest only that the two works are separated by a considerable distance, measured not only in time but also by spiritual experience, thought, and perhaps also reading. However, so much theory and general principle has been added to practical guidance in the second treatise that a special purpose should be supposed. Possibly Hilton had been asked to expound his doctrine of contemplation in closer relation to theology,[2] or, perhaps he simply saw the need for this. Other indications, particularly the way he discusses souls at various stages, suggest that he had the assistance of spiritual directors and confessors in

---

[1] *Epistola ad Solitarium*, Royal 6 E III, fol. 122v. b.

[2] It seems likely the writings of the fourteenth-century contemplative writers were closely scrutinised by other theologians. There is a hint of this in the *Epistle of Privy Counsel*: "I hear some men say—I mean not simple lewd men and women, but clerks of great knowledge—that my writing to thee and to other is so hard and so high . . . that scarcely it may be conceived of the most subtle clerk or witted man or woman in this life, as they say" (*Cloud of Unknowing*, ed. Dom Justin McCann (London, 1952), p. 105). Both treatises of Hilton's *Scale* were translated into Latin "per quemdam sacre theologie doctorem"—the Carmelite Thomas Fishlake.

mind, as did St. John of the Cross in the *Ascent of Mount Carmel*. Hilton is eminently judicious, continually analysing "how thou mayst know." In chapter 27 he remarks how ignorance of spiritual matters is a hindrance to a soul's progress:

> There are many devout souls that through grace come into this murkness and feel the knowing of themselves, and yet wit they not fully what it is; and that uncunning in part hindreth them.[1]

There are also passages which show that the book was intended for the *use* of the individual person: "If thou wilt know when thou art in this secure murkness and when not thou mayest assay thus. . . ."[2] In most circumstances such teaching on the discernment of spiritual states would be better placed in the hands of a spiritual director. But Hilton was aware of the needs of people deprived of capable direction. In his letter to Adam Horsley on the Religious State, where he stresses at some length the benefit of subjection to a Superior, and the dangers of seculars left to their own untaught desires, fervours, graces, efforts, deceptions and temptations, he says:

> I speak of those seculars who do not fear to set out on the way of the spiritual life without a director or capable guide, whether a man *or a book*, obeying their own impulse . . . if not even the least of the arts can be learned without some teacher and instructor, how much more difficult it is to acquire the Art of Arts, the perfect service of God in the spiritual life without a guide?[3]

This consciousness of people without a guide, without even a suitable *book* to help them, seems to me to throw light on part of Hilton's aim in the second treatise of the *Scale*, and on some of the methods which distinguish this work from his other writings. Even if Hilton's sheer eminence as a teacher of the spiritual life is left out of account, this broad concern of his may partly explain the enduring usefulness and wide reach of the *Scale* through several centuries.

The second treatise of the *Scale* appears to be the culmination of Hilton's spiritual teaching, written out of abundant experience and in closely considered relation with theology. But it is written to meet the spiritual needs of all, *pusilli et magni*. It is a treatise on the supernatural life as such, disembodied, one might say,

[1] *Scale II*, Ch. 27, p. 336.   [2] *Ibid.*, Ch. 25, p. 325.   [3] Bod. Lat. th. e 26, fol. 127.

from the outward "states," and concerned with everything from stirrings of grace in an habitual sinner to the greatest graces of union in the contemplative life. Hilton looks only at the interior condition of the soul, the capacities with which it has been endowed by God and the stage of grace at which it has arrived.

It is this work, even more than *Mixed Life*, that contains Hilton's teaching on contemplation for active men and women with secular responsibilities. When Hilton answers the question why so few come to the experience of contemplation, he has little to say about impeding outward circumstances but much about a lacking inward will:

> [They] *set not their hearts to profit* in grace, nor to seek none higher state or good living through busy travail in praying and thinking and other bodily or ghostly working . . . thus perchance do some of the chosen souls that lead in the world active life; and it is little wonder of them, for they are so occupied with worldly busyings that needeth for to be done, that they may not *fully set their hearts* to profit in ghostly working.[1]

Hilton speaks of the "life" reformed in Faith alone in phrases such as "perilous," "excusable" and "blame":

> Nevertheless it is *perilous* to them, for they fall out and in all day, and are now up and now down, and may not come to stableness of good living. Nevertheless they are somewhat *excusable* because of their state of living . . . now sayest thou, since it is so that reforming in Faith is so *low* and so *perilous* to rest in . . .[2]

It is the Christian life of the majority of men and women, not merely of contemplatives, that Hilton stresses as a "beginning life." "Perilous" though it be, it is an exacting life, which many of us would be happy to truly live:

> if they fall lightly as it were against their will through frailty or uncunning, anon their conscience grieveth them and paineth them so grievously that they may have no rest till they be shriven and may have forgiveness . . . in that trowth they keep them in love and charity to their even-Christian . . . and flee all deadly sins after their cunning, and do the deeds of mercy to their even-Christian.[3]

The active "state" is still regarded as an impediment, with a realistic understanding of what it is to earn a living and maintain

[1] *Scale II*, Ch. 18, p. 290. [2] *Ibid.*, pp. 291, 297. [3] *Ibid.*, Ch. 10, pp. 255, 257.

a family; but in chapter 18 there is a trace of regret, and an
eagerness still to influence such seculars as he may:

> But other men that are free from worldly business if they *will*,
> and may have their needful sustenance without great bodily busi-
> ness, as specially religious men and women that bind themselves
> to perfection, and other men also in secular estate that have mickle
> reason and great kindly wit, and might, if they *would* dispose them
> thereto, come to mickle grace; these men are *more to blame* for that
> they stand still as they were idle, and *will* not profit in grace, nor
> no further seek to come to the love and the knowing of God.[1]

In this early section of the second treatise there is a general wish
to encourage all men to come to a deeper and more generous
love of God in a life of spiritual effort and prayer. I should not
wish my own interest in these points, and the emphasis of
selective quotation, to mistranslate Hilton's apostolic concern
with *all* into some particular concern with people in secular life.
Indeed, in the passage last quoted he spoke first of those who
bind themselves to perfection in religion. Yet in this second
treatise there is no theoretical restriction of people in an active
"state" to the antechamber of "devotion." Perhaps in the mature
illumination of his own spiritual experience Hilton no longer
cared to express himself in the same categoric, and perhaps
derivative way. Rather he will say:

> There may be many sundry ways and divers works leading
> sundry souls to contemplation; for after sundry disposings of men,
> and after sundry states, as are religious and seculars, that they are
> in, are divers exercises in working. Nevertheless, there is no gate
> but one; for what exercise it be that a soul have, but if he may come
> by that exercise to this knowing and to a meek feeling of himself,
> and that is that he be mortified and dead to the world as in his love,
> and that he may feel himself set sometimes in this restful murkness
> . . . soothly he is not yet reformed in feeling, nor hath not fully
> contemplation.[2]

And after his own account of the beginning and purgative way
he adds:

> And I expect well that He worketh otherwise also, that passeth
> my wit and my feeling. Nevertheless, whether he work thus or
> otherwise, by sundry means, in longer time or shorter time, with

[1] *Scale II*, p. 291.   [2] *Ibid.*, Ch. 27, p. 341.

mickle travail or little travail, if all come to one end, that is to the perfect love of Him, then is it good enough. For if He will give one soul on one day the full grace of contemplation and without any travail, as He well may, as good is it to that soul as if he had been examined, pained, mortified and purified twenty winter time.[1]

The emphatic passages of chapter 18 show his hopes of greater spiritual endeavour in *any* state of life and his wish to put an end to "Ho, I will no more of this" in the mouth of any person.

To those of us who might protest with the anchoress of *Scale I* that this teaching is "too high" and that we are not "able to take it nor fulfil it," Hilton gives an effective answer when he tells how the Church, like the woman of Chanaan:

asketh help of Our Lord for simple uncunning souls, that are travailed with temptation of the world and cannot speak perfectly to God by fervour of devotion nor burning love in contemplation; and though it seems that Our Lord repelleth her first because they are as it were alien from Him, nevertheless for the great trowth and desert of Holy Church He granteth to her all that she will.[2]

I have explained how Hilton was exceptional among writers of his time in giving close attention to the problems of the contemplative life lived in an active state, and I have shown also how different features of the second treatise in the *Scale* illustrate concern with the spiritual progress of all Christians, no matter what their state of life. It remains to say something about his teaching on the relation between the interior life of contemplation and outward works of charity. The most relevant passage on this subject is in the additions to his translation of the *Meditationes Vitae Christi* by James of Milan, in a chapter called "How a man in all his doings may be contemplative":[3] Hilton's additions show how he has absorbed the teaching and made it his own:

Yea, a blessed man were he that might in active life serve our Lord with Martha, yet nevertheless rest at our Lord's feet sitting with Mary. For thus do angels perfectly that serve us in earth and yet they see aye God's face in heaven. Right so doth such a man that travaileth, and serveth an "holy" man or a sick or doth any other

---

[1] *Scale II*, Ch. 31, p. 366.   [2] *Ibid.*, Ch. 10, p. 259.
[3] *The Goad of Love*, ed. G. Kirchberger (Faber, London, 1952), p. 126. Hilton's additions are marked here by double inverted commas.

work to worship of God, and only beholdeth "our Lord Jesus Christ" in him. "He feedeth his brother and he is fed of God. ..."

[Hilton wishes such a man to] yield him and relent him all into God, that he nothing see, nor feel, nor regard but God, "as if there were nothing else but God and he." And that he were "so turned" and transformed into God "through such a deep printing of thought in him" that on each quick side he turned him he should not feel nor understand but "Jesus Christ." And what manner work he did to man "specially or generally before men" he should fully feel "and ween" that he did it to God. ... "Lo this form is properly that a man thinketh himself ever in God's presence."[1]

Surely here is contained the teaching made explicit by Père Garrigou-Lagrange in *The Three Ways of the Spiritual Life*:[2] "the illuminative life appears under two normal forms, the one definitely contemplative ... the other active, as in a St. Vincent de Paul, a contemplation which by the light of the gifts of wisdom and counsel constantly sees in the poor and abandoned the suffering members of Christ." To the objection that this ideal may seem difficult or even impossible, Hilton adds "as it *is* to any man that hath been long *blind* in sin."

[1] *Ibid.*, p. 128.   [2] Anon. trans., Burns Oates, 1942, p. 61.

16. JULIAN OF NORWICH

Anna Maria Reynolds

VERY LITTLE is known, though much has been conjectured, about the author of *Sixteen Revelations of Divine Love*,[1] the anchoress Julian of Norwich; only a few stray references in contemporary documents remind us that she really was a person and not just a name. From wills we learn that she was a recluse at the Church of SS. Julian and Edward, Conisford, Norwich, from at least 1403 onwards, and that she was still living in 1416. The scribe of the oldest known manuscript of her writings refers to Julian as "a devout woman," a description corroborated by Margery Kempe of Lynn, who went to consult Julian about her soul "because the anchoress was expert in such things and able to give good counsel."

Of her identity nothing is known: her very name could be an adopted one, taken from the church to which her cell was attached. Neither is there any clue as to whether she was or was not a nun before becoming a recluse, whether she was or was not already a recluse when she experienced her revelations, whether she was or was not a native of Norwich. The obscurity is complete.

The anchoress herself gives the setting of the "Revelations of Divine Love" which form the subject of her book:

> These revelations were shewed to a simple unlearned creature living in this mortal flesh, in the year of our Lord one thousand three hundred and seventy-three, on the thirteenth day of May. And when I was thirty years old and a half, God sent me a bodily sickness . . .

After languishing three days and three nights Julian received the last sacraments; for two more days and nights she continued to grow weaker, until everybody around her, and herself too,

---

[1] The critical edition for the Early English Text Society is now being prepared. The quotations in this article are taken from a partially modernised edition by Fr. James Walsh, S.J., to be published shortly by Burns and Oates.

believed her last moments had come. Then she was suddenly and completely cured. The figure of Christ on the cross upon which she had fixed her gaze, became alive before her eyes. Blood trickled down from under the crown of thorns "hot and fresh and right plenteously."

This was the first Revelation or "Shewing." Fourteen others followed in succession, six of them concerned directly with Our Lord's Passion, the remaining eight with other spiritual truths. All fifteen took place between about four o'clock in the morning and three in the afternoon of the same day. The sixteenth and last Shewing—the indwelling of the Blessed Trinity in the soul—was made on the night following.

Julian has left to her "even-Christians" two separate accounts of these revelations, a short account[1] and a much fuller one. It is now generally supposed that the short account was the first to be written, probably soon after the Shewings were experienced. Julian, in the longer narrative, remarks that for fifteen years after and more she pondered and prayed over the Shewings and received new light on their significance. The longer account obviously incorporates these further reflections and illuminations, which generally develop at length points dealt with more concisely in the earlier version. Both versions are written in the first person and follow the chronological order of the Shewings. The tone of the narrative is conversational, and the treatment of subject informal: a record of personal experience rather than a schematised treatise.

Towards the end of her book, Julian summarises both the content and the purpose of the Shewings made to her:

> It belongeth to us to have three knowings. The first is that we know our Lord God. The second is that we know ourselves— what we are by Him, in kind and in grace. The third is that we know meekly what we are with regard to our sin and our feebleness. And for these three was made all this Shewing, as I understand it.

Julian is well aware that no genuine private revelation could add to the sum-total of revealed knowledge, the deposit of faith. She insists that she was shown nothing that does not belong to the faith of Holy Church. The content of her Revelations concerns the chief mysteries of faith: the Unity and Trinity of God, and

[1] Cf. Sister Anna Maria Reynolds, C.P., *A Shewing of God's Love* (Longmans 1958).

the Incarnation. What the mystics receive when it is given to them to see what no man can utter is a stronger personal grasp of these truths, an acuter awareness of God's relationship with His creature, the reality of the Divine impact. They do indeed receive a new sight, but it is of the same truth which they already know by faith. Hence, when Julian sees the immensity of God and His spirituality—"seeing God in a point" she calls it—what is brought home to her is the exquisite refinements of the Creator-creature relationship, the profundities implicit in that rather over-worked word "Providence." And she succeeds in transmitting to her readers something of her own wonderful sense of security and rest in this all-wise and loving care:

> See, I am God. See, I am in all things. See, I do all things. See, I never lift my hands off my works, nor ever shall, without end. See, I lead all thing to the end that I ordain it to, from without-beginning, by the same might, wisdom and love that I made it with. How should anything be amiss?

Julian's sight of the Blessed Trinity might be termed the classical mystical experience beginning as it does with the imaginative vision of Christ's suffering humanity, and culminating in the penetrating grasp of the Godhead revealed in and through Christ. "For where Jesus appeareth, the Blessed Trinity is understood, as I see it." The revelation is followed by the typical ecstatic reaction; but this is expressed so simply and engagingly that it almost escapes our notice. "In the same Shewing, suddenly the Trinity filled full my heart with the utmost joy (thus I understood it shall be in heaven without end unto all that come thither)." Here again, the Shewing confers a deeper awareness of the union between the sinful creature and the God who reveals Himself as "our everlasting lover, endless joy and bliss."

The Divine wisdom and truth were shewn to Julian as it were in reflex, in the soul of our Blessed Lady. The extent of Mary's knowledge of God is the measure of her greatness who is "more in worthiness and in fullness of grace than all that God made . . . except the blessed manhood of Christ." And her wisdom and truth consists in "this knowing of the greatness of her Maker, and the littleness of herself that is made." For Julian, then, there is no distinction between the right knowing of God and the knowledge of self. Wherever her Shewings begin, they always end by offering a new look at the ineffable union between the Godhead and every soul in grace. He is the Maker, the Lover, the Keeper: the Father, the Mother, the Husband even: "And in the knitting and the oneing He is our very true Spouse, and we His loved wife and His fair maiden. With which wife he was never displeased; for He saith: 'I love thee, and thou lovest me, and our love shall never be parted in two.' "

For Julian, all the divine attributes, all that is revealed of God, are aspects of His love. "Charity unmade is God": this is the most important message both of the Shewings and of her comments on them. At the very beginning of her narrative she declares:

> Our soul is preciously loved by Him that is highest, in a way that passeth beyond the knowing of all creatures. That is to say, there is no creature made that can know how much and how sweetly and how tenderly our Maker loveth us.

Julian is at a loss for words and images to convey the concrete reality and all-embracing nature of this love. It is courteous; it is homely; it comes down to our lowest needs; it enwraps and envelops us more closely than our very skin and flesh; it is a love which is never slaked, a personal love, a love which makes all things profitable to us. God is the Maker, the Keeper, the Lover, who is always with us, in us, leading and sustaining us. And when, more than fifteen years after her shewings, she was finally enlightened, in contemplative prayer, about their meaning, these were the words she heard "in ghostly understanding"; "Love was His meaning. Who sheweth it thee? Love. Wherefore sheweth He it thee? For Love."

Not surprisingly, Julian sees all our ills summed up in the unknowing of this God who is love. In fact, if we look for a practical, everyday message in the high teaching of the *Revelations*, it is stated simply enough:

> For some of us believe that God is almighty and may do all; and that He is all-wisdom and can do all; but that He is all-love, and will do all—there we fail. And it is this unknowing that most holdeth back God's lovers, as I see it.

Though Julian says more than once that her revelations were granted for profit of us all, for all her fellow Christians, she does, in fact, effectively reduce her audience to those who "deliberately choose God in this life, for love." In the shorter version of the *Revelations*, the limit is set even more precisely, as "every man and woman who desires to live contemplatively." That she unconsciously directs her words to those who are "proficients" in spiritual living is clear from her teaching on prayer. Her very definition of the prayer of petition, "Beseeching is a true and grace-giving, lasting will of the soul which is oned and fastened to the will of our Lord, by the sweet and secret working of the Holy Ghost," indicates that she is speaking in the contemplative context of the *castissima oratio*. It is significant also that Julian has no reference to the penance and mortification which are the beginner's first lesson in self-renunciation. But she has a good deal to say of the suffering which afflicts the soul in the consciousness of its own sinfulness, when it "sees truly that sin is worse, more vile and more painful than Hell"; and particularly of the pain that mortal life itself is for those who long to be dissolved and to be with Christ—the third and final "night" of St. John of the Cross. She speaks of self-renunciation with the uncompromising simplicity of St. Ignatius in his *Principle and Foundation*:

> We need to have knowledge of this—that we should reckon as nought everything that is made, to love and have God who is unmade. For this is the reason why we are not all in ease of heart and of soul: that we seek here rest in this thing that is so little and where no rest is in, we know not our God that is Almighty, all-Wise and all-Good. For He is very rest. It is His will to be known and it is His pleasure that we rest us in Him. All that is beneath Him sufficeth not to us. And this is the reason why no soul can be in rest until it is naughted of every thing that is made. When the soul is willingly naughted, for love, so as to have Him Who is All, then is she able to receive ghostly rest.

Julian says that it is easier for us to come to the knowing (by which she means contemplative knowledge) of God, because "God is nearer to us than our own soul." Yet "by the gracious leading of the Holy Ghost, we shall come to know them both in one," for the reason that "our soul is in God." Julian is at one with traditional spiritual doctrine in her insistence that mystical knowledge is a special foretaste of the Vision of the Blessed:

And there shall we see God face to face. Homely and all-abundantly the creature that is made shall see and endlessly behold God who is the Maker. For no man may see God and live after, that is, in this mortal life. But when He will shew Himself here, of His special grace, He strengtheneth the creature above the self, and measureth the shewing, according as this is His will and is profitable for the time.

Julian tells us how her own vision was restricted, how the Shewing was measured in her own case: " . . . the working of creatures was not shewed; but only of our Lord God in creatures"; and (a limitation vitally affecting any theological judgment of the *Revelations*):

I speak of them that shall be saved. For in this time God shewed me no other . . . For in mankind that shall be saved is comprehended all, that is to say, all that is made, and the Maker of all. For man is in God, and in God is all.

Julian never "saw" any individual creatures except our Blessed Lady. When she desired to know whether a friend was making spiritual progress, she received the traditional answer, *ne plus sapere quam oportet*. "Take what your Lord God shewed to you as spoken [*sc.* the word, "all shall be well"] generally, beholding His courtesy. For it is greater worship to God to behold Him in all things than in any particular thing."

The constant term of Julian's sight throughout her revelations, and afterwards whenever she was favoured with infused graces, was the whole Christ. He is the focal point of her every vision:[1] Christ in His Suffering Humanity, in His Divinity, in His Loving tenderness for the creature, in His union with all that is. "Oftentimes our Lord said . . . 'I it am that is all. I it am that Holy Church preacheth and teacheth thee'": "our Mother, Holy Church, that is Christ Jesus." Just as she "saw in Christ that the Father is," so in Christ she sees every soul that shall be saved "as it were one soul." Theologians have taken her to task for her unorthodoxy in apparently attributing impeccability to the predestined: "in every soul that shall be saved there is a godly will that never consented to sin and never shall." But in the context of her teaching on the Mystical Body, the Indwelling of the Blessed Trinity and Incorporation, the recapitulation of all creation in Christ the Head, the godly will is that "blessed will"

[1] Cf. Paul Molinari, S.J., *Julian of Norwich* (Longmans, 1958), pp. 151-6.

which is kept whole and safe in our Lord Jesus Christ: it is in man's *kind* (*i.e.*, all those that shall be saved, in general and not in special), which "is so knit and oned to Him that in it must be preserved a substance which never could nor should be separated from Him." She has nothing to say of the precise manner in which the individual predestined soul, in this life, participates in this blessed work. This was never shewed. She never even raises, let alone answers, the question posed by the theologian, "How can a man sin and yet not lose grace?"

Knowledge of the self, "what we are by Him, in kind [nature] and in grace" seems to have been given to Julian in those times of "high and ineffable prayer . . . when our courteous Lord, of His special grace sheweth Himself to our soul . . . when, of His special grace, we behold Him plainly." It was then that she "saw and felt that His marvellous and superabundant goodness filleth full all our powers . . . beyond all that we can explain or even conceive." In her attempts to give expression to her special beholding of "what our true self is," Julian had recourse to the popularised form of Augustinian psychology used also by her contemporaries, Walter Hilton and the author of *The Cloud of Unknowing*. Augustine, distinguishing two levels in the Reason, held that the human mind is true to itself as the image and glory of God, only in so far as it contemplates the truth in God, by the operations of the higher reason. This true knowledge of God, which re-forms the soul to its pristine image, is contemplative knowledge, *sapientia*. Discursive knowledge, *scientia*, is proper to the lower part of reason, which is concerned, to use a phrase of Hilton, "with the knowing and ruling of earthly things." Julian has several pairs of terms which correspond to the Augustinian distinction. She speaks of the true and change-able self, of the outward and inward parts of the soul, as well as of higher and lower; but most often she speaks of "substance" and "sensuality."

Man's kind, human nature, which Julian says is the noblest thing ever God made, with all its gifts of nature and of grace, was created for Christ, even as it was redeemed in Christ: "For Him was this fair kind prepared: for the worship and nobility of man's making and for the joy and bliss of man's salvation." The higher part of man, his substance, is united inseparably to the Godhead, made in His image and likeness, "the thought of

His heart" from all eternity, enclosed in the power of the Father, the wisdom of the Son, the goodness of the Holy Ghost. "For our substance is whole in each person of the Trinity, which is one God." Substance and Sensuality are readily identified with St. Paul's description of conscience and the lower self.[1] But Julian has little to say about the "beastly" side of the sensuality (except to remark, with St. Paul, that, of itself, it can do nothing good), for the reason that she was never shewn the lower part in control: "that the outward part could draw the inward to its own assent—this was not shewed to me; but that the inward part, by grace, draweth the outward part, and that both shall be oned in bliss without end by the power of Christ —this was shewed." The sensuality is brought into harmony with the substance in the Incarnation, in the perfection of human nature which is Christ:

> For in that same time that God knit Himself to our body in the Maiden's womb, He took our sensual soul. In taking which, having enclosed us all in Himself, He oned it to our substance. In this oneing He was perfect man; for Christ, having knit in Himself every man that shall be saved, is perfect man . . . These two parts were in Christ—the higher and the lower; which is but one soul. The higher part was ever in peace with God, in full joy and bliss; the lower part, which is sensuality, suffered for the salvation of mankind.

The post-Tridentine theologian will naturally find a certain looseness of thought and imprecision of expression in Julian's teaching on the nature of the soul. She makes no precise distinction between natural and supernatural, between the various moments and effects of creation, supernatural elevation and redemption. But within her own terms of reference there is no confusion nor obscurity, least of all unorthodoxy. She is not concerned with building abstract theological hypotheses concerning the purely "natural" man and his existence in an order in which he would never have been destined for participation in the Divine Nature. What she saw was the shadow of Eternal Wisdom from without-beginning, the Divine order as it was, is, and shall be:

> By the endless purpose and decision, and the full accord of the Trinity, the second Person was to be the ground and head of this

[1] Romans 6, 14-25.

fair human kind; of Him we are all sprung, in Him we are all
enclosed, to Him we shall all go; finding in Him our full Heaven
in everlasting joy; according to the foreseeing purpose of all the
Blessed Trinity from without-beginning.

Truly to know our soul is to know the whole Christ, "in
whom is the Father and the Holy Ghost"; to know Him in His
Church. So she speaks of the blessed soul of Christ as "knit and
oned to God, in which oneing it is made endlessly holy"; and
adds:

> Furthermore He means us to know that all the souls that shall be
> saved in heaven without end, are knit in this knot and oned in this
> oneing, and made holy in this holiness.

Again, we need to remind ourselves that Julian is seeing, *sub
specie aeternitatis*, the completed growth of Christ.[1] She did not
see herself amongst the number of the saved. But every one
who chooses God, for love, may be sure that he will be loved
without end. We owe it to God, she says, to be "as sure, in hope,
of the bliss of heaven whilst we are here, as we shall be, in
certainty, when we are there." She distinguishes, then, between
Christ as head, who is glorified and impassible, and the body of
Christ, "not yet fully glorified nor entirely impassible." The
members of His body are to achieve a glory and perfection
proportionate to His by suffering in Him and with Him: "in
this life, as our Lord sees it, we are on His Cross, dying with
Him in our pains and our passions."

Julian's sixteenth and last revelation, which she calls the
conclusion and confirmation of all that was shewn, was again
a knowing of her soul as the dwelling of the Trinity:

> And then our good Lord opened my ghostly eye, and shewed me
> my soul . . . so large as it were an endless word . . . a worshipful
> city. In the midst of that city is our Lord Jesus, true God and true
> man . . . He sitteth in the soul, established in peace and rest. And
> He ruleth and maintaineth heaven and earth and all that is. The
> soul is all occupied with the Blessed Godhead which is sovereign
> Might, sovereign Wisdom, sovereign Goodness.
>
> The place that Jesus taketh in our soul—He shall never remove
> therefrom without end. For in us is His homeliest home and His
> endless dwelling.

[1] Julian consistently re-echoes and enlarges upon the great Pauline christo-
logical and ecclesiological texts.

Julian is here striving to reduce to imaginative terms the doctrine
of the Indwelling of the Blessed Trinity in the souls of the just.
She sees the life of faith as a growing consciousness of this divine
dynamic possession of the soul, and the reciprocal nature of
this possession—we must desire to "have God" even as He
desires to have us. All the elements of this high doctrine, so
emphasised in St. John's Gospel and his first epistle, are developed
in the *Revelations*.[1] Knowledge of the self thus inevitably becomes
knowledge of the Maker dwelling therein. For Julian there are
various types of this "beholding of the self and of God."[2] Her
own beholding in the time of her Revelations was of "His
special grace," the grace of infused contemplation, when God
so acts in the soul that it "can do nothing more but behold Him
and enjoy Him." Below this "high unperceivable prayer," in
which the soul "finds" God, there are various stages of seeking, which Julian calls "believing prayer." It is not an experiential
knowledge of God and the soul, but an attachment of the will,
in the knowledge of faith, to the word of God: "if any man
love me, he will keep my word . . . " In all its prayer, the loving
soul should achieve a more or less constant conscious awareness
that it lives with, dwells in, God. By living faith we can "perceive
Him wisely, receive Him sweetly, keep us in Him faithfully";
and by frequent acts of love, co-operate with the Holy Ghost,
"endless life dwelling on our soul" who "keepeth us and worketh
therein a peace and bringeth it to ease by grace and accordeth
it to God."

We have already noticed that though Julian addresses herself
to all her fellow-Christians, she does in fact take it for granted
that her readers will be as fully committed to Christ as she is
herself: "His dear friends and lovers, whose hearts, like hers,
burn in the love of our dearest Jesus," as the scribe of the Sloane
Manuscript writes in his colophon. Julian's teaching on "what
our self is as regards our sin and feebleness" is directed to them.
They are to understand that "of ourselves we are right nought
but sin and wretchedness." We need to see our sin, "and by the
sight we should be made ashamed of ourselves, and broken down
with regard to our pride and presumption," so that "by this
meek knowing, we shall be broken off from all things that are

[1] Cf. James Walsh, S.J., *God's Homely Loving*, THE MONTH, April, 1958.
[2] Cf. Molinari, loc. cit. pp. 104–39.

not our Lord." This knowledge is itself a grace. "For our sin is so foul and horrible that He, of His courtesy, wills not to shew it us except by the light of His mercy." Hence, though in this life we realise that we do naught but sin, there can be reason and moderation in our mourning and sorrow. There are, however, many good souls who fall into a kind of despair at the sight of their own sin and feebleness:

> For even when we begin to hate sin, and to amend us by ordinance of Holy Church, there dwelleth in us a dread that is an obstacle to us, through the beholding of our selves and our sins committed in the past. Because of our sins of every day, because we (or some of us) hold not to our promise, nor keep to the cleanness that our Lord setteth us in, but fall often-times into so much wretchedness that it shames us to mention it—the beholding of this maketh us so sorrowful and so heavy that we can scarcely see any comfort. This dread we mistake sometimes for meekness. But it is foul blindness and a wickedness. And yet we cannot despise it as we do any other sin that we recognise, though it cometh through lack of judgment, and is against truth.

Margery Kempe's witness of Julian's contemporary reputation as a spiritual director finds certain corroboration in this lucid diagnosis and confident prescription. The whole weight of Julian's mystical experience lies behind her teaching on true humility. Her own problem, during the course of the Revelations, as well as before and afterwards was (as it is for all who strive to love God) the fact that sin and evil seem to challenge and success- fully defy the power, wisdom and love of the Blessed Trinity. God's lovers are very acutely aware that they are sinners in a sinful world.

For Julian .with her magnificent sense of solidarity with Christ in His Church, the problem resolved itself into a clash between conscience, reinforced by the teaching of the Church, which indicated that her sinfulness put her far away from God, and the Shewings, which constantly proclaimed God's ineffable nearness. The problem was solved for her through the gradual elucidation of the parabolic allegory of the Lord and the servant, which forms the centre-piece of her book, an unfolding of the "marvellous high deepness" of the humility and charity of Christ. She saw a servant standing before his Lord, ready and eager to do his Lord's bidding. She saw him quickly come to grief, but kept safe in his Lord's love even in his falling; and eventually restored and rewarded. It is a true medieval allegory, an "action-picture" with scriptural analogies apparent throughout: the suffering servant of Isaias, the parable of the Prodigal Son and the Lost Sheep. The servant, she learnt, was shewed both for Christ and for Adam; and Adam is "every man that shall be saved," the "long-lived seed" of Christ, in Whom the Father is: the seed brought forth, nurtured in mercy and grace at the Incarnation, in Christ, God and man; Who fell, with Adam, into the Maiden's womb, taking our Sensuality, and reforming it in us by mercy and grace. There are times, then, when we feel the weight of doom, which is sin and its consequences, hanging over us. We are to accept this sight of our own sinfulness and weakness, "our ghostly blindness," as "the penance that God Himself giveth us," as our suffering with Him in His Church; and also as an invitation to "turn into the beholding of His mercy, cleaving to His love and goodness."

Time seems to have proved that there is no better imagery for depicting the reality of God's love for His chosen creatures in all its intimacy than that of the relationship between mother and child. There is little scriptural warrant for it; but we recall how effectively it is used by Isaias, and how striking is Our Lord's own image of the hen and her chicks, as He weeps over the city of Jerusalem. Julian develops the image out of her Shewing of the parable of the Lord and the servant with great boldness and freedom; and her use of it, with the constant overtones of Christ in His Church, and of the *Speculum Justitiae*, rounds off, logically and naturally, the main thesis of the *Revelations*, knowledge of God and ourselves:

> I understood that there is no higher stature in this life than childhood —in the feebleness and failing of might and understanding—until the time that our gracious Mother hath brought us up to our Father's bliss. And there shall truly be made known to us His meaning, in the sweet words where He saith: "All shall be well; and thou shalt see, thyself, that all manner thing shall be well."

17. MARGERY KEMPE

Edmund Colledge

IT IS IMPOSSIBLE TODAY, five hundred years and more after she dictated it, to read Margery Kempe's *Book* with indifference. Many will share the exasperation, the revulsion, even, which, she cheerfully admits, she provoked in her contemporaries. "Some said it was an evil spirit which afflicted her, some said it was a sickness, some said she had drunk too much wine; some cursed her, some wished her in the harbour, some would have liked her out at sea in a bottomless boat." But there will surely be others who will conclude that when all the evidence has been taken into account which she herself furnishes of her many physical and mental disorders, still we have in her *Book* the autobiography of a soul which loved God, after its own extraordinary fashion, with a rare and pure single-mindedness.

There is nothing about Margery which is not sensational: the very circumstances of her *Book's* rediscovery startled the academic world. Until the mid-1930's all that was known of her was contained in a little pamphlet printed by Wynkyn de Worde, seven short pages of prayers "taken out of the book of Margery Kempe of Lynn." The pamphlet was reprinted in 1521 by Henry Pepwell, who in his title and colophon called her a "devout anchoress." So that in the standard works on the enclosed religious life in England, Margery's name always appeared as "anchoress of King's Lynn in Norfolk," and it was generally supposed that her lost *Book* had contained little to distinguish it from many other such "short treatises of contemplation." as Worde had styled his extracts; though the discerning might have observed that this "anchoress" had a special devotion to the Holy Places, they could not have known that the phrase "as was granted to you when you were in Rafnys" showed that Margery had been at Ramleh, half way between Jaffa and Jerusalem. But when the indefatigable American connoisseur of medieval English mysticism, Hope Emily Allen, on one of her frequent visits to Europe for material for her studies, one day in 1934 called at the Victoria

and Albert Museum, there was put into her hands a manuscript
of the mid-fifteenth century, which its owner, Colonel William
Butler-Bowdon, had sent to the Museum for repairs to its
original binding. Soon we were told that this was the lost "Book
of Margery Kempe" which was found again, that the Carthusians
of Mount Grace had formerly owned it, and that it had been
piously preserved by the recusant Bowdon family "from time
immemorial." When Hope Allen first announced her find, she
indicated that Margery was no enclosed solitary, and that the
like of her *Book* had never been seen; and when students were
able to read it, first in 1936 in a modernised version made with
admirable speed and accuracy by Col. Butler-Bowdon, then in
1940 in a learned edition of the original English, by Hope Allen
and Professor Sanford Brown Meech, with much critical appara-
tus, they were confronted by a truly extraordinary document. Its
reappearance must count as one of the major events in medieval
English scholarship, and however much one may disagree with
Hope Allen's subsequent treatment of her material, it must be
said that at the time no-one was better fitted than she to identify
this work and to find a way through its labyrinthine narrative.
But now let Margery and her *Book* speak for themselves.

She was born *c.* 1373, the year in which Bridget of Sweden,
whose life and writings were to be her guides through life, had
died in Rome. She was a native of Kings Lynn, then called indifferently "Lynn" or "Bishop's Lynn," on the estuary of the Ouse
into the Wash, one of the chain of East Coast ports which faced
the great cities of the Hansa and the Netherlands across the North
Sea, grew rich by trade with them and reflected some of the
splendour of their public and private buildings. Her parish church,
St. Margaret's, which so often appears in her *Book*, stands as a
memorial to the wealth and pride of Lynn's citizens; and as one
walks through the town, its streets still narrow and thronged,
one finds everywhere ruins and relics of the many chapels and
religious houses which Margery frequented. In her day Lynn contained a Benedictine priory, friaries of the Franciscan, Augustinian, Dominican, Carmelite and Sack orders, a hospital for lepers
and several anchorholds. Her father, John Brunham, was four
times mayor, and in her early twenties she married John Kempe,
a freeman who later held civic office. But of all such circumstances as these, we learn only in passing; the *Book* itself opens

P

with a headlong dive into the troubled sea of her spiritual voyage through life. "By the leave of our merciful Lord, Christ Jesus, and to the magnifying of His holy name, Jesus, this little treatise"— it makes in fact a very long book—"will deal in part with His wonderful works, how mercifully, how benignly and how lovingly He moved and stirred a sinful wretch to His love, which sinful wretch for many years wanted and meant, by the stirring of the Holy Spirit, to follow our Saviour, making great promises to fast and to perform other acts of penance. But always when she was tempted she was turned back again, like the reed which bends to every wind and cannot stand firm unless there is no wind, until the time when our merciful Lord, Christ Jesus, having pity and compassion upon the work of His hand and His creature, turned health into sickness, prosperity into adversity, honour into shame and love into hatred." It was then that Christ in His goodness led her along His own way of perfection, "every step of which He had trodden before her," visiting her with bodily infirmity, mental affliction, the loss of her possessions and the enmity of her friends and family.

A long period of madness was only ended when Christ Himself appeared to her; and after that "it seemed to her that she was bound to God and that she wanted to be His servant." But she was still held fast by worldly vanities, and especially by her love of ostentatious finery; and when her husband took her to task, she replied that though she had married beneath her, still she had to think of her family's good name. Not satisfied with her husband's sufficient but modest means, she went into brewing, with disastrous results. She promised God and her husband that this would be the end of her ambition, but it was not so. She took to milling, and this also was an inexplicable failure, so that people began to say that she was under a curse, though wiser men, whom she at last believed, said that this was the compassion of God. "Then she asked God for mercy, and forsook her pride, her greed, her longing for worldly honours, and did great bodily penance, and began to enter into the way of everlasting life." Then for the first time she heard miraculously the sounds of heavenly melody, and she longed to live chastely if her husband would agree.

"For the first two years when this creature was thus drawn to our Lord, she had great peace in her soul from all temptations. Fasting was no effort, she hated the joys of the world, and she felt no rebellion in her flesh. She seemed so strong to herself that she feared no devil in hell, because she performed such great bodily penances. She thought that she loved God more than He loved her. She was smitten with the deadly wound of vainglory and did not feel it, for many times she longed for the Crucified One to free His hands from the cross and embrace her in token of love."

But Christ then mercifully sent her three years of cruel temptation. She had thought that all fleshly desires were extinguished in her, but she was bitterly tried by lust, for all her prayers and penances and tears. Added to this, she was convinced that God had forsaken her. Then, on a Friday before Christmas, Christ appeared to her as she was weeping and saying her prayers in St. Margaret's Church, and granted her the first "revelation" of which we are told.

It is at this point that her "second conversion" begins, when Christ promises her "You will be devoured and gnawed by the people of the world as a rat gnaws the stockfish: but do not be afraid, daughter, for you will have the victory over all your enemies, and I shall give you grace enough to answer every scholar who questions you about the love of God."

Presently her husband agreed to their taking a vow of chastity, and when Christ approved her desire to go abroad on pilgrimage, He commanded her to wear white, as if she were a dedicated virgin. She was constantly visited with violent fits of weeping in prayer, but it was not until she reached Jerusalem, that on Mount Calvary she for the first time fell on the ground and shouted aloud in her agonising ecstasies. In Rome, on the return journey, she at last had a white habit made and wore it. Later she suffered one heavy reverse, when she refused to believe that her unwelcome visions of the damned were sent to her by God, so that He in His displeasure withdrew her consolations and favours, and for twelve days she was horribly oppressed by impure images and ideas. Still later, when her weepings and cryings had made her so intolerable to the people of Lynn, who were being led against her by a famous Franciscan preacher (whom a fifteenth-century annotator of the manuscript identifies as William Melton), that she was advised by her friends to leave the town, God caused her cryings to cease; and the people, to whom she was no longer a cause of annoyance, said that this showed that she was a hypocrite and an impostor. For long she and her husband had given up housekeeping, and lived in separate parts of the town; and when he suffered the accident which led to his paralysis and fatal illness, she was blamed for having neglected him. Yet her account of how she cared for the dying old man, no longer able even to control his natural functions, tells much of her resigned and mortified way of life.

> She had to work harder, washing and wringing out clothes, and it cost her more for fuel, and it was a great hindrance to her contemplation, so that often what she had to do would have been irksome, but she remembered how in her youth she had enjoyed many pleasurable thoughts, fleshly delights and inordinate love for her husband's person. And therefore she was glad to be punished by the same person, and she took it more easily, and cared for him and helped him, it seemed to her, as she would have done for Christ Himself.

How seriously are we to take Margery Kempe and her *Book*? She in her candid accounts of what her friends and her enemies said and did to her provides us with a whole range of judgments from which to choose. At one end of the scale there was a man who had her under arrest who said to her "If ever you are a saint in Heaven, pray for me" (to which she humbly and adroitly answered, "I hope that you will be a saint yourself, and every other man who gets to Heaven"). Yet this very man was leading her to the Archbishop of York to be interrogated on charges of heresy, and there were several occasions, notably once in Leicester, when she was in real danger of being burned as a Lollard. And between these two extremes there were those who dismissed her as an hysterical epileptic, said that she was merely a self-deluded exhibitionist, accused her of hypocrisy and fraud, consulted her as a clairvoyante, took her counsel as that of a true contemplative and revered her as an ecstatic visionary who had been admitted to the divine privities.

The charge perhaps easiest to acquit her of is that of heresy. The picture which she draws for us of early fifteenth-century England is an ugly one, only too reminiscent of the techniques of religious and political repression we have seen employed in so many quarters of the globe in our own day; and the worst feature which they all share is the sudden, violent outbreaks of a rage compounded of fear and hatred among people too ignorant and stupid to know what it is they are denouncing to the professional persecutors. To quote the Scriptures in English was enough to be called "Lollard," for the laity to speak with any show of authority about religious matters was sufficient to brand them as "false hypocrites," to criticise the clergy adversely was the mark of a heretic; and since Margery never stopped doing these things, she was constantly courting danger. A typical instance is her adventure in the Cathedral Church at Canterbury. She had been praying and weeping in church almost the whole day, until the monks and the laity had had enough of it and "greatly despised and reproved her" (which probably means that they told her to be quiet or go away). At this her husband pretended that he did not know her, and made off for the rest of the day. An old monk who had been a great personage in the world asked her "What can you say about God?", and when she answered that it was her wish to speak and hear about Him, and repeated a story from the Scriptures by way of illustration, the old monk said "I wish you were shut up inside a house of stone so that no-one could talk to you." A young monk said that she must be either filled with the Holy Spirit or possessed by a devil "because what you are telling us here is out of Holy Writ, and that you did not acquire yourself." The end of this altercation, in which, as is usual in Margery's narratives, she came off best, was that as she went out of the church the monks and the others followed, shouting "You will be burned, you false Lollard! There is a cartful of thorns ready for you here, and a barrel to burn you with!"; and so she stood outside the town gates as night came on, some people gaping at her and the rest shouting "Take her away and burn her!"

But in fact she was no heretic, and her whole *Book* is a remarkable and valuable witness of the degree of theological and scriptural knowledge to which an illiterate laywoman could attain. And it must also be said that when she was involved not in a mere public brawl but in a properly-conducted enquiry into her religious beliefs, she was always acquitted of charges of heresy, because she expounded her faith with singular clarity, and because she was always treated with strict justice. Her exposition, for instance, before her judges at Leicester, of the Catholic doctrine of the Mass could serve in any age as a model, and the mayor of the town, who had brought her to trial, was reduced to saying "She does not mean in her heart what she says with her mouth."

Then he goes on to make a further remark: "I want to know why you go around dressed in white, because I think you have come here to entice our wives away from us and lead them off with you." We owe the elucidation of this dark saying to the learning and ingenuity of Hope Allen and her collaborators, who, reminding us that Margery had just returned from overseas, observed that sixteen years earlier, in 1399, there had been a royal proclamation to all the ports and counties of England, warning the civic authorities of the danger that "a new sect of people dressed in white robes and claiming for themselves great sanctity" might attempt to enter the Kingdom. These were the Flagellants, sometimes known as the *Albi*, *Bianchi*, a great company of whom had in that year once again been on the move across Europe, gathering followers as they went. "We want no religious crack-pots here," the mayor is in effect saying, "and it says in my regulations that people coming from abroad dressed in white are not allowed."

In the end, Margery was permitted to go free from Leicester, but on condition that she went to Lincoln for a certificate of good character from the bishop. Yet she found it impossible to keep out of trouble: within a very short time exactly the same chain of events was taking place at York. Her account of her misfortunes there well illustrates her peculiar gifts as a raconteur: the simplest incident, as she describes it, becomes vivid and immediate, and she sees herself always as the figure of fun she appeared. In the Minster a priest took hold of the collar of her white habit and said "You wolf, what is this clothing you have on?" She refused to answer him, but some little novices walking past said "Please, sir, it's wool." So the priest began to curse, and she rebuked him, and reminded him of the Commandments, and presently the whole city was in a tumult, and she was summoned to appear before Archbishop Henry Bowet at his country house at Cawood for interrogation as a heretic. A great crowd had gathered in the archbishop's chapel to listen to this, "and she made her prayers to our Lord God Almighty to help and succour her against all her enemies, spiritual and bodily, for a long time, and her flesh trembled and quaked amazingly, so that she was glad to put her hands under her clothes so that it would not be noticed," But God helped her to give the right answer, as He had promised long ago that He would, and the archbishop said "She knows her Faith all right. What shall I do with her?" His clerics replied "We know that she knows the articles of the Faith, but we will not tolerate her living amongst us, because the people have great faith in her talk, and she might pervert some of them." The archbishop said to Margery "I have bad reports about you— I hear that you are a very wicked woman," to which she made the incomparable reply "And I hear, sir, that you are a wicked man, and if you are as wicked as they say, you'll never get to Heaven unless you mend your ways here." Finally, however, she was pronounced no Lollard, and set free on the usual condition: that she went away and left the archbishop and his people in peace.

The young monk at Canterbury had pronounced a judgment entirely characteristic of the epoch when he said that Margery's religious knowledge, in particular her knowledge of the Bible, must have been supernaturally acquired; but we know from her *Book* (and the testimony upon this subject is of unique value to students of medieval spirituality) much of how Margery taught herself and was taught by others. It is beyond any reasonable doubt that she could neither read nor write. One recent commentator has questioned this, drawing attention to the words of one "revelation" in which Christ is made to say to her "I have often said to you that whether you pray with your lips or think in your heart, whether you read or listen to reading, I shall be pleased with you." But the language here echoes, probably deliberately, the "read or hear read" formula so often found in indulgences attached to prayers and books, a formula itself deriving from the opening phrase, *Omnibus visuris vel audituris*, of the medieval writ. We can see from another such "revelation" how precisely Margery understood the terms and forms of indulgences: "Daughter, as often as you say or think 'Honoured be all those holy places in Jerusalem in which Christ suffered bitter pain and passion,' you shall have the same indulgence as if you were physically present there, both for yourself and for all those for whom you wish to gain it." There is, however, another place in the *Book* which at first sight may seem to throw further doubt upon its author's illiteracy. This is where she is describing how she was miraculously saved from injury when she was struck by a fall of stones and wood from the vault of St. Margaret's Church in Lynn as she knelt at prayer, "holding down her head and with her book in her hand." But very probably Margery is here indicating that she did as we know that many other pious persons, among them in England notably Godric of Finchale, used to do, that she possessed some devotional manual with pictures in it, and that she used the pictures as a guide to her prayers and thoughts. That she could not herself read in this book is placed beyond question by much that she says, and particularly by her story of how she prayed to God, asking that He would send her a scholar to fill her soul with His word, and how a young priest came to Lynn who for several years "read to her many a good book of exalted contemplation as well as other works—the Bible, with commentaries upon it, St. Bridget's book, Hilton's book, Bonaventura, *Stimulus Amoris*, *Incendium Amoris* and others such." And it is with characteristic shrewdness and complacency that she ends this story by observing that these years were of profit to the young priest, as well as to her, because "afterwards he obtained a benefice, with great cure of souls, and then he was very glad that he had read so much before."

What she heard read she for the most part retained and could reproduce, as illiterates so often can, with great accuracy. The words and stories and applications of the Scriptures are never out of her recollection. She is able to rebuke her enemy, the Mayor of Leicester, with the words:

> "Sir, you are not fit to be a mayor, and I shall prove that by Holy Writ, for our Lord God said Himself, before He would take vengeance upon the cities, 'I shall come down and see'; and that, sir, was only to show such men as you that you ought to carry out no punishment unless you know before that it is deserved."

Or, again, take her account of her "revelation" of how Christ appeared to her and Mary Magdalene (to whom she had great devotion) as He did on Easter Day:

> She heard and saw how our Lord Jesus Christ appeared to her in the likeness of a gardener, saying "Woman, why do you weep?" Mary not recognising Him, all inflamed with the fire of love, answered to Him: "Sir, if you have taken away my Lord, tell me, and I shall take Him back again." Then our merciful Lord, having pity and compassion upon her, said: "Mary." And at that word, she, recognising our Lord, fell down at His feet and would have kissed them, saying: "Master." Our Lord said to her: "Do not touch Me."

Then it seemed to this creature that Mary Magdalene said to our Lord: "Ah, Lord, I see clearly that You do not wish me to be so familiar with You as I used to be. . . ."

This conflation of St. John chapter xx with minor details from St. Matthew and St. Mark, and its ingenious cross-reference of St. Matthew xxviii 9 to the story of the sinful woman, traditionally identified with Mary Magdalene, who anointed and kissed Christ's feet at the feast, may not be original to Margery; but it is perhaps significant that she uses St. John for her main source, the account used in the Easter Week liturgy, and she does show very clearly the precise point at which she departs from Scripture and begins her own imaginative reconstruction of the scene with herself as participant.

Such reconstructions, with her recollections of Scripture or the liturgy as their framework, form, it will be found, the stuff of almost all her "meditation" or "contemplation," terms which she uses indifferently. In her first "revelation," Christ had commanded her not to use so much vocal prayer, to "speak to Me in your mind, and I shall give you exalted meditation and true contemplation." Her "meditations," when she describes them, are usually constructed after the classical models devised for women such as she by St. Anselm: indeed, the very first, describing how she became handmaiden to St. Anne and helped to rear the infant Mary, is taken straight from Anselm's meditation upon the Nativity. We may deplore its emotional ebullience, we may think that it is too much centred upon Margery, but we must concede that its theology is impeccable and that it demonstrates, with such touches as its *Domina, non sum digna*", wisdom and skill in its deployment of her material. So too with the scenes in which she describes her participation in the Epiphany and the events of the Passion. Margery's Passion narratives, indeed, are altogether of their time. The story of the Gospels is very faithfully given, but there are many additions. When she writes: "Our merciful Lord saying to them as a meek lamb: 'Whom do you seek?', they answered in anger: 'Jesus of Nazareth'. Our Lord replied: '*Ego sum*' "—the Latin is used by Margery—"and then she saw the Jews fall down upon the ground . . .," what she describes had very probably been made vivid to her by the Good Friday ceremonies which she had annually seen enacted. She is, it should be observed, a most accurate commentator upon the liturgical uses of her time. For example, her description of the Palm Sunday ceremonies looks, to a modern reader, like an addle-pated mixture of Corpus Christi and Good Friday; but we can learn from such contemporary liturgists as Clement Maidstone that she is recounting with the greatest accuracy the ceremonies of the procession of the Host and the unveiling of the crucifix which were then observed upon that day.

But there is added, especially in her stories of the Passion, a wealth of further detail, describing Christ's torments, which derives from another source, the great body of late medieval literature, poems, treatises and prayers, and of paintings and sculpture which catalogue in horrifying items the physical sufferings of the Passion. On Mount Calvary, Margery writes, "she had before the eyes of her soul contemplation as true as if Christ had hung in His humanity before her bodily eyes . . . His precious, tender body all ragged and torn by scourges, fuller of wounds than ever was dove-cote of holes, hanging upon the Cross with the crown of thorns upon His head, His blessed hands, His tender feet nailed to the hard tree . . . " In Leicester "she came into a fair church where she beheld a crucifix, piteously painted and lamentable to behold, through the sight of which the Passion of our Lord entered her mind." In Norwich "this creature saw a fair image of Our Lady called a *pité*, and through beholding of that *pité* her mind was all wholly occupied in the Passion of our Lord Jesus Christ and in compassion for our Lady St. Mary, by which she was compelled to cry out aloud and to weep very bitterly, as if she would have died." Here we are in the world of St. Bridget's *Revelations*, of Mathias Grünewald, of *Christi Leiden;* but, morbid neurotic though Margery may have been, she had in her conversion indeed lost her heart of stone, as the celebrated end of this Norwich anecdote shows. A priest came up to remonstrate with her, and said: "Damsel, Jesus has been dead a long time," and when she could speak she replied: "Sir, His death is as fresh to me as if He had died today, and it seems to me that it should be so to you and to all Christian people."

On this occasion she had been in Norwich to pray for favours at the tomb of Richard Caister. She had visited Norwich previously, and had talked with Caister when he was vicar of St. Stephen's. Caister, it is plain, enjoyed already in his lifetime a reputation for great sanctity; and Margery describes how she

accosted him in his church and asked him if he could spare an
hour or two after dinner to talk with her about the love of God,
"and he, lifting up his hands and blessing himself, said 'God bless
my soul—what could a woman find to say about our Lord's love
that would take an hour or two? I shan't eat till I hear what you
have to say.'" This ancedote is cautionary, if we remember that
the saintly Richard Caister was living a few streets away from
Julian of Norwich in her anchorhold. Those who indulge in the
kind of speculation which forms so much of the scholarship of
Hope Allen and her school, assuming that because A and B both
lived in C one of them must have "influenced" the other, would
do well to ponder Richard's evident indifference to the *Frauenbe-
wegung* of which Julian and Margery are held to be such outstanding English members. When, a few pages later, Margery tells
of her visit to Julian and of the counsel she had from her, there is
nothing in their "holy dalliance" which reflects the profundities
of Julian's own *Revelations*.

It is clear, however, that they talked about the "discretion of
spirits," that Margery received from Julian the assurances she
constantly needed that she bore none of the marks of diabolical
possession, and that they then discussed Margery's weeping-fits.
Julian had said: "When God visits a creature with tears of contrition, devotion or compassion, he may and he should believe
that the Holy Spirit is in his soul . . ." The rest of this passage,
with Hope Allen's learned identifications of the authorities whom
Julian cited, is of great interest, and it should be added that in the
phrases just quoted there is very likely an allusion to Hugh of St.
Victor's famous words about tears as *charismata*, from *De Arrha
Animae*. Margery's interview with Julian shows beyond doubt
what the critics have always told us, that Julian, despite her protestations of ignorance, was a woman well-informed in mystical
theology; and it also shows that Margery was busy accumulating
opinions upon the "theology of tears." This underlies her special
devotion to Mary Magdalene, patron of weepers; and in another
place she tells how a priest who was convinced of her fraudulence
was converted to her support after he had read in Jacques de Vitry's
Life of Mary of Oignies, from which Margery quotes chapter
and verse, of that ecstatic's gift of "tears of pity and compassion."
And all that Margery Kempe had learned, from the lives of other
holy women and from her own speculations, is summed up in

the "revelation" in which she finds authority and reason and utility for this mysterious gift which had brought her so much affliction and persecution.

> She said: "I ask nothing at all, Lord, but what You may well give me, and that is mercy which I ask for the people's sins. Again and again every year You tell me that You have forgiven me my sins. Therefore I now ask mercy for the sins of the people as I would ask for my own, for You are all love, Lord, and it was love that brought You into this wretched world and caused You to suffer cruel pains for our sins. . . . I wish I had a well of tears to constrain You with, so that You would not take complete vengeance upon man's soul by separating him from You for ever, for it is a grief to think that any man should ever commit any sin through which he ought to be separated from Your glorious sight for ever.

Flere est orare, Margery is telling us here, and the Church, which still retains a votive mass "for the gift of tears," tells us that Margery is right. Others can do great things for the salvation of souls, but the best that this poor woman could do was to weep, so she wept to God's glory and to keep sinners out of hell.

Did she, however, "weep by the book"? Sceptics will doubtless say that if she had not heard of Mary of Oignies and the other Netherlands ecstatics, if no-one had ever read the *Stimulus Amoris* and Rolle and Hilton to her, if, more than all, she had not become fired with ambition to become England's Bridget, her vapourings would probably have followed other, less reputable modes. They will point to the many clear indications which her own descriptions of her "ravishings" give that she was a hysteric, if not an epileptic; and they will suggest that her "revelations" are subjective, imitative, excogitated. All of this may be true, and any *promotor fidei* could with ease demolish Margery's claims for the consideration of her sanctity. But we today have Thérèse to remind us that to aspire to sainthood is not in itself an obstacle to sanctity or sanctification; and before we dismiss Margery as the dupe of her own ambitions, let us remember her virtues. There is great honesty and sincerity: she could not be more frank about her own sinfulness. She showed wonderful patience and constancy and faith: it is hard to credit that any fraud, however pious, could have displayed her endurance. She does not love God at the expense of His creatures: throughout her *Book* we find a beautiful compassion for the weak and ailing and afflicted. She may indeed have looked and acted like a fool, have wearied men to death with her obsessive talk of heavenly things, have driven them to distraction with her screaming and tears, but all this she did, so far as she could control her own actions, because she truly believed that God had told her that this was what He wanted of her. She was, all too typically, a child of her own Gothic times; but one may believe that in any age she could have said, with St. Edmund Rich, "I have sought You, I have preached You, I have loved You."

18. ST. THOMAS MORE

Germain Marc'hadour

"IF WE BE, not only simple as doves, but also prudent and wise as serpents."[1]

When St. Thomas More englished this text, which Père Lagrange called "the gem of St. Matthew," he shifted its emphasis, no doubt deliberately. The Gospel would seem to stress, if anything, dove-like simplicity, by putting it at the end of the sentence to linger as an echo in the mind's ear. But More found the Catholics of his day so guileless that they were too easily beguiled, so simple that they were apt to behave like simpletons: "Our Saviour saith that the children of darkness be more politic in their kind than are the children of light: and surely so seemeth it now."[2] Let innocence, then, let the spirit of childhood be preached to a more sophisticated generation. The vital need of his own age was discretion, that maturity which corresponds to the completed growth of Christ. It is this virtue which More singles out in the preface to his first published work.[3] The Fathers called it the mother of all virtues, and the importance which More attached to it is signalised by what he says of it, thirty years later, on the last page of his last book: "An adder so long rubbeth his old withered skin among thorns and briars till at last he casts it quite away, and so leaving it in the hedge cometh forth fresh and young again: so if we, according to Christ's counsel, become wise as serpents, and rubbing off this old rivelled body of ours as the adder doth his skin, among the thorns of tribulation for the love of God, leave it behind us in the world, we shall therewith become fresh and young again, and so be shortly carried up into heaven, where we shall never wax old again."[4]

[1] More's rendering of Matt 10, 16 (*Estote ergo prudentes sicut serpentes, et simplices sicut columbae*) is found in his *Confutation* (*English Works*, 1557 edition, p. 763. All references are to the pages of this edition). For More's Correspondence we have used the edition of E. E. Rogers (Princeton University Press, 1947).

[2] p. 355; cf. p. 1371.

[3] Dedicatory letter (to Thomas Ruthal) of More's translations from Lucian, Rogers no. 5.

[4] *Expositio Passionis, ed. cit.*, p 1403.

In More himself wariness shone brighter than artlessness. Such was the unflagging caution with which he endeavoured to ward off the final blow, to dodge the horror and ignominy of a traitor's death, that many historians have accused him of a prudence which approximates to lack of generosity, if not cowardice. This is to ignore—which More never did—Christ's command to His persecuted disciples to seek safety in flight, and Christ's counsel that, before we make a war or build a tower, we should "sit and reckon what the charge will be."[1] We are, however, concerned here with More's spiritual attitudes and principles as they are expressed in his works, particularly his letters and devotional treatises rather than as reflected in his own behaviour. Were it not for his writings, we would never have suspected that some of his views, which seem exactly typical of the Londoner, the lawyer, the scholar or the statesman, were in fact dictated by specifically Christian considerations. The light he has thus thrown on several episodes of his life, even if we are still baffled by others, should at least teach us to suspend our judgment about his motives.

Simplicity can be overdone. Since the Gospel itself is a rather complex key to the complex lock of man's soul, any rule of life that ignores this complexity will be found wanting when it comes to the practical test. Vowed celibacy may achieve a great simplification by ruthlessly discarding everything save the one thing that matters, and the solitude of the cloister even more so. But Thomas More's lot was thrown with those who push their way towards God through the tangled undergrowth of worldly concerns. He personally tried a number of approaches: some that were neat and straight as the dove's flight, others that were hardly less tortuous than the snake's path; some that were gentle and attractive, others that required nothing less than heroic faith and energy. He is a perfect guide for the Christian layman, since he possessed that manifold experience of the world and of God which is, as he says himself, "the very mother and mistress of wisdom."[2]

An obvious danger for the layman is to be unduly attached to the things of earth. Tribulation, generously provided by life itself, is the ideal means of preventing this. It is one point on

1 Rogers, *ed. cit.*, 206, 210; cf. pp. 1354-8.
2 *History of King Richard III*, ed. J. R. Lumby (Cambridge 1883), p. 89.

which medieval writers, Catholic humanists and Protestant reformers, at least before Calvin, never disagreed.[1] More's originality lies in treating the subject more elaborately and more exhaustively than anyone else before or after him: chiefly, though not exclusively, in the three books of his *Dialogue of Comfort against Tribulation*. Temptation is the Christian's severest test, the only one of which St. Paul complained repeatedly.[2] Yet More says with St. James, "esteem and take it for a thing of all joy when you fall into divers and sundry manner of temptations."[3] The devil, for all his being now in a humiliated and hampered position, is still a formidable adversary. "Our wrestling is not here against flesh and blood,"[4] but against someone stronger and cleverer than we are. And if he wins, our fate is that death which alone fully deserves the name of death, because it separates, not the body from the soul, but "the whole entire man . . . from the fruition of the very fountain of life, Almighty glorious God."[5]

The fear of the devouring monster should not paralyse us, however. Though he is more than a match for us, he is never a match for God. There is no danger as long as we cling to God, whose truth is our shield: "a long large pavise that compasseth us round about, and covereth all along the body."[6] We cling to God by faith, for which we must pray continually, saying with the apostles, "Lord, increase our faith," or with the father of the dumb child, "I believe, good Lord, but help thou the lack of my belief!"[7] We must keep ourselves on the alert, ready to fight and, with God's grace, labour for the things we ask in prayer.

The Christendom into which More was born had lost its militant spirit. Knighthood had degenerated into an elaborate etiquette; it was more a ritual than a function. The fencing sword, the tilting lance, were not so much weapons as toys, with their carved hilts and gilded sheaths. The decay of chivalry was symptomatic of a general softening of the soul's fibre. Erasmus, largely under the influence of Colet, heralded the doom of the rather passive, acquiescent, sentimental and retiring

---

[1] See especially Boethius, Gerson, the "Short Treatise" printed by Caxton in 1491 on *The Twelve Profits of Tribulation*, and St. John Fisher's *Spiritual Consolation*. William Tyndale, in his *Obedience of the Christian Man*—"a wicked book," More says—writes that "Prosperity is a right curse. . . . The Spirit, through tribulation, purgeth us . . . and filleth us full of the wisdom of God." (1st ed., 1528, fol. 7).

[2] 2 Cor. 12, 6-10.　　[3] *Works, ed. cit.*, p. 1178.　　[4] *Ibid.*

[5] *Ibid.*, p. 1286.　　[6] *Ibid.*, p. 1180.　　[7] *Ibid.*, p. 1143.

spirituality then prevailing, when he published his *Enchiridion*, the "handbook" or "hand-dagger" of the Christian knight, meant to be used, not in pageants, but in the warfare of daily life. More was the embodiment of this new type of Christian man, enlightened and enterprising; the secular arm of the Church for peaceful defence and conquest. He did not merely describe the Christian soldier's equipment, he demonstrated it.

He reminds the faithful of their responsibility. The Church had become almost synonymous with the clergy. More himself held that "ye be the salt of the earth" was spoken "for the priests and bishops only."[1] Yet he also held that "God hath given every man cure and charge of his neighbour."[2] The laity must therefore be apostolic and co-operate most whole-heartedly with their priests: "I would have them love well and agree together, as the body and the soul of one man." More hinted that other Englishmen should share with him the labour of confuting Protestant pamphleteers. "As the true disciples of Christ were in slumber and fell asleep in Christ's company, while Judas the traitour was waking and watching . . . so true believing men, able in writing to much more than overmatch them, if they would wake and pray and take the pen in hand, be now so forwearied with the sorrow and heaviness to see the world wax so wretched, that they fall even in a slumber therewith and let these wretches alone."[3]

If we are to help in spreading or defending the Gospel, we have to be fully informed about it, "according to the counsel of St. Peter, bidding us be ready to give a reckoning, and to show a reasonable cause to every man of the faith and hope that we have."[4] Some pastors in pre-Reformation England—and maybe to-day too—would warn their flock against wanting to know too much: did not "inordinate appetite of knowledge" drive Adam and Eve out of paradise?[5] Books such as *The Cloud of Unknowing* and *The Image of Love* also entertained a distrust of the intellect, with their picture of blind love groping its way to the God of love.

More knew the dangers of intellectual passion, and may have felt the temptation himself. He translated the famous passage where Pico, "the Phoenix of geniuses," whilst writing his *De*

[1] *Ibid.*, p. 143; and cf. pp. 226 and 937.   [2] *Ibid.*, p. 279; and cf. pp. 1217 and 1276.
[3] *Ibid.*, p. 356.   [4] *Ibid.*, p. 106.   [5] *Ibid.*, p. 242.

Q

Ente et Uno, suddenly turns to his friend Angelo Poliziano, and sighs, "Alas! How mad of us to keep seeking by knowledge that which love alone can reach and grasp!"[1]

The more common danger, however, is intellectual sloth. More fully endorses the adage of St. Anselm, *Fides quaerens intellectum*. True faith is soundly inquisitive. Mary, the believer *par excellence*, is witness to this: "the cause of her question was faith" when she asked the angel, "How may this be?"[2] Secular knowledge, besides being noble and profitable in itself, is an essential prerequisite for a full understanding of revealed truth. In his devastating letter to the Louvain Divine, Martin van Dorp, More denounces the arrogant folly of some theologians who fancy they can dispense with grammar, literature and the study of languages, simply because they are expert logicians. The time they have wasted on logic they ought to have devoted to drinking deep from the pure sources of Divine Revelation.[3]

The Bible alone offers a boundless field for our investigation. As an appendix to his *Life of Pico*, More singled out a letter in which, among many other things, the Earl of Mirandula urged his nephew to learn from God Himself how to pray: "Thou mayst do nothing more pleasant to God, nothing more profitable to thyself, than if thine hand cease not day nor night to turn and read the volume of Holy Scripture. There lieth privily in them a certain heavily strength, quick and effectual, which with a marvellous power transformeth and changeth the reader's mind into the love of God."[4]

The lesson was not lost on More himself, and he could rely upon his own experience when he repeated it in the introduction to his treatise on the Four Last Things: "Remember the last things, and thou shalt never die." The book purports to be nothing more than variations upon this single inspired sentence. "This only text, written by the wise man in the seventh chapter of *Ecclesiasticus*, is such that it containeth more fruitful advice and counsel, to the forming and framing of man's manners in virtue, and avoiding of sin, than many whole and great volumes of the best of old philosophers, or any other that ever wrote in secular literature."[5] Our Lord's own pronouncements on the same

1 "*Heu! malumus semper quaerendo per cognitionem nunquam invenire quod quaerimus, quam amando possidere id quod, non amatum, frustra etiam amaretur.*" *Ibid.*, p. 7.
2 *Works, ed. cit.*, p. 1060.   3 Rogers, no. 15.   4 *Works*, p. 13.   5 *Ibid.*, p. 72.

subject in the New Testament are even more efficacious. But the whole Bible, from Genesis to Apocalypse, is a heavenly feast. "The very strange familiar fashion thereof may to good men and wise well declare that, as it was written by men, so was it indited by God . . . It is, as a good holy saint saith, so marvellously tempered, that a mouse may wade therein, and an oliphant be drowned therein."[1]

This rich and vital manna is obviously meant for all the children of God. Consequently, More unambiguously "shewed his mind that it were convenient to have the Bible in English."[2] Inevitably some lewd fellows will be found "to handle Holy Scripture in more homely manner than a song of Robin Hood"; it pertains to the "wisdom and discretion" of the bishops to make some provision against such abuses, but let us not forfeit the use for fear of the abuse. More himself never tires of perusing and quoting the inspired authors, not merely for arguments against the Lutherans, but for spiritual edification. Many chapters of his *Dialogue of Comfort* are mosaics of Scriptural texts. Where Boethius wrote a *Consolatio Philosophiae*, and Gerson a *Consolatio Theologiae*, More wrote a *Consolatio Scripturarum*.[3] How shall we learn to "consider tribulation as a gracious gift of God?"—"If we lay first for a sure ground a very fast faith, whereby we believe to be true all that the Scripture saith, understanden truly as the old holy doctors declare it, and as the Spirit of God instructeth his Catholic Church."[4]

This sentence is not merely a thrust at those heretics who, for all their learning and their zeal, misconstrue the word of God because in their quest for the truth they ignore, or even defy, the "perpetual apostle" of Christ, the Catholic Church.[5] Quite apart from controversial purposes, More's intense devotion to the mystical Body of Christ is undoubtedly the most striking feature in his own spiritual portrait, and the central piece of his doctrinal construction. The life abounding and the fulfilment that we seek are in God, whose fullness dwells in our fellow-man Jesus Christ. Christ is present with us chiefly through His written Word and in the Blessed Sacrament, but this double manna is served to us from the hands of Mother Church. Christ promised

---

[1] *Ibid.*, pp. 156, 159, 162. [2] *Ibid.*, pp. 240-247.
[3] Cf. Rom., 15, 4. [4] *Works, ed. cit.*, p. 1168.
[5] *Ibid.*, p. 458.

to be with her until the end of the world, and promised that His Spirit should lead her into all truth.[1]

More was too much and too consciously a layman to have that clerical mind which R. W. Chambers claims to find in him. "Ecclesiologically minded" would describe him better. He paid less heed to the diversity of organs and functions in the Church than to her being one body. True unity, that is, oneness of mind and heart, is a thing of such beauty that it always betokens the presence and the action of God. More never tires of quoting St. Matthew, "Where there are two or three gathered together in my name, there am I also in the midst of them,"[2] or, with broader implications, Psalm 67, 7, *Deus qui inhabitare facit unanimes in domo*, interpreting it with the Liturgy as "the Holy Spirit which maketh all of one mind in the house of God, that is in the Church."[3]

It is significant that More's wording of this verse is usually taken, not from the Vulgate (*unius moris*), but from the Introit for the eleventh Sunday after Pentecost. He probably makes his boldest comment on the blessings of unanimity when he writes that "if the Church of Christ, intending well, do all agree upon any one thing concerning God's honour or man's soul, it cannot be but that thing must be true."[4] Common consent is a sufficient touchstone and guarantee of the assistance of the Spirit of Truth.

Communion is not an idle word: the Eucharist was from the beginning called *Synaxis* because its primary fruit is the wonderful "communion of men together with God. . . . The *thing* of the Blessed Sacrament is the unity and society of all good folk in the mystical body of Christ. . . . Our Saviour is the worker of this communion: in giving his own very body into the body of every Christian man, he doth in a certain manner incorporate all Christian folk and his own body in one corporation mystical."[5] Sacramental feeding of the soul is not the only, or even the principal, fruit of Holy Communion; the increase of vitality results from a richer, freer, closer connection between the Head and the rest of the body.

More's amazing insistence upon this mystery places him nearer to St. Paul and St. Augustine, and again, nearer to modern

[1] Both these promises (Matt. 28, 20, John 16, 13) are cited more than fifty times in More's works.
[2] *Ibid.*, pp. 1235 and *passim.*
[3] *Ibid.*, p. 179, and cf. pp. 168, 456, 1095, etc.
[4] *Ibid.*, p. 192. Cf. 1 Cor. 1, 10.
[5] *Works*, pp. 1332, 1336 and 1347.

theology and devotion, than to his contemporaries. His vivid awareness of the mystical belonging-together was grafted upon a keen sense of human solidarity. It is never good for a man to be without companionship; he becomes fully himself by being integrated in a community, or rather in a system of more or less concentric communities. Whatever one may think of many details in the *Utopia*, there is no doubt that the book denounced individualism whilst it was still in its cradle, and advocated some measure of socialisation. The city of men ought to be one big family, where civic relations are controlled not by rigorous justice, but by that gentler daughter of justice, *piety*, in its true theological sense.[1]

"If the Roman playwright is rightly praised for saying that, being a man, he could not be indifferent to anything human, how can we Christians sleep and snore unashamedly, while our fellow members of Christ, in countries occupied by the Turks, are exposed, not only to suffering, but to great spiritual dangers?"[2] We must wake up and pray for them. The "silly souls" in Purgatory have a still better claim upon our active sympathy, for "none is there, yet living, that is more very member of Christ's mystical body . . . nor no man living that hath more need of help."[3] Devotion to the Church Suffering is a corollary of the doctrine of the Mystical Body which the modern Catholic is sometimes slow in drawing. The two books of More's *Supplication of Souls* convey to us the mighty clamour of an entire prison whose inmates are bound to us with the double bond of nature and grace, besides various other "pieties" arising from kin or friendship.[4] Theirs is a collective experience, totally unlike the *animula nudula* of some medieval complaints, or Newman's Gerontius, who dreams of his soul throbbing all alone in God's palm. And Heaven, too, is a *socia exsultatio*, where we shall be "merry together" with "the Trinity in his high marvellous majesty, our Saviour in his glorious manhood sitting on his throne with his immaculate Mother and all that glorious company."[5]

If the Pauline image of the Body suffered a sort of eclipse in

[1] On piety as the equivalent of filial obedience and its paramount importance in More's spirituality, see my article "Obedient unto death: a key to St. Thomas More," in *Spiritual Life*, Milwaukee, 1961, pp. 205-222.
[2] Latin Works—*Opera Omnia*, Frankfort, 1689, p. 165, and cf. *Works*, p. 1379.
[3] *Ibid.*, p. 327.   [4] *Ibid.*, p. 288.   [5] *Ibid.*, p. 1261.

More's day, the Gospel similes, popularised by the Mass and the homily, retained their appeal. More frequently cites Our Lord's saying: "I am the true vine, and you are the branches." He often alludes to the "parables of the Kingdom," and points out that the mixture of good and evil in the Church Militant is rather reassuring than disturbing, since it agrees with the Founder's own description of it. "Therefore, as I say, in Christ's field here upon earth, there shall never lack cockle among the corn: and yet shall it still be Christ's holy Church, and his holy field, so holy that he calleth it the Kingdom of Heaven. For be there never so much cockle in that field, yet doth God continually out of the field with his fan cleanse from the cockle good corn, and sendeth it pure and clean unto heaven; and in that field, like as the devil turneth the corn into cockle, so God turneth again much cockle into corn. . . . Let us labour that we may be corn ourself."[1]

"Let us labour," then, and "not look to go to heaven on featherbeds: it is not the way, for Our Lord himself went thither with great pain."[2] We are not Stoics striving to be captains of our souls: we are Christians, one with Christ, longing to be with Him, and eager meanwhile to be like Him. "The same way that Christ walked, the same way must we walk."[3] The call to the imitation of and conformity with our Head lies at the root of our vocation: "Let dead men alone with dead men, follow thou me. Dead be they that live not to God, and in the space of this temporal death laboriously purchase themselves eternal death."[4] Baptism and Holy Communion make us "quick, lively members"[5] of one who is waiting for us in "the land of the living." If we allow His grace to work freely in us, it will lead us to accepting, or even embracing, a life of hard work and poverty, of prayer and self-denial, until eventually we "set the world at nought" and live the full paradox of the Gospel, including the folly of the Cross.

Work, or at least manual labour, is not, it seems, a precept of God "binding every man."[6] For most of us it is a necessity, of which we shall be wise "to make a virtue."[7] But, far from being a virtue in itself, work can be a temptation: *negotium*, "business," in Psalm 90, is the name of a devil. So let the disciple of Christ beware of being a "work addict"; to the "meat" of

---

[1] *Ibid.*, p. 826.   [2] Roper's *Life of More*, Early English Text Society, p. 26.
[3] *Works*, p. 1260.   [4] *Ibid.*, p. 16.   [5] *Ibid.*, p. 1349.   [6] *Ibid.*, p. 304.   [7] *Ibid.*, p. 1206.

virtue and study, let him always add play as a "sauce."[1] As wanton work may be a vice, so the *negotiosum otium* of mental prayer is a most virtuous occupation. Remember Mary Magdalen, "whose idle sitting at her ease and hearkening Our Saviour accounted and declared for better business than the busy stirring and walking about of his good hostess Martha."[2] Though life imposes Martha's lot on most of us, there are quieter hours when we must make up for it by emulating Mary, especially after receiving Jesus in holy communion: "Let us by devout prayer talk to him, by devout meditation talk with him. . . . And let us with Mary hearken well what Our Saviour, being now our guest, will inwardly say unto us."[3]

Humbler forms of recreation may and should be added to these indispensable pauses of the soul. "That proper pleasant talking, which is called *eutrapelia*, is a good virtue."[4] One grace More prayed for, in prison, was "recreations not necessary to cut off."[5] But necessity is an elastic notion, and it takes into account the needs of others, so that time seemingly wasted in conversation may in fact be wisely and charitably bestowed. Even when starting in a light vein, it is possible, out of the heart's abundance, to end up speaking about God, hope in whom is the one solid foundation of our joy, the one permanent ground of our comfort. "The ease of his yoke standeth not in bodily ease, but in the sweetness of hope."[6] "I beseech him make you all merry in the hope of heaven."[7] Cheerfulness need not be cultivated for its own sake, any more than one would cultivate apple-blossom.

More would not have put his name to the apocryphal text in which he is supposed to have prayed, among other things, for a good digestion and a sense of humour. He was not a "jolly fellow." Although he was good at dispelling gloom by very amusing banter, and could be extremely witty in his own dry way, he never advocated hilarity. Why is it then that his writings are so exhilarating, as his presence obviously was? Because they teach us the art of transmuting everything—the drab, the tedious, the tragic—into gladness, through "clearness of conscience" and the conviction that the Almighty is also the All-loving: "Nothing can come but that that God will. . . . Whatever that be, seem it

---

1 *Roper, loc. cit.,* p. 7.   2 *Works,* p. 304.   3 *Ibid.,* p. 1268.   4 *Ibid.,* p. 1171.
5 *Ibid.,* p. 1416.   6 *Ibid.,* p. 143.   7 *Rogers, ed. cit.,* no. 201.

never so bad, it shall indeed be the best."[1] A perfect definition
of Christian optimism. Life is hard, there's no denying it, "but
then against that grief Seneca teacheth us a good remedy:
Semper da operam ne quid invitus facias. Endeavour thyself evermore
that thou do nothing against thy will. . . . The thing that we see
we shall needs do, let us use always to put our good will thereto."[2]
My own ill-will, coming athwart God's will, is the only thing to
lament, or to redress. The malice of others can kill me, not trouble
me "Though I might have pain, I could not have harm . . .
In such a case a man may lose his head, and suffer no harm."[3]
This *riddle*, as he himself calls it, was the leit-motif of More the
prisoner; his unusually high spirits showed that he had solved it.
The deep, "peaceable" happiness of a Christian, however, need
not be expressed by laughter. "*Est tempus flendi*, saith the Scripture,
et est tempus ridendi: there is time of weeping, and there is time
of laughing. . . . To prove that this life is no laughing time, but
rather the time of weeping, we find that our Saviour himself
wept twice or thrice, but never find we that he laughed so much
as once."[4] This is More's way of reminding us that the ways of
God are often thorny.

The ways of God? More exactly, the ways of fallen man; and
it happens that the paths of vice are even thornier than those of
virtue. "Many a man buyeth hell with so much pain that he
might have bought heaven with less than the tone half,"[5] "If
thou ween that I teach thee wrong, when I say that in virtue is
pleasure and in sin is pain, I might prove it by many plain texts
of Holy Scripture," which he proceeds to do. Is it not therefore
"madness to take sinful pain in this world, that shall win us
eternal pain in hell, rather than pleasant virtue in this world,
that shall win us eternal pleasure in heaven?"[6] Spiritual high-
brows may frown upon this ignoble arithmetic of pleasure, but
More knows what there is in man and he is catering for all
sorts: even the noblest find themselves in low spirits at times.
St. Thérèse of Lisieux expressed some dislike for verse 112 of
Psalm 118, because it ends with *propter retributionem.* But to the
Lutheran Bugenhagen, who had attacked the doctrine of merit,
More wrote: "You are looking down upon the Prophet, since he,
less fastidious than you are, was not ashamed to confess that he

[1] *Works*, p. 206.   [2] *Ibid.*, p. 1239.   [3] *Rogers, ed. cit.*, nos. 206, 210, 216.
[4] *Works*, pp. 1154-1155.   [5] *Ibid.*, p. 1205, and cf. p. 12.   [6] *Ibid.*, p. 98.

served God with a view to retribution."[1] With those who have
no faith at all, he reasons in the spirit of Pascal's dialectic wager.
In doubt, he says, "the far surer way is to believe. . . . Any wise
man will take the surest way," that is, will bet on the existence
of God and some reward in the after life. Then, like the austere
friar in the "merry tale," he will gain on all counts, even in this
life.[2]

When he comes to satirise the bitter, weary, cumbrous,
laborious folly and tyranny of the deadly sins, More pours his
most acid scorn upon "peevish pestilent pride, the head and root
of all sins, the mother of all heresies.[3] "Beware of the least spice
thereof." All forms of pride are analysed and ridiculed in More's
writings. "Such a pestilent serpent is ambition and desire of
vainglory."[4] "What is fame but the blast of another man's
mouth, as soon passed as spoken?"[5] "An high spiritual pride"
is such a stinking disease that "one foul act of lechery," if it
cures it, is a blessing.[6] More's elaborate letter about the education of his children[7] is an essay on not coveting praise, "this
shadow of glory."[8] Wicked envy, "the daughter of pestilent
pride,"[9] is hardly less pernicious and shameful than her mother.

"The good manner mean,"[10] that is, the sensible middle way,
must be found between peevish (reckless) pride and pusillanimity,
whose daughter, a silly puling creature called Scrupulosity,
refuses to do anything for fear of doing things amiss; and so
she wastes her time and frays other people's nerves.[11] It is better
to walk briskly, and stumble at times, than to creep. "Let us
with an holy ambition be proud! . . . Let us fence us with faith,
and comfort us with hope, and smite the devil in the face with
the firebrand of charity."[12] Let each pursue excellence and mastery
in his own craft and calling. Although we are but unprofitable
servants, and "all the justice of man is like a foul spotted clout,"[13]
there is in store for us a reward "wonderful huge and great,"[14]
"a good measure, shaken together, heaped and running over,"[15]
out of proportion with our achievements.

In our heaven-bound voyage, elementary prudence teaches
us to fear the excessive ballast of earthly riches. "God in the

[1] *Rogers, ed. cit.*, no. 63. [2] *Works*, pp. 329-330. [3] *Ibid.*, p. 1273.
[4] *Richard III*, Lumby ed. cit., p. 10. [5] *Works*, p. 1221. [6] *Ibid.*, p. 272.
[7] *Rogers, ed. cit.*, no. 63. [8] *Works*, p. 7. [9] *Ibid.*, p. 1273.
[10] *Ibid.*, p. 206. [11] *Ibid.*, p. 1182. [12] *Ibid.*, pp. 16 and 1263.
[13] *Ibid.*, pp. 140, 269, *Rogers, ed. cit.*, no. 83. [14] *Works*, p. 1259. [15] *Ibid.*, p. 263.

Gospel counselleth the rich folk to buy in a manner heaven."[1]
Read the story of the dishonest steward; or hear the warning
of Christ which Mother Church broadcasts each year on Ash
Wednesday. "Hoard not up your treasures in earth, where the
rust and the moth fret it out, and where thieves dig it out and
steal it away. But hoard up your treasures in heaven, where
neither the rust nor the moth fret them out, nor steal them away.
For where is thy treasure, there is thine heart too."[2] More also
often quotes the strong words in St. Luke: "Thou fool! This
night shall they take thy soul from thee; and then these things
that thou hast gathered, whose shall they be? And holy saint
Bernard saith that it may be said unto him further: 'Thou that
hast gathered them, whose shalt thou be?'"[3]

Even by the standards of wealthy society, More, until the King's
service impoverished him, enjoyed almost untold affluence, and
this seems to have made him somewhat uneasy. Staying rich,
and at the same time winning heaven, is like walking on a tight
rope: who will escape Christ's plain threat, however hyperbolic
may be his simile of the camel and the needle's eye? Yet Scripture
mentions several wealthy persons who were God's special friends.
Our Lord's hosts at Bethany had so much money that Mary,
in a few seconds, could spill ten times the amount that Judas got
for his traitorous bargain. Lazarus the beggar, after dying "for
pure hunger and thirst at the rich glutton's door," found "comfort and rest in Abraham the wealthy rich man's bosom."[4] And
Job, the perfect pattern of equanimity in alternate wealth and
woe, speaks in the letter More sent to his wife on hearing that
all his barns had been burnt: "He sent us all that we have lost,
and since he hath taken it away again, his pleasure be fulfilled.
Let us never grudge thereat, but heartily thank him as well for
adversity as for prosperity. . . . Take all the household with you
to church, and there thank God both for that he hath given us,
and for that he hath taken from us, and for that he hath left us."
More wrote this letter from Court on 3 September 1529.[5]
Less than three weeks before, on 13 August, Erasmus, a refugee
in Freiburg from the iconoclast violence of Basel, confessed to
his friend Canon Botzheim that his painful adjustment to reduced circumstances was a far cry from Job's attitude: *Quantum
adhuc absumus a formula beati Jobi.* The perfect ease with which

---

[1] *Ibid.*, p. 1206.   [2] *Ibid.*, p. 1232, and cf. p. 92.   [3] *Ibid.*, p. 94 and *passim.*
[4] *Ibid.*, pp. 1159, 1263.   [5] *Rogers, ed. cit.*, no. 174.

More rose to the occasion, the heroic detachment evinced by the provisions he dictates concerning the other victims of the fire, the obvious confidence he has that his family will follow suit and face the prospect of sheer destitution, illustrate both the incomparable quality of his virtue and the influence of his saintly example.

More was inspired by the truth that every man is welcome to God. Listen to Jesus: "He that cometh to me, I will not cast him out."[1] And look at Jesus, "who spread his arms abroad upon the cross, lovingly to embrace all them that will come."[2] Maybe you are deterred by what Christ expects from His followers: "Called he not them to watching, fasting, praying, preaching, walking, hunger, thirst, cold and heat, beating, scourging, prisonment, painful and shameful death?"[3] You sag at the mere prospect of this "light burden," your will-power is weakened by original sin, marred by faulty training and the contagion of false principles, but you are nevertheless really free and responsible. Your eternal destiny lies in your own hands. Those who preach the bondage of man's will blaspheme God and rob man of his most royal prerogative. You will prove them false prophets by acting freely. If you feel restive, ask God to break you: "pray him strain your jaws with a bit and a bridle, and draw you by the cheeks, maugre your teeth."[4] "Never forget these two things: that both the Son of God died for thee, and that thou shalt also thyself die shortly . . . With these two spurs, the one of fear, the other of love, spur forth thine horse through the short way of this momentary life to the reward of eternal felicity."[5]

The "spur of love," the figure of Christ's Cross, is always in the picture: not on the horizon, but in the foreground, with the Word of God written across it in bold letters of blood. *Stat crux dum volvitur orbis* is the Carthusian motto. There stands forever the Tree of Life; and More stood gazing at it, questioning it, reading the riddle of the Crucifix. He wrote two voluminous treatises on the Passion, both unfinished. Since his own and his family's sufferings were more of the heart than of the body, he exhorted them and himself "in all our agonies and troubles devoutly to resort prostrate unto the remembrance of that bitter agony, which Our Saviour suffered before his Passion at the Mount."[6] Jesus was never so pathetically human as in His

1 *Works*, p. 1042 and *passim*.   2 *Ibid.*, p. 1174.   3 *Ibid.*, p. 143.
4 *Ibid.*, p. 1054.   5 *Ibid.*, p. 13.   6 *Rogers, ed. cit.*, no. 202.

darkest hour, with "his flesh shrinking at the meditation of pain and death": when one remembers that He was the Son of Man, "the great horror and fear" He experienced then lose their strangeness.[1]

Although his spiritual director John Colet showed great devotion to the Child Jesus, More, in apparent reaction against his time, hardly ever alluded to the sweet mysteries of Christ's infancy. St. Joseph, for instance, is practically absent. Our Lady, whom More loved tenderly and visited at her shrines in Willesden, Muswell Hill and elsewhere, is mentioned only incidentally: her Immaculate Conception, because this was a good instance of a "traditional" truth slowly emerging by unanimous consent; the Annunciation, to demonstrate by the example of Mary, "so discreet and circumspect," that it is lawful to vow virginity, and that once having taken it one is bound to keep the vow. The very popular cult of the Name of Jesus was not altogether free from a sentimental bias or a semi-magical nominalism. Instead of "Jesus" More usually says "Our Saviour," which means the same. The Christ he saw was a grown-up man, sweet and loving-kind—and we too "shall in this world be each to other piteous and not *sine affectione*, for which the apostle rebuketh them that lack their tender affections here"[2]—yet capable of anger and defiance, scorn and biting irony. Christ used the familiar symbols and gestures of His fellow men: to signify that the Jewish Passover was henceforth gone and buried, "he drank to it with his apostles, to wash it away, so to speak, for a final end thereof."[3] In fact, we must, with St. Paul, know Christ "not according to the flesh," but according to the Spirit, through which He rose from the dead and makes us partakers of His contest, His victory and His inheritance. In Holy Communion, He is the risen Crucified, the same who bade Magdalen not to cling to His humanity. The sweetness of His presence counts less than our sharing in His immolation, and our being "by his Spirit more firmly knit and uned quick lively members in the society of saints."[4]

More's balanced piety, like the Liturgy, always addresses God with a mixture of affection and awe. So in the long prayer at the end of his *Pico*, the first line is, "O holy God of dreadful majesty," and the last, "As a very tender loving father." This is

1 *Works*, p. 1235.   2 *Works*, p. 1169.   3 *Ibid.*, p. 1323.   4 *Ibid.*, p. 1349

the very phrase he uses as a *Vale* when writing to his children from the Tower.[1]

"The spur of fear" proves to be, eventually, another "spur of love." Death, at first sight, is a grim and grisly vision; as it becomes familiar, its horror decreases. It is "near, at hand," since not only shall it soon dispatch us hence, but it is already at work in us: decay is a daily, hourly process. All the world is at once a prison and a stage, on which all the actors are prisoners sentenced to death. "Every man universally is a very prisoner in very prison without any sophistication at all."[2] God is "our chief gaoler."[3] A gruesome comparison? It might be, if it did not come from a happy prisoner, looking forward to the moment when his bodily ailments would loosen his fetters and "hance him up to heaven,"[4] into the fatherly embrace of that loving gaoler. He "longed to be out of this world and to be with him . . . Whoso long to be with him shall be welcome to him."[5] He was never sorry when he felt the cold fingers of death gripping his heart, but "rather sorry when I saw the pang past."[6] Meanwhile it was good to remember that the Lieutenant of the Tower, and the King's Highness, and the devil himself, were after all but under-gaolers. "The celestial joy standeth in blessed beholding of the glorious Godhead face to face," but it is also a warm personal encounter, with "special gifts" for each elect, "specified in the second and third chapter of the Apocalypse."[7] Of the four last things, Heaven is the "real thing," alongside which death and the devil dwindle into insignificance. If we learn to "see heaven open, and Jesus Christ there standing, as did the blessed St. Stephen," we shall "not regard a rush all the rest";[8] we shall be "in haste to meet the Great Spouse."[9] One of the special joys More expects from heaven is to meet the anonymous young man who, at the time of Christ's arrest, "let his sheet fall from him and fled himself naked away." How sweet it will be to know a youth so simple—just one garment loosely cast about his limbs—yet so prudent, and to hear him talk about the events of that night, and about Him by whose bitter death the gates of everlasting life were opened to all men of good will.

1 *Rogers, ed. cit.*, nos. 202, 216. See also the various *fervorini* in his *History of the Passion*, e.g., *Works*, p. 1305: "O my sweet Saviour Christ, inspire the marvel of thy majesty, with the love of thy goodness, so deep into my heart . . ."
2 *Works*, p. 1242.   3 *Ibid.*, p. 1245-6   4 *Ibid.*, p. 1250.   5 *Rogers, ed. cit.*, no. 208.
6 *Ibid.*, no. 214.   7 *Works*, p. 1259.   8 *Ibid.*, p. 1407.   9 *Rogers, ed. cit.*, no. 206.

19. BENET CANFIELD

Gerard Sitwell

THE SUBJECT of this article, though his name is now hardly known, had in his own day and for some time later a great reputation as an authority on the spiritual life. He was an eminent exponent of a particular tradition, the tradition of the contemplative life, or as it is often called the mystical way of life, a school of which it might be said that it was concerned only with the attainment of contemplation. The statement as it stands needs some explanation. Contemplation as understood by these authors was recognised as a free gift of God, and it was further recognised that to look for its attainment other than as the culmination of a life of mortification and prayer was to tempt God. The soul must put itself to the best of its ability in the appropriate dispositions, and this it could only do by a strict self-discipline and the cultivation of prayer. Even granted all this a certain natural disposition is still required, and the attempt to cultivate contemplation without this is both unwise and unprofitable. But subject to these provisos the authors of this school did hold that one should directly and consciously aim at the attainment of contemplation. This tradition had a long history, but there is no doubt that it originated in the early monasticism of the fourth and fifth centuries in the Eastern Roman Empire, that it was given its intellectual background in the schools of Alexandria, and that this was at least coloured by Neo-Platonist ideas of contemplation as the end of life. It was not till the high Middle Ages that this spirituality made any considerable impact on Western Europe, but after Thomas Gallus had made the works of pseudo-Denis well known in the first half of the thirteenth century, we find spiritual treatises more and more stressing the attainment of contemplation as the sole end of the spiritual life. The fourteenth-century English mystics came in on the full flood of this movement, which had already swept the Rhineland and the Low Countries, and was later to reach Spain

and France. This spirituality always retained the essential characteristics of the monasticism of the desert, and showed not a little
of the Neo-Platonic influences which lay behind it. It is not
merely that there was no place for what we call "good works"
—active charity for one's neighbour—but the individual was to
be sanctified by a programme aimed solely at the attainment of
contemplation. Reading, prayer, and meditation was to constitute the activity of the anchoresses for whom most of the treatises
were written. If they were obliged to say the Divine Office,
that was to have the first call on their time, but the prayer in
which the authors were interested started when that was finished.
It was indeed the eremitical life for which this spirituality catered,
and in which alone it could be fully carried out. It was essentially Christian in as much as it presupposes devotion to Christ
and meditation on His life, but this of its nature could not enter
into the higher reaches, and though the sacraments and the
Mass are, of course, taken for granted, it could not be said that
they are put forward as principal means of sanctification.

In the fifteenth century another school of spirituality arose,
based on the systematic consideration of the whole scheme of
life from a Christian point of view. It began as a means of reform
within the religious Orders, and, with the development of the
retreat and the method of mental prayer we know as meditation,
it became the great instrument of pastoral and missionary
activity of the Counter-Reformation. This is the spirituality
with which we are familiar, for it is the one which came to
predominate, but during the sixteenth and most of the seventeenth centuries the two streams flowed side by side with almost
equal force. The reason that the earlier school, which aimed
deliberately at the cultivation of contemplation, came to be
largely discredited was that certain inherent dangers in it were
not sufficiently guarded against, and it was eventually led to
the extremes of Quietism. The condemnation of Molinos, however, which marks the final disintegration of this system of
piety, did not take place till 1678, and at the period when Benet
Canfield was writing, the turn of the sixteenth century, the
school which he represented, if it was beginning to be a little
suspect in certain quarters, had still great influence.

Such is the background against which Benet Canfield's contribution to spiritual literature needs to be seen, but a word must

be said about the facts of his life and the world in which he lived. He was born in 1561, the son of John Fitch of Canfield in Essex.[1] When he became a Capuchin and took the name of Benet in religion, he was called according to the custom of the Order Benet Canfield, and that is the name by which he is more widely known. In the year 1585, when he was a law student in London, he was converted to the Catholic faith, and it happens that there has come down to us an account of his early life and conversion, which he wrote at the order of his superiors in 1596. It was printed in the 1614 edition of his works, and is generally known as the *Autobiography*. There is no space here to describe his conversion in detail, but the significant thing is that it was in the first place a conversion of life, not a conversion to Catholicism. It was effected by the chance reading of a book, and it had all the symptoms of contemporary religious enthusiasm as manifested among Protestants—fear of hell rather than love of God was the predominating motive. Very soon after this—a matter of days—he began to be tormented with doubts as to whether he should become a Catholic, but it is certain that a general religious conversion took place first and independently. After a further violent emotional crisis, accompanied by prayer, and fasting, and sleeping on the floor, he decided to become a Catholic, and this he believed to be the result of a direct inspiration from God. From the circumstances which he describes it is evident that he was in touch with both Catholics and Puritans before his conversion, and he must almost certainly have had previous thoughts about becoming a Catholic for the issue to have arisen so quickly and in so urgent a form. This enthusiastic conversion accounts no doubt for his going to France within six months in order that he might have the free practice of his religion, though the break with his family evidently did not pass unnoticed. That he should have sought to enter a religious Order was only the logical follow-up of his first conversion, and from the start apparently it was the Franciscans with their ideal of poverty and asceticism who attracted him. That six months after landing he decided to join the Capuchins rather than the Cor-

---

[1] Fr. Optat de Veghel's book, *Benoit de Canfield: Sa vie, sa doctrine et son influence* (Rome 1949) is invaluable as a well-documented source of facts, but less satisfactory as a commentary on his teaching. All the biographical matter here is taken from it.

deliers, and in March 1587 entered their noviciate, he again attributed to the direct inspiration of God.

He became, then, a Capuchin in the France of 1587. It is worth recalling briefly what this meant. The long drawn-out agony of the Wars of Religion was approaching a paroxysm, but it must be remembered that however great the evils caused by these wars may have been, and they were very great, there was another side to the picture. It was the time when, with the final achievement of the Council of Trent, the tide of the Counter-Reformation was beginning to flow with its full force. Much remained to be done, particularly in France, where the reform of the clergy, which had to be the basis of all reform, had not yet begun, but there was a tremendous enthusiasm among the *élite* and in joining the Capuchins, a branch of the Franciscans which was practically a new Order and one founded under the influence of the movement for reform, he would encounter that enthusiasm in one of its most vigorous manifestations. This background of intense religious feeling in which he seems to have participated both before and after becoming a Catholic probably largely accounts for his reactions when he entered the religious life, for he appears to have spent half the time in his noviciate in a state that was at least semi-ecstatic. Mystical manifestations of this kind in a modern novice would be highly suspect, and they were in fact of some concern to his brethren, who subjected him to some of the more bizarre medical treatment of the time—freshly killed pigeons were split open and put on his head. This is not the place to attempt any assessment of his early mystical experiences, but that he was directed through them with skill, and that there was underlying them a high degree of grace, is shown by the rapidity with which the physical manifestations were shed, and with which he advanced to a condition in which he was obviously perfectly balanced, and indeed a master in the spiritual life. For it seems that as early as 1592 he had already been ordained priest, had produced the first draft of what was to be his main literary work, *The Rule of Perfection*, and that he had been called in to settle the doubts of Mme Acarie, the remarkable leader of a sort of devout *salon* in Paris, upon the sanctity of whose life the Church was later to set her seal by beatification.

It should perhaps be mentioned that in 1599 Benet Canfield

R

went to England. The fact of this well-known mystic going on the English mission would have been of great significance, if it were not for the fact that there is more than a little suspicion that he left France because of difficulties with the Parliament of Paris. He was captured immediately on landing, and after spending three years in Wisbech and Framlingham was allowed to return to France.

To turn now to his teaching in *The Rule of Perfection*; the form in which he presents this makes it seem at first sight new and original, but fundamentally it is traditional. He makes the attainment of perfection consist wholly in conformity with the will of God. This of course in a wide sense it does. Sin is sin precisely in so far as it is a voluntary transgression of God's will, and a human life will be perfect in so far as it not only avoids deliberate transgression of this will but is sensitive to its lightest touch. The question is how this will of God is to be known. Canfield divided his book into three Parts in which he treats of what he calls the exterior, the interior, and the essential will of God, and by this he means to indicate three ways in which God's will is manifested to the soul. In the first it will be—though not entirely—by exterior means, in the second by direct inspiration involving a truly contemplative experience, while in the third the soul becomes united with the essential will of God, which, he says, is God Himself. This Part, therefore, is specifically concerned with the highest form of contemplative union. There is, of course, no division in the will of God; the distinctions which Canfield draws are in the various ways in which this will is apprehended by the soul, and even so the distinctions are arbitrary, but that does not detract from their pedagogic value in providing a framework within which the development of the soul can be studied. In effect the first Part is a treatise on mortification, the necessary groundwork of all spiritual life, and Canfield makes it consist solely in the inner conformity of the will, what Augustine Baker called interior as distinct from exterior mortification. This is, of course, the heart of the matter, and Canfield's application of it is searching in the extreme. The second and third Parts deal with the mystical experiences that the soul may expect to undergo as the outcome of the preliminary discipline.

Part I. The first stage, then, which he equates with the active life, is one in which the soul learns to conform perfectly to the will of God as manifested exteriorly. That so far as it goes presents no difficulty. The will of God is evidently to be seen in all lawful authority, and this must be obeyed. But in the ordinary business of living our lives we necessarily perform many actions which are neither commanded nor forbidden by any particular decree of authority. Even the religious living under a vow of obedience must have many small personal decisions left to him, but Canfield will not allow these matters which are neither commanded nor forbidden to escape his general rule of doing everything for the will of God, and he lays down minute rules for judging them. Such actions may be either contrary to nature, that is to our natural inclinations or preferences, or they may be according to nature, and the rule is that, if they are contrary to nature we make ourselves do them, and if they are in accordance with our natural inclinations, we deny ourselves and refrain from doing them. The principle involved is simply the necessity of mortifying our fallen human nature, but stated as uncompromisingly as that it is a hard doctrine demanding something like heroic courage, and not to be put in practice without a high degree of grace. He does in fact say that discretion must be used, and if for serious reasons such as health, it is expedient for us to do something that we like or to refrain from something we dislike, then we must act reasonably and it becomes a matter of making a prudent judgment. But even when this test has been applied there is another class of actions which has slipped through the net, actions that in themselves neither attract nor repel us—we are simply indifferent as to whether we perform them or not, or we have no preferences in a choice but must do something. In that case, he says, we just have to come to a reasonable decision, and he gives sensible advice. "Then must hee dispatche and choose the one way or the other, allwayes with the intention above said of the will of God, rather then with distraction and breaking his braines, and losse of tyme, make too long discussion."[1] The important thing is that in these cases we make the

[1] There are two English editions, 1608 and 1609, both published at Rouen. Neither contains the third Part. References here are to the 1609 edition. In 1878 Fr. Collins published an abridgment of the first two Parts together with the treatise on meditation of the Passion.

deliberate intention of acting for the will of God. This must always be done. If, for example, a man is commanded to do something which is congenial to him, he must make the intention of doing it for the will of God, and try to distinguish this motive from the natural pleasure he takes in the action.

He goes on to say that there are six degrees of perfection in carrying out God's will. In the first place the intention must be *actual*, that is we must advert to the fact that we are performing a particular action because it is God's will that we do it. Then there follow: *only*, our intention of performing the action because it is the will of God must exclude all other intentions; *willingly*, the action must be performed whole-heartedly and generously even if it is menial; *assuredly*, with conviction that it really is the will of God, and this, he says, we must judge by an interior discussion; *clearly*, with lively faith to see it as God's will; and *speedily*. The use of these qualifications and the analysis they involve is, of course, good teaching technique, but an over-great preoccupation with them might easily lead to scrupulosity and anxiety. Canfield, however, shows admirable discretion in the way he inculcates the directing of our intention in practice. We must avoid being oblivious of the divine will,

> yet to eschew this extremitie of Oblivion, a man must not fall into the contrarie excesse of overmuch Remembrance, in multiplyeng so many acts and rectifieng so often his intention as to trouble the braine. And therefor when I say that a man must direct his intention in all works, I meane not of every little action done by every part and sence of the body or power of the soule, but of such works as are distinguished and separated in them selfes; but particularly and above all, we must not forget those which we feele to please or displease nature very much; for it is thear (as they say) whear the Hare goeth away, and wherein consisteth true advancement.[1]

Of the first degree of intention he says, "a man must not be scrupulous if hee faile in this degree and some others, as though he had committed some synne, seing the desire he hath to practise this Rule doth add no new obligation."[2] That is important advice which ought not to be overlooked.

All this is set out in great detail; difficulties and objections are forestalled and methods proposed, including a sort of examen, by which the practice may be furthered. As has been shown, Benet

[1] p. 57.   [2] p. 58.

Canfield displays a wise discretion in the application of his method, but even so it would require an experienced man to guide himself or anyone else according to such rules. It is not in practice the sort of thing that can be learnt out of a book.

Part II. In the first Part the will of God was made known to the soul by exterior means, but at this further stage it is manifested in the interior of the soul itself by "inspirations, illuminations, and the like other attractions of God." Canfield is explicit that this manifestation of Himself to the soul by God should be the outcome of the purity of intention inculcated in the first Part. The cultivation of purity of intention brings about the mortification of the passions and affections of the soul, and this mortification brings a great tranquillity, the tranquillity a profound silence, and in this silence God speaks to the soul.[1] It is the standard teaching of the mystics on the necessity of reducing the soul to a state of passivity. To have this intention of acting only for the will of God means that by a free choice of our will we adhere to what we believe to be God's will quite independently of our natural feelings and desires. By a simple act of the superior part of our will we turn away from creatures and turn towards the Creator, we must "cast our thought and all our spiritual sight on God with all tranquilitie and repose, sweetly, serenely, and without all maner of stresse or violence."[2] All the divisions he makes in his book, the degrees of perfection in carrying out the will of God, the stages by which God manifests Himself to us, are to be transcended in practice. Their purpose is to instruct the beginner and provide an intellectual background. Even if there is turmoil in our lower nature from the passions, and we are harassed by external difficulties, that need not prevent us from adhering peacefully to the will of God, "and this ought to be great comfort, and encouragement to all such as are combated by theyr passions, and agitated with temptations."[3] The result will be this manifestation of God's will. He uses all sorts of metaphors to describe it, seeing, hearing, touching, tasting, but they are all meant to illustrate the soul's reception of an infused knowledge. It is a state which is to permeate the whole of a man's life, and it is clear that he envisages the soul arriving at a fairly advanced stage of contemplation. It would be idle to

[1] p. 37. [2] p. 134. [3] p. 135.

attempt to equate this with any of the accepted categories, but he speaks of the soul "hearing his sweet voyce, his delicious and mellifluous speaches unto her," of its "reioycing in his amourous and alluring aspect, sweet kisses, chaste embracements," and "feeling this efficacious inaction, and lively touch of his good pleasure and will."[1] All this is something to be cultivated; the soul must cut off all superfluity of exterior and interior activity in order that the divine action may be unhindered in it, and if this is done further effects will be produced which he enumerates as admiration, humiliation, exultation, and elevation. Finally at the end of this Part he gives advice on prayer. Here again the only thing to be sought is the will of God, and in particular the soul must guard against desires which are good in themselves, such as to feel fervour, devotion, illumination, etc., but which would hinder the purity of its intention. He gives no detail as to the method of prayer.

Part III. The third Part of *The Rule of Perfection* is a treatise concerned entirely with the higher reaches of the mystical life. It is as long as the first two Parts put together and no more can be done here than to give a brief summary with some comment on certain outstanding points.

He makes it clear that by the essential will of God he means God Himself, the Godhead, and it is man's union with this with which he is concerned. He begins by giving what may be called the ordinary teaching on the necessity for avoiding the use of both the imagination and the intellect in the endeavour to reach God. *The Cloud of Unknowing* gives perhaps the classical exposition of this doctrine, and Canfield's teaching agrees with it entirely, but is much less clearly expressed. What has to be achieved is really the concentration of the mind on the simplest idea of God, and Canfield advocates the use of the word *God* or *Essence* as a focus in the same way that the *Cloud* does. This concentration and simplification of the activity of the intellect is all that man can do of himself by way of preparation for the divine action, but it is this latter which Canfield unlike the author of the *Cloud* is interested in. The divine action which may be expected to ensue, for, of course, nothing that man is able to do can ensure it, may, according to Canfield, take place in two ways, or produce a twofold effect. In either case a very high degree of

[1] p. 136.

union will be reached, but the routes are apparently alternative. This is a very curious distinction which Canfield introduces, and it leads to a certain obscurity in his teaching at the start. In one of these ways the soul is entirely passive under the divine action, in the other there are "certain most subtle activities" on its part. The rest of the book is based on this distinction. In chapters 4 to 7 the course of the soul which follows the first way is traced in four stages to a state which seems to be the equivalent of the Spiritual Marriage—a continual awareness of the presence of God. The same end is apparently reached by the alternative route, and its significance will be commented on later. In chapters 8 to 15 he describes the development of the soul which takes the second way, which itself bifurcates into what he calls passive and active annihilation. Chapters 16 to 20 form a sort of appendix on the subject of meditation on the Passion, on which Canfield has a doctrine peculiar to himself among mystical writers. Canfield is discursive, he uses unaccustomed distinctions and terms, and he does not use them consistently. To attempt to reconcile and elucidate every statement in this Part would require a very long and detailed commentary, and it is doubtful if even then the result would be satisfactory. Here it is only possible to draw attention to one or two points.

It was inevitable that at the end of the seventeenth century in the violent reaction against mysticism caused by the condemnation of Molinos, Canfield should have been accused of Quietism, and his work was even condemned, but it is clear that he was far removed from the real Quietist mentality. He makes the point that the discipline of the active life is to be maintained throughout, and this is far from the sort of surrender leading to complete antinomianism which was the real bane of Quietism. He speaks of the soul being passive in the hands of God as all the mystics do, but he is explicit when treating of his first way that this passivity is to wait on the elevation and attraction of God, and that those are deceived who cease from all activity without this —the characteristic error of the Quietists (Chap. 6).[1] The distinction which he makes in the third Part between the two ways in which the soul is united to God is far from being clear. The subtle activities in the soul must be themselves the work of God,

[1] There were many Latin and French editions containing the third Part in the seventeenth century (none since), but they are all hard to come by and I have given only general references to chapters.

for he is insistent that this whole state is far beyond the reach of any human activity, and yet it seems that it is for the soul in some way to make a choice. It shall be for each soul to take up (*assumere*) that which is best suited to it, and the two ways are not to be confused, he says (Chap. 3). When he describes the parallel way in which the soul attains this highest union he introduces an important distinction which is somewhat obscured by his unusual terminology. Within this way, in which, it will be remembered, he speaks of the soul engaging in certain subtle activities, it may achieve either what he calls passive or active annihilation. He uses the word annihilation because the soul is possessed by a profound sense of its own nothingness as compared with God, and of the nothingness of all creatures. Other writers of course use the term to describe this as one of the effects produced by a certain degree of union, but Canfield uses it with the qualifications active and passive to describe two different conditions in which the soul may find itself. Passive annihilation occurs when God actually makes Himself present to the soul in contemplation, and is in effect some kind of ecstasy. But it is his teaching on active annihilation which is of greater interest. In this state the soul is able to contemplate God, or at least to have some sort of continual awareness of His presence, even when engaged in active works. It is the characteristic of St. Teresa's Seventh Mansion, when the soul experiences the so-called Spiritual Marriage, and it is interesting to observe the stress which Canfield lays on this state. Although many of the most famous mystics among the saints had great outward achievement to show for their lives, the mystical or contemplative tradition described at the beginning of this article had no place for such achievement, and so Canfield writing within this tradition, but at the same time as a member of an Order most actively engaged in saving souls, is at pains to point out that the contemplative need not necessarily sacrifice his contemplation if he engages in good works. He condemns those who refuse to take on outward good works on the pretext that these would interfere with their spiritual lives. To the person truly "annihilated" the thing taken on is "nothing" and harmless, and if he refuses, his error involves him in a twofold darkness. The work itself is turned to darkness in the spiritual sense, and his fear engenders a further spiritual darkness of its own.

Finally a word must be said about his teaching that considera-

tion of the Passion of Christ was not to be given up at any stage,
even the most advanced, of the mystical life. The way he puts it
is that Christ is to be contemplated in His divinity and His
humanity together *uno simplici conspectu*. From the way in which
Canfield himself goes on to interpret this remark he becomes
involved in a dilemma from which there seems to be no escape.
The humanity can only be considered by means of images, and
for the divinity to be contemplated these must be discarded, so
that it seems that a man must, as he says, at the same time receive
and reject images. He is content to leave it at that, and say that it
is necessary to transcend reason and take refuge in faith (Chap. 17).
It is very curious that Canfield should have tied himself up in
this dilemma, for it does not seem necessary. The author of the
Cloud had said that the soul cannot meditate on Our Lord's life
during the actual time of the work, as he calls it, of contemplation, but that it must occupy itself with this at other times, and
this is the teaching of St. Teresa.[1] But Canfield, who in Chapter
20 refers to St. Teresa in general terms as favouring his thesis—
without of course giving a reference—does not seem to have
been content with this, and it would seem that he must have had
in mind a passage in the same chapter, where she says that in the
seventh Mansion the soul never ceases to walk with Christ Our
Lord, but is ever in the company of both His human and divine
nature. This is evidently a mystical state in which the soul finds
itself, and it is not capable of an explanation in terms of ordinary
human experience. St. Teresa said that, if she remembered, she
would say more about this when she came to write of the seventh
Mansion, but unfortunately she forgot! As it is her single sentence
is as enlightening as Canfield's five chapters!

The Rule of Perfection as a whole is something of a *tour-de-force*.
The fact is Canfield was pushing the Dionysian tradition too far
and adopting too narrow a conception of it. He was inculcating
a direct pursuit of contemplation by what amounted to a technique, but the real end of the Christian life is charity, the love of
God and the love of one's neighbour in and for God, and if a
sufficiently high degree of this is reached, the soul may well
experience the highest union, but the ancient Christian tradition
in the West was to wait for this to happen if and when God
willed.

[1] *Interior Castle*, Mans. VI, chapter 7.

20. AUGUSTINE BAKER

Renée Haynes

THOUGH AUGUSTINE BAKER wrote in the main for men and women wholly dedicated to the contemplative life, it is no more necessary to be one of them before reading his work than it is to study hermetic philosophy before enjoying the poems of his contemporary and fellow-countryman, Henry Vaughan; poems whose transparent mysterious paradoxical imagery set the self wondering and stretching out towards that imageless awareness of which the Benedictine wrote, noting carefully that "we should not take . . . spiritual matters as corporal or sensible things, albeit they be expressed to us under such terms, otherwise can they not be expressed."

> I saw Eternity the other night
> Like a great Ring of pure and endlesse Light
> All calm, as it was bright.

> . . . and feel through all this earthly dresse
> Bright *shootes* of everlastingnesse.

> There is in God, some say
> A deepe and dazzling darknesse; as men here
> Say it is late and dusky because they
> See not all clear.
> O for that Night, that I in Him
> Might live invisible and dim.

Here words, reflecting as they must the sensory perceptions by which men live, are yet so used as to suggest a significance deeper than any analysis could yield, and to stimulate an understanding both above and below the level of definition. The process of communication involved is the precise opposite of that used in deliberate allegory, the basis of the Baroque, where imagery, figures, groups, gestures may all too easily harden as it were into a stylised marble exuberance too heavy, too decorative, too dramatic to do anything but attract attention to itself rather than to the meaning with which it should be charged.

I write "may," because of course the effect is not inevitable, not automatically produced. Some temperaments thrive on allegory and drama, some do not. Some can follow with devotion the singing of a High Mass to the music of Mozart, while others find the very beauty of that music an almost irresistible distraction from prayer. Allegory and the use of set imagery (and most other forms of expression) are like George Herbert's "window" on which "a man may stay his eye, or look right through." It is impossible to generalise, but one may hazard that the assumption of vivid equivalence between image and reality, of "this equals that," is on the whole more congenial to Southern Europe with its classical tradition, its permanent bright colour, its extraordinary clarity of outline than to the North, whose loved understated landscapes, raindrops and trees, rivers and blown grass are set glowing by the "heavenly alchemy" of unexpected light. Perhaps for such reasons as these baroque art has never flourished in this country. The age of Fr. Baker was the age of its glory in the rest of Europe. It was also the age when Catholicism in England was an underground movement preoccupied with missionary work and with survival. The great centres of contemplation were in ruins or had been taken over as country houses. The contemplatives had long been scattered; martyred, dead, fled or absorbed into the new order. The clergy who came in gay courage from overseas thought inevitably in the Southern idiom. For styles in art do not affect art alone, they pervade every mode of human communication, from slang to opera, from etiquette to ritual, secular or sacred. To cite an instance from another context, it is plain to the stranger at Chevetogne that the wonderful Byzantine liturgies sung there spring from the same root of collective being, feeling and expression as gave rise on other levels to the classical Russian ballet and to the painted toys, one within the other, of the old régime. It is also painfully plain to him that he finds it hard to yield attention to this beautiful alien fantastic idiom as to an idiom of prayer. Ikons and robes and processions, the flames on multiple candlesticks slanting to this side and to that as they are moved in blessing, the chant of *Gospodye pomelya*, Lord have mercy, recurring like waves in a cavern, all are so fascinating in themselves as to deflect that very desire to perceive the interfusion of time and eternity which they were designed to stimulate.

One of the by-products, as it were, of Fr. Baker's humble and transparent life was the restoration of the continuity in English spiritual writing which had been interrupted by the Reformation. In the kind of language that came naturally to himself and to the majority of his fellow-countrymen (language exemplified— religion apart—in the sphere of poetry by Vaughan, Traherne and Herbert) he set forth the truths more easily conveyed to Southern temperaments by baroque imagery, showing to those daunted by it the reality that lay beyond. He revived interest in the work of English and Flemish mystics (so oddly linked by the medieval wool trade and weaving guilds) and kept alive among the English men and women here and in exile the knowledge of the kind of prayer taught in the fourteenth and fifteenth centuries by the *Speculum Perfectionis*, *The Cloud of Unknowing* and *The Ladder of Perfection*, and recognisable in our own time in *The Spiritual Letters* of Dom John Chapman and in Dom Bede Griffiths' *The Golden String*.

Augustine Baker's own life falls into three periods, so far as his own being (rather than exterior happenings) is concerned; from his birth to his "first conversion"; from his first conversion to his "second"; and thence to his death of a fever, possibly the plague, which saved him from the hands of the pursuivants.

He was born in Abergavenny in 1575 and christened David. His parents were conscientious Protestants, his mother the daughter of the local vicar, Lewis ap John, his father the agent of the local landowner. An intelligent, quick-witted child, he was educated at Edward VI's new foundation, Christ's Hospital, and left at the age of fifteen to go up to Oxford. Here, at Broadgates Hall (now Pembroke) he is said to have been "frivolous." One remembers that passage in the University Statutes which forbids undergraduates to bowl hoops down the High or to play marbles on the steps of the Bodleian! At seventeen he returned to Abergavenny for four years, and negotiations were made for his marriage, but they fell through, and in 1596 he was sent to London to read law. Like his fellow-townsman Blessed David Lewis nearly forty years later, he spent some time at the Middle Temple; like St. Thomas More before him, he was a member of Lincoln's Inn, the Bishop of Lincoln's Inn where St. Hugh had lived when he was in London. On the death of his brother David, Baker went home again, and was presently made Recorder of Abergavenny.

Until his middle twenties this lively, sensitive young man seems like many others to have been fully and joyfully occupied in living, in learning, and in exercising his mind, a mind formed by a classical education, by the traditions of an Oxford not quite sixty years away from the Church, and by the exact and stimulating discipline of law. The question of religion seems to have been ignored. There were so many other things to do and to think about. It is probable that his brother's death shook the foundations of this attitude. It is certain that the immediate possibility of his own destroyed them. As he was riding on some legal business over a damaged footbridge he saw his danger, realised that he could not turn and should not go on, and vowed that if he came safe to land he would study the evidence for the existence of God. The horse made its way somehow on to firm ground and the rider kept his word. After wide reading and objective consideration of evidence and argument, he came quietly to the conclusion that he must join the Catholic Church, and was reconciled to it by a missionary priest, Fr. Robert Floyd. His mother and sisters followed him. In 1603, at twenty-eight years old, he went to London hoping there to meet priests from overseas from whom he could find out how to become one himself. It was thus that he travelled to Italy, and entered the Benedictine novitiate at a monastery in Padua, taking Augustine as his name in religion, and exemplifying his namesake's saying "our hearts are restless till they rest in Thee."

Presently he became unhappy, not understanding how to practise the prayer to which he was called and unable to make much headway with the methods he was taught; to make a vivid mental picture of some scene in the life of Our Lord, to reflect on its every aspect, and to apply its moral to himself. He wrote later that "No working of the imagination or understanding could any longer produce any effect on the will."

This made him all the more miserable because he had once been given an intense and immediate sense of the Presence of God, lasting over many months, and he longed above all things for its restoration. He was "in ignorance of the state of desolation or privation that usually followeth contemplation"; his superiors did not speak of it; he did not know that others had suffered and recorded it; he had no idea that to be resigned to lie fallow, like a writer between books, might help him, so long as he made "a right use of" his state. Not for many years did he discover that "the will is the guide and captain, and the understanding doth but attend the will, going whither he goes and following him." In the meantime, not knowing what else to do, he "continued only with vocal prayers and exterior observances" and became "wholly tepid," frustrated, and finally ill. It was thought best that he should go home. He set out restless and uneasy, meaning to make his journey a leisurely one, so that he could at any rate see and enjoy the sights of the countries through which he went. But something impelled him willy-nilly to make haste. He arrived in England to hear that his father was mortally sick, and travelled on into Wales in time to comfort him, to reconcile him to the Church, and to be with him when he died.

Once more he set himself to "pure internal prayer"; once more he found he could not keep it up. The year 1609 linked him with a Community that had prayed in London for more than five centuries. Dom Sigebert Buckley, a very, very old monk of Westminster, his brethren all gone, had spent the whole long reign of Elizabeth I in prison as in a hermitage, living on to see at last the fulfilment of his prayer that the line of the English Benedictine should not die out. He was about ninety when two English priests trained overseas were professed and admitted in his ancient fragile presence to the Abbey of Westminster. Two years later Augustine Baker was given leave by his Italian Superiors to join them.

For the time being, however, neither this nor the grace of the priesthood, from which he had hoped so much, seemed to help him in his main desire. He lived in London till 1620, fulfilling his religious duties, acting as a sort of poor man's lawyer, helpful to others, stultified in himself and continually tempted to reflect that he was after all no worse than anyone else. About the end of this period he came across a copy of the *Speculum Perfectionis* which reflected the causes of his state and sparked off what he called his second conversion.

Sent at the same time to the depths of the Devonshire countryside to be private chaplain to a Catholic squire, he missed the stimulus of London but resisted his impulse to return, resolving (as he writes in that part of his *Secretum sive Mysticum*, a com-

mentary on *The Cloud of Unknowing* which has been edited as
his *Confessions*) by God's grace to give himself wholly to Him,
and to make internal prayer his daily and most important
business, never to be omitted, neglected or postponed to any
other affairs whatsoever. Here, praying at first for as long as
eleven hours a day, he ceased to diffuse his attention either upon
exterior affairs or upon "an interior so bepainted with images
that she (the soul) can see nothing but them," and learned in
stillness to focus it upon God "not enquiring what He is, but
believing Him to be that incomprehensible Being which He is."

He was not granted that immediate happiness in God which
had illumined his youth. However, he writes as if from
experience (his whole narrative is cast in the third person, as
a master describing the development of a "poor scholar") of the
state of mind of those who "are come to a stability in prayer,"
have shed "the stupidity or dullness that doth possess them who
are . . . in an exercise of the will towards contemplation" and
now "grow to have free use of their wits . . . in greater clearness
and perfection than before" without distraction from their
settled love.

The irritability that might have been expected to go with his
extreme concentration and its concomitant "dullness" does not
seem to have been allowed to show itself; though a passage
elsewhere about the necessity to control anger against flies and
"inanimate creatures like pen and ink" seems to indicate some
experience of it. He peacefully fulfilled his duties as chaplain,
and moreover made converts—including one particularly prickly
and resentful old lady—not by "disputation" but, as Dom Justin
McCann writes, "by praying for them and inviting them to pray
with a sincere resignation to obey the truth when God should
reveal it to them." Recalled to London, he spent some time in
compiling material for a history of the English Benedictines.
Then, in 1624, began the nine most fruitful years of his life, both
in direction and in writing. He undertook the first regarding
himself and all directors as no more than "God's usher," or
under-schoolmaster, "to the soul." The second he did because
those he had directed wanted to keep a record of his teaching.

Twelve months before this some English Catholic girls had
gone beyond seas to Cambrai to establish with the help of three
nuns from Brussels a group of English Benedictines (now at

Stanbrook). It was financed by the dowry of one of them, Helen More, great-great-grand-daughter of St. Thomas More. She took the name in religion of Gertrude, and she was a vivacious, affectionate young woman "of a good sharp wit and quick judgment" who loved reading and rhyming, and seems at first to have had little notion of the reason why contemplatives withdraw from the world. She was probably homesick. She found meditation very difficult. She grew bored with the routine of the house, which seemed to her to subserve no particular purpose. Boredom made her unhappy. Unhappiness made her unkind. Unkindness made her bitterly remorseful, yet preoccupation with her own faults made her no better. The vicious circle of behaviour was pain and weariness. She felt that she could not return to the world because the others depended on her financially, and yet that she could hardly bear to be professed and follow till the end of her days the life she was leading.

Augustine Baker was sent to train the community, and the novice was advised to go and talk to him. She was reluctant to do so because he was known to recommend solitude and silence, which she found particularly irksome. In the end she went as a matter of obedience to her mistress, and she was much struck by his reading aloud a passage to the effect that those in her state "can do no better than in their poverty of spirit and aridity to be contented, doing the best they can." He said, she wrote later on, "that I must give all to God without willing reservation of any inordinate affection to any creature . . . then that I must use mental prayer twice a day"; which she did, without much feeling but "profitably" so that "within fifteen days I found myself so quieted in mind and thought that I wondered at it myself."

Once shown clearly the end to which her life was dedicated and the means to be used she was enabled peacefully to use them and to seek it. "Fr. Baker for a long time encouraged me not to be daunted with my sins and imperfections, assuring me that it would all turn to my good if by prayer I would endeavour to tend to God." Her previous argumentativeness subsided and she began to realise that, in the words of her nineteenth-century biographer Fr. Collins, "it is the sight of the infiniteness of God given to the soul by His own light that alone can humble her. Till she has experienced this she cannot know what humility is."

She came to accept her own temperament without anxiety; "all was to be done more by quietness than by extraordinary force . . . the way for me to overcome myself was as I could, not as I would." She acknowledged freely that she could not pray well "without much and often diverting myself with indifferent things" (particularly conversation after meals) and asked only "let all this imperfection humble me . . . to adhere wholly to Thee is my only desire in all I do."

Certain Benedictines seem to have been worried about her methods of prayer, and an enquiry was made into them. At the Chapter held on 1 August 1633, however, all was cleared up, and they were approved; and public thanks were moreover given to Fr. Baker. It was as if her work were done. The next day she fell ill; then she developed smallpox. She died in the Infirmary on 17 August "in peace and quiet until her last breath," though the flies were buzzing around her sores and her throat was so painful that it must have been agony to speak as she did to tell the Lady Abbess that "God has given me peace in my soul, and what can one desire more, coming to die? . . . I have nothing to do but leave myself wholly to Him." She was twenty-seven years old.

A quarter of a century later her writings were published in Paris. The title page is inscribed "The Spiritual Exercises of the most Virtuous and Religious Dame Gertrude More of the holy order of St. Bennet and the English Congregation of Our Lady of Comfort in Cambray; she called them An Ideot's Devotions (*Amor ordinem nescit*), but her only Spiritual Father and Director Fa. Augustine Baker stiled them *Confessiones Amantis*, a lover's confessions." The frontispiece depicts a sweet, intelligent, handsome face with a smile diffused over it, though the lips are closed. Opposite, there is a long anonymous poem beginning:

> Renowned More, whose bloody Fate
> England ne'er yet could expiate
> Such was thy constant *Faith*, so much
> Thy *Hope*, thy *Charity* was such
> As made thee twice a Martyr prove
> Of *Faith* in Death, in Life of Love.
> View here thy Grandchild's broken Hart
> Wounded with a Seraphick Dart
> Who while she liv'd mortals among
> Thus to her Spouse Divine she sung

S

> "Mirror of Beauty, in whose Face
> The Essence lives of every Grace
> True lustre dwells in thy Sole Spheare.
> Those glimmerings that sometimes appeare
> In this dark vayle, this gloomy night
> Are shadows tipt with glow-worm light. . . ."

It would be interesting to know who wrote it. The "song" attributed to Dame Gertrude herself has a certain flavour of Vaughan again. The dedicatory letter to her sister, the Reverend Mother Bridget More is signed only with the initials F.C. The reminiscence of St. Teresa and the "Seraphick Dart" is a curious, alien intrusion. Dame Gertrude's own verses, which were many but not very good, show no capacity for projecting inner experience in visible, tangible, physical shape. She writes rather of dying to ourselves and all things else so that our souls may tend to their "dear Centre" as naturally as flames fly upward, and reflects in a hurdy-gurdy rhythm that yet somehow conveys an extraordinary awareness,

> . . . and seeing that my *God* is rich
> How can I say I'm poore?
> And *thee* more myne than I mine own
> What can I wish for more?

Fr. Baker's *Confessions* have a more personal note than the great collection of writings known as *Sancta Sophia*, Holy Wisdom, and the personality of the author emerges all unconsciously here and there in various phrases, as when he notes that the nuns, living together need not envy him the ascetic freedom of the solitary existence he has described, since they will of necessity have more mortifications than he in keeping their Rule, and may even "hope to have a good cross superior if you pray hard for one." Thus the mature man with a twist of humour. But what echoes of childhood, of shepherd and pipe and ancient traditional round, resound in the strange, evocative, archaic imagery of "You have had in him" (the poor scholar) "in some sort as it were the bell-wether of the flock, a king-leader unto you of the spiritual dance."

It was at the request of this same Cambrai community that Fr. Baker set down the majority of those manuscript treatises—

there were over forty of them—which were edited and published
in 1657, sixteen years after their author's death, by Dom Serenus
Cressy.

This Benedictine, a generation younger than he, had been
converted in 1646 after a brilliant Anglican career as Fellow of
Merton, chaplain to Lord Falkland, Canon of Windsor and Dean
of Leighlin. He owed much to Fr. Baker's teaching, and readers
of *Sancta Sophia* in turn owe much to him. Treatises written
ad hoc without thought of publication have been put together,
much inevitable repetition has been pruned, and the book is
integrated into a single whole. It is still at times long-winded—
the result perhaps of a legal desire for exactness—and it still
stresses various points over and over again where it is felt that
they are likely to recur in the experience of the interior life. But
it is full of memorable expressions ("of how gluey and tenacious
a nature corrupt self-love is in the soul!") and it is down to earth
as well as up to heaven, as simple, practical and unsentimental
as a manual of carpentry. Here is the basis of your life. Here is
its meaning. Here is your aim. Here is how to work towards it.
Here are the obstacles you will find, the mistakes you may make.
Realise that the way is long, hard, up and down. "Many changes
the soul must expect, many risings and fallings; sometimes light
and sometimes darkness; sometimes calmness of passions and
presently . . . fiercer combats than before; and these successions
of changes repeated God knows how oft before the end
approacheth."

He posits that man was made for "eternal beatitude . . . a
returning to the divine principle from Whom he flowed, and
an inconceivably happy union with Him, in mind, will and
affections": that "the means to happiness and the end in itself
are essentially the same, to wit, the union of the spirit with God":
that though there is "naturally in all souls a certain propension
to seek God," after the Fall their powers and faculties were
disordered" and "all circumstant creatures . . . seduced their
affections from Him"; that the Redemption brought both new
light into our understanding and "divine charity in our hearts";
that the duty of all Christians is "daily to aspire, assisted by grace,
to the same perfection for which we were first created . . . by
faith contemplating Him and by love ever adhering to Him";
and that grace will conduct souls "suitably to their several

dispositions by an almost infinite variety of paths and fashions" towards the beatific vision.

He discusses different kinds of temperament, and the activities suitable to each, and then notes that he is especially concerned with those called to contemplation, even though some of them may be living in the world. Incidentally he warns those who wish to enter monasteries against any romantic "imagining the outward habit and interior virtues inseparable companions," and adds that they should not be actuated either by general vague good will or by a liking for routine, a liking which may bring them to "a stable course of most dangerous tepidity." The only valid reason for entering is a desire for "the union of the spirit with God in recollected constant prayer," a desire most easily fulfilled there because though God is present everywhere the soul most perfectly "enjoys and contemplates Him" in a place where it can concentrate its attention on so doing without constant interruptions.

He records that the first effect of prayer is "a tender sensible" (*i.e.*, conscious) "devotion," but that it later throws a disconcerting light on "a thousand secret and formerly invisible impurities of intention, hypocrisies and self-seekings." These are to be repented but not chewed over. "The soul must with patience and quietness bear with her own imperfections as she would with those of others," pray for their cure but not "ransack" her conscience, avoiding self-occupation, and thinking of Christ rather than brooding upon past sins. As a maxim she is given that of Walter Hilton's pilgrim, "I have nothing, I am nothing, I desire nothing but to be with Jesus in Jerusalem," the vision of peace.

It would be ridiculous to pretend to summarise in a brief article the gentle, direct, humble, matter-of-fact teachings of *Sancta Sophia*. What can be said is that they are stamped throughout by a clear and constant distinction between the end of prayer and the means undertaken to achieve it. Again and again Fr. Baker insists that those means have no *automatic* virtue in themselves; that they should not be practised mechanically, or with a cold-bath glow of virtuous achievement, or even with the priggish intention of setting a good example. The soul may become badly distracted from her main Object by becoming entangled in a "multiplicity" of burdens and customs. (One remembers the curious primitive reliance on mathematical magic that seems to lurk in the human mind, making Aldous Huxley's "Eupompus give splendour to Art by numbers" and convincing Maria Chapdelaine in the French-Canadian novel that she was acquiring merit by repeating the prayers of the rosary hundreds and hundreds of times, counting as she did so.)

Austerities can be undertaken in the spirit of those challenged by the "try your strength" machines at fairs. Carried out "without prayer and purity of intention," writes Fr. Baker, they "do rather tend to self-esteem," and are all too easily linked with "self-love, self-judgment, and the satisfaction of nature even by crossing it." He sets out the main ascetic practices which will be found useful, and gives the reasons for them, thus. By humility, prostrations, and the acknowledgment of secret imperfections, pride and self-love are expelled. By perfect obedience, self-judgment and self-will are abated. By fasting and lack of sleep, sensuality is deadened. By religious poverty, worries about material things are expelled. All these, pride and self-love, self-judgment and self-will, physical desire and financial anxiety are very powerful distractions. Once they are out of the way, the mind has greater liberty to pursue its final End—an End for which its attention is further set free by solitude, silence, and lack of contact with the world.

It must of course be recollected that all this was written for people who had already undertaken the three great vows of poverty, chastity and obedience and were wholly dedicated to contemplation.

A chapter in Section III sets out how "secular people living in the world" may, with modifications, use the book. The main proviso is that they should carry out all their duties "in order to God," allowing a certain amount of solitude and silence every day for prayer, setting a greater value on "precious time," and accepting quietly "all interior and exterior mortifications" that may come upon them. This is amplified in a short essay on "A Spiritual Life in a Secular State," which insists that a man (women do not seem to have been considered) "must have a reasonable care for his family," especially for the education of his children, and play his part in affairs of Church and State, but without getting too much absorbed in them. He should avoid unnecessary distractions, pursue his daily recollections and frequent the sacraments. Though he must not make himself conspicuous, he will probably find himself thought peculiar, and "less liked and esteemed" than before. "But this and more too (if need be) he must be contented to digest . . . *propter amorem Dei*." There is held up as an example, "the devout Liv-er and holy Dy-er and Martyr, Sir Thomas More."

Fr. Baker did not himself die in the calm of a cloister but in London, where he was sent again on the English mission in 1638. In 1641, having moved from one address to another, time and again, in order to avoid arrest—eighteen priests, two of them Benedictines, were condemned to death that year—he fell ill of "a contagious fever" which frightened away the pursuivants, and died four days later. It was in the house of a Mrs. Watson, mother of one of the Cambrai nuns.

NOTES ON CONTRIBUTORS

PROFESSOR EMILE J. ARNOULD, M.A., Ph.D., D.Litt. (London), D. ès L. (Paris), has been Head of the French Department in the University of Dublin since 1945, after lecturing on Anglo-Saxon in Paris, and on French Language and Literature in the Universities of Edinburgh, Manchester, London and Exeter. He has also lectured on Medieval Latin at Trinity College, Dublin. Professor Arnould's main field of research was Anglo-Norman, and more particularly the religious literature in that dialect and in Middle English, e.g. in: *Le Manuel des Péchés* (the French original of Robert of Brunne's *Handlyng Synne*), *étude de littérature anglo-normande*, Paris and Geneva, Droz, 1940; *Le Livre de Seyntz Medicines, the unpublished devotional treatise of Henry of Lancaster*, Anglo-Norman Texts II, Oxford, Blackwell, 1940; *Etude sur le Livre des Saintes Médecines du duc Henri de Lancastre*, Paris, Didier, and Geneva, Droz, 1948. Professor Arnould's interest in Richard Rolle was originally aroused by the suggestion then put forward by some scholars that Rolle had been a student at the Sorbonne and, therefore, influenced by French medieval culture and the French language. This he soon discovered, and proved, to have been a grave error. Professor Arnould contributed a number of articles relating to the life and works of the great English mystic and ultimately published a critical edition of his most original work, the *Melos Amoris* (Oxford, Blackwell, 1957), drawing on all the other writings of Rolle's for the presentation of this essential work.

EDMUND COLLEDGE, O.S.A., has specialised in the study of the devotional literature, Latin and vernacular, of England, the Low Countries and the Rhineland in the later Middle Ages. He is the author of studies and modern English translations of Ruysbroek, Tauler and Suso; he published in 1957, in collaboration with Joyce Bazire, a critical edition of *The Chastising of God's Children*, and, in 1961, an anthology, *The Medieval Mystics of England*. He taught English Language and Philology at Liverpool University from 1937 until 1963 when he resigned his Readership there, and entered the English novitiate of the Augustinian Friars Hermit. He made his simple profession in September 1964.

WILLIAM OWEN EVANS was born and brought up in Cardiff and educated by the De La Salle Brothers at St. Illtyd's College. He served in the Royal Signals in Germany, Egypt and Palestine (1944–48). A student at University College, Cardiff (1951–55), he was awarded the Lord Glanely Postgraduate Studentship which he held at Merton College, Oxford (research in Middle English under Professor J. R. R. Tolkien, 1955–57), where he took the degree of Bachelor of Literature. He was Assistant Lecturer in English Language at Sheffield University

(1957–59), and then returned to University College, Cardiff, to a Lectureship in English Language and Literature. He is 38 years of age, married with two children.

Fr. Hugh Farmer, O.S.B., monk of Quarr Abbey, Isle of Wight, was born in London, 30 January 1923. Educated at Blackfriars School, Laxton, he was solemnly professed at Quarr in January 1946, and ordained priest in August 1949. He lectured at Quarr in fundamental theology 1950–54, in medieval Church history 1957–58 and 1961–62. Leverhulme Research Scholarship 1959–60. F.S.A. 1962. He has published *The Monk of Farne*, London 1961; *Magna Vita Sancti Hugonis* (with D. L. Douie) 1961–62. He is a contributor to *Analecta Bollandiana*, *Journal of Ecclesiastical History*, *Revue d'Histoire Ecclésiastique*, *Dictionnaire de Spiritualité*, *Dictionnaire d'Histoire et de Géographie Ecclésiastique*, *Wiseman Review*, *The Month*, *Life of the Spirit*, *Clergy Review* and *Analecta Monastica*, of which he is associate editor. His hobby is designing and weaving ecclesiastical vestments. At present he is chaplain at Redrice School, Andover.

Fr. Benedict Hackett, O.S.A., was born in Limerick, Ireland, in 1921, and entered the Augustinian Order in 1939. He took his Bachelor's degree with first-class honours, at the National University of Ireland in 1943. H.Dip.Ed. 1951. Graduated as Ph.D. in 1955 under the direction of Fr. Aubrey Gwynn, S.J., with a doctoral thesis entitled *William Flete, O.S.A. and St. Catherine of Siena*. He pursued further historical researches at Paris, Rome and Siena 1956–60. He is a contributor to the *Dictionnaire de spiritualité* and presently engaged on editing the earliest statutes (*c.* 1250) of the University of Cambridge. He has been Sub-Prior and Master of Novices at Clare Priory, Suffolk, since 1960. His published works include: *The Spiritual Life of the English Austin Friars of the Fourteenth Century; William Flete and the De Remediis Contra Temptaciones; Blessed John Stone, Austin Friar, Martyr.*

Fr. Peter Hackett, S.J., was born in Bournemouth in 1924. After joining the Society of Jesus in 1942, he was called to serve in the Royal Navy until the end of the War. On his return, he completed his noviceship, and took an honours degree in English Language and Literature at Campion Hall, Oxford. After his ordination in 1957 and the completion of his priestly studies, he was appointed assistant Headmaster at the Catholic College, Preston. He is now Headmaster at the Campion School, Hornchurch in Essex.

RENÉE HAYNES, a great grand-daughter of T. H. Huxley and eldest daughter of G. S. P. Haynes, was educated at various private schools, including the Lycée Française du Royaume Uni, and at St. Hugh's College, Oxford. After reading law for a year, she took a final degree in history. She is married to Jerrard Tickell the novelist and has three sons. Brought up an agnostic, she became an Anglican at Oxford and a Catholic in 1942. She has published three novels, contributions to several collective volumes, a sketch of *Belloc* in the *Writers and their Work* series, an essay *Pan, Caesar and God*, and a full-length study of extra-sensory perception in relation to biology and to religion, *The Hidden Springs* (1961). She also edited with a memoir her father's posthumous volume *The Lawyer: a Conversation Piece*. She contributes articles and book reviews to various periodicals and occasionally broadcasts.

C. HUGH LAWRENCE is Reader in Medieval History in the University of London. Born in December 1921, he served as an officer in the Bedfordshire and Hertfordshire regiment from 1940–46, and commanded a Company in Burma. He took a first-class honours degree in History at Oxford University (Lincoln College) in 1948, and was awarded his doctorate in 1955. He was elected a Fellow of the Royal Historical Society in 1959, and has lectured at Bedford College since 1951. Publications: *St. Edmund of Abingdon, A study in hagiography and history* (1960); articles and reviews on Church history in *English Historical Review, Journal of Ecclesiastical History, Bulletin of the Institute of Historical Research, Encyclopaedia Britannica*, etc. He edited, in co-operation with Professor David Knowles, *The English Church and the Papacy in the Middle Ages* (1965). He was brought up an Anglican and was received into the Church on leaving school in 1940. He is married and has five children.

ABBÉ GERMAIN P. MARC'HADOUR, born in Brittany on 16 April 1921, was ordained priest on 18 June 1944. He was a high-school teacher from 1945 to 1952 in his native diocese of Vannes and in 1952 was appointed to teach English Philology at the Catholic University of the West, Angers, founded in the fourteenth century. He went to the U.S.A. in September 1960 as a Fulbright Travel Grantee, and worked for a year within the *St. Thomas More Project* of Yale University, editing More's *Supplication of Souls*. He returned to America in June 1963 for the summer vacation, as guest of the Folger Library, Washington, D.C. He has been International Secretary to the *Amici Thomae Mori*, since December 1962 and is editor of *Moreana*, 29, rue Volney, Angers, France.

DONALD NICHOLL was born in Halifax, Yorkshire, in 1923. He was educated at Heath Grammar School, Halifax, and Balliol College, Oxford, where he read history. He served in the army during the War, mainly in the Far East. After teaching for several years at Edinburgh University he moved to Keele University, where he is now Senior Lecturer in History. He is author of *Recent Thought in Focus* (1952), editor and translator of Dante's *Monarchy* (1954) and of several German philosophical and theological studies. His latest book is *Thurstan, Archbishop of York* (Stonegate Press, York, 1964). He is a frequent contributor to Catholic periodicals. He is married and has five children.

FR. HUMPHREY PAWSEY is a Carthusian monk at St. Hugh's Charter-house, Parkminster, Sussex.

SISTER ANNA MARIA REYNOLDS, C.P., is headmistress of the Margaret Clitherow Grammar School for Girls, Bradford, Yorks. She specialises in English medieval literature and has been doing research on the writings of Julian of Norwich for nearly twenty years. Her published work includes an article on literary influences in the *Revelations*, and a partially modernized edition of the shorter text of Julian's book. In collaboration with Father James Walsh, S.J., she is preparing a critical edition of the *Revelations*.

JOY D. M. RUSSELL-SMITH was born in New York in 1929, and was educated at the Assumption Convent, Ramsgate, Kent. A scholar of St. Anne's College, Oxford, she took a first-class honours degree in English (1952). She was appointed to her present post of lecturer in English, Birkbeck College, University of London in 1954. Her special interests are the medieval English religious writers, particularly the *Ancrene Riwle* and Walter Hilton. She is at present editing the shorter Latin and English writings of Walter Hilton.

DOM GERARD SITWELL, O.S.B., was born in 1906, and was educated at Ampleforth and St. Benet's Hall, Oxford. He received the Bene-dictine habit at Ampleforth in 1924, was professed the following year and ordained in 1933. From 1933–47 he taught at Ampleforth, where he was Assistant Procurator and Sub-prior 1945–47. He was Master of St. Benet's Hall, Oxford, from 1957–64. Publications: Walter Hilton, *The Scale of Perfection*, translated into modern English with Introduction and Notes (1953); *Life of St. Odo of Cluny*, by John of Salerno and *Life of St. Gerald of Aurillac* by St. Odo, translated with Notes and Introduction (1958); *Medieval Spiritual Writers*, Faith and Fact Series (1961), and of the new edition of Serenus Cressy's compilation of the spiritual teaching of Augustine Baker, *Holy Wisdom* (Orchard Series 1964). He studies in outline and seeks to relate the main trends in spirituality from *c.* 1000 to the eve of the Renaissance in the late fifteenth century; and has published numerous articles in *Downside Review, Clergy Review, Month,* etc.

C. H. TALBOT, Ph.D., F.R.Hist.S., F.S.A., was born in Portsmouth, 1906. He became interested in medieval spirituality when the late Dom André Wilmart encouraged him to edit Saint Aelred's work, *De anima,* which was published in 1952 by the Warburg Institute, University of London, where he was on the library staff. He has since published a number of other medieval texts, including the *Sermones inediti Aelredi abbatis Rievallensis,* the *Centum Sententiae Walteri Daniel, Florilegium morale Oxoniense* and many others connected with monastic and particularly Cistercian spirituality. He collaborated from 1947 to 1959 with Dom Jean Leclercq on the new edition of the works of St. Bernard, of which three volumes have so far appeared. He is now on the staff of the Wellcome Historical Medical Museum, where he has compiled a biographical dictionary of English medieval physicians and is now writing a history of medieval medicine. He has recently published two volumes of documents relating to England and Poland under Queen Elizabeth I; a third will appear shortly. He was Birkbeck Lecturer at Cambridge, 1962–63, on Ecclesiastical History, the subject of which was *Cluniac Monasticism from Saint Odo to Peter the Venerable.*

FR. JAMES WALSH, S.J., born in Lancashire in 1920, was educated at the Catholic College, Preston, Lancashire. He joined the Society of Jesus 1938, took an honours degree in the Classical languages and English language and Literature at Oxford University, and was ordained priest in 1952. After taking a doctorate in Ascetical and Mystical Theology at the Gregorian University, Rome, in 1957, he was appointed assistant editor of *The Month.* In 1961 he founded *The Way,* a quarterly periodical of spirituality, with Fr. William Yeomans, S.J., and remains its editor. He is also Vice-Postulator for the Cause of the English and Welsh Martyrs, and for the Cause of Mother Cornelia Connelly, Foundress of the Society of the Holy Child Jesus. His special study is fourteenth-century English spirituality. He has published *The Revelations of Divine Love of Julian of Norwich* (Burns & Oates Orchard Series 1961, and Harper, New York), and *The Knowledge of Ourselves and of God* (Mowbrays Fleur de Lys Series 1961). He has published articles on Medieval Spirituality in the *Revue d'Ascétique et de Mystique* and *Archives d'Histoire Doctrinale et Littéraire du Moyen Age,* as well as contributing regular articles on spirituality to *The Month* and *The Way*. He is at the moment preparing an edition of the works of the author of *The Cloud of Unknowing*, which will be published in 1965.

DOM AELRED WATKIN, O.S.B., the son of E. I. Watkin, philosopher and writer, was born in February 1918. He was educated at Blackfriars School, Laxton, and Christ's College, Cambridge, where he took a first class in both parts of the historical tripos. After a short period with Sheed and Ward, the publishers, he entered the Benedictine abbey of Downside in 1936. He was House Master at Downside School from 1948 to 1962, when he became Headmaster. He has edited the Glastonbury Chartulary, Register of the Archdeacons of Norwich, etc.; and has published the *Heart of the World* (London and New York 1954) and *The Enemies of Love* (London and New York 1958). He is a Fellow of the Society of Antiquaries and of the Royal Historical Society.

BIBLIOGRAPHY

GENERAL

Great Western Mystics: Their lasting significance, by David Baumgardt. Columbia U.P., New York; O.U.P., London, 1961.

The Cistercian Heritage, by Louis Bouyer. Mowbray, London, 1958.

The English Mystics, by Gerald Bullett. Michael Joseph, London, 1950.

Western Mysticism, by Cuthbert Butler, O.S.B., Constable, London, 1922. Second edition, 1951. Also as a paperback in Hutchinson's Grey Arrow Series.

On the Continuity of English Prose, by R. W. Chambers, E.E.T.S., O.S., 191A. Reprinted 1957.

The Hermits and Anchorites of England, by Rotha Mary Clay. Methuen, London, 1914.

English Mystics of the Fourteenth Century, by T. W. Coleman. Epworth Press, London, 1938.

The Mediaeval Mystics of England, ed. and with an introduction by Eric Colledge. Murray, London, 1962.

The English Medieval Recluse, by F. D. S. Darwin, S.P.C.K., London, 1940.

English Spiritual Writers, ed. by Charles Davis. Burns & Oates, London, 1961.

The Pre-Conquest Church in England, by Margaret Deanesly. Black, London, 1961.

Saint Bernard et la Bible, par P. Dumontier. Présentation par J. M. Dechanet. Desclée de Brouwer, Paris, 1953. (Bibliothèque de spiritualité médiévale.)

The Light and the Rainbow, by Hilda Graef. Longmans, London, 1959.

English Mystics, by G. E. Hodgson. Mowbray, London, 1922.

Studies of English Mystics, by W. R. Inge. Murray, London, 1906.

A City not Forsaken: studies of the English masters of the Spiritual Life, by Edith L. Kendall. Faith Press, London, 1962.

The English Mystical Tradition, by David Knowles. Burns & Oates, London, 1961. Paperback ed. 1964.

The English Mystics, by David Knowles. Burns & Oates, London, 1927.

The Monastic Order in England, by David Knowles. University Press, Cambridge, 1940. 2nd ed. 1963.

The Religious Orders in England, by David Knowles, 3 vols. University Press, Cambridge, 1948–59.

La Spiritualité du moyen âge, by J. Leclercq, F. Vandenbroucke and L. Bouyer. Aubier, Paris, 1961. An English translation is to be published by Burns Oates in 1965.

Literature and Pulpit in Medieval England, by G. R. Owst. University Press, Cambridge, 1933.

Preaching in Medieval England, by G. R. Owst. University Press, Cambridge, 1926.

The English Church in the Fourteenth Century, by W. A. Pantin. University Press, Cambridge, 1955.

The English Religious Heritage, by Conrad Pepler, O.P. Blackfriars, London, 1958.

Late Medieval Mysticism, ed. by Ray C. Petry. S.C.M., London, 1957.

Quatre Mystiques Anglais: Richard Rolle, Juliane de Norwich, Dom Augustin Baker, Gertrude More, by P. Renaudin. Editions du Cerf, Paris, 1945.

Medieval Spiritual Writers, by Dom Gerard Sitwell (Faith & Fact, 40). Burns & Oates, London, 1961.

English Spirituality, an outline of ascetical theology according to the English pastoral tradition, by Martin Thornton. S.P.C.K., London, 1963.

The Mystics of the Church, by Evelyn Underhill. Clarke, London, 1925.

Medieval Spirituality, by Felix Vernet. Trans. by the Benedictines of Talacre. Sands, London, 1930.

The English Way, ed. by Maisie Ward. Sheed & Ward, London, 1934.

Poets and Mystics, by E. I. Watkin. Sheed & Ward, London, 1953.

Auteurs spirituels et textes dévots du moyen âge latin, by A. Wilmart. Paris, 1932.

Three Middle English Mystics, by R. M. Wilson. English Association, London, 1956.

BEDE

Bibliography:

A Bede bibliography: 1935-1960, by W. F. Bolton. Traditio 18, 1962, pp. 436-45.

The long article by Mgr. Cecchetti in *Bibliotheca Sanctorum II*, Rome, 1962. Coll. 1006-74 includes a detailed bibliography.

A Hand-list of Bede Manuscripts, by M. L. W. Laistner, with the collaboration of H. H. King. Cornell U.P., New York, 1943.

Texts: Works in PL 90-5.

The complete works of Venerable Bede in the original Latin, collated with the manuscripts and various printed editions, accompanied by a new English translation of the historical works, and a life of the author by J. A. Giles. 12 vols. Whittaker, London, 1843-44.

A critical edition is being issued in the series *Corpus Christianorum*. Three volumes have already appeared.

The standard edition of the historical works is: *Venerabilis Baedae Opera Historica*, ed. by C. Plummer, 2 vols. Clarendon Press, Oxford, 1896.

They are also in the *Loeb Classical Library* (vols. 246 and 248) with a trans. by J. E. King.

The Ecclesiastical History of the English People. Translated out of Latin into English by Thomas Stapleton. Ed. by Philip Hereford with an introduction by Bede Jarrett, O.P. Burns & Oates, London, 1935.

A History of the English Church and People, trans. and with an introduction by Leo Sherley-Price. Penguin Books, Harmondsworth, 1955.

The Ecclesiastical History of the English Nation and other writings. Introduction by David Knowles (Everyman's Library 479). Dent, London, 1958.

Expositio Actuum Apostolorum et Retractatio, ed. by M. W. Laistner. Mediaeval Academy of America, Cambridge, Mass., 1943.

Bedae Opera de temporibus, ed. by Charles W. Jones. Mediaeval Academy of America, Cambridge, Mass., 1943.

Bedas metrische Vita sancti Cuthberti, ed. by W. Jaager. Mayer and Müller, Leipzig, 1935.

Two lives of St. Cuthbert: a life by an anonymous monk of Lindisfarne and Bede's prose life. Texts, trans., and notes by Bertram Colgrave. University Press, Cambridge, 1940.

Studies:

The Venerable Bede, his life and writings, by G. F. Browne. S.P.C.K., London, 1919, 2nd ed. 1930.

The Venerable Bede, his spiritual teachings, by Sister Thomas Aquinas Carroll. Catholic University of America Press, Washington, 1946.

Bede, his Life, Times and Writings; Essays in commemoration of the twelfth centenary of his death, ed. by A. H. Thompson. Clarendon Press, Oxford, 1935.

EARLY ENGLISH RELIGIOUS LITERATURE—I AND II

Texts:

The Homilies of the Anglo-Saxon Church, ed. by B. Thorpe, 2 vols. London, 1844 and 1843.

The Blickling Homilies, ed. by R. Morris, 2 vols. London, 1874–80.

An Ancient Manuscript (the Nunnaminster Book), ed. by W. De Gray Birch. London, 1889.

Bede, *Historia Ecclesiastica*, ed. by C. Plummer. Oxford, 1896.

The Book of Cerne, ed. by A. B. Kuypers. Cambridge, 1902.

Die Vercelli-Homilien, ed. by M. Förster. Hamburg, 1932.

The Dream of the Rood, ed. by B. Dickins and A. S. C. Ross. London, 1934.

The Exeter Book, ed. by G. P. Krapp and E. van K. Dobbie. New York, 1936.

The Battle of Maldon, ed. by E. V. Gordon. London, 1937.

Regularis Concordia, ed. by T. Symons. London, 1953.
Bede, *Homilies*, ed. by D. Hurst, in Corpus Christianorum Series Latina 122, 1955.
Murphy, Gerard, *Early Irish Lyrics*. Oxford, 1956.
The Homilies of Wulfstan, ed. by Dorothy Bethurum. Oxford, 1957.
The Benedictine Office, ed. by J. Ure. Edinburgh, 1957.
The Seafarer, ed. by Ida Gordon. London, 1960.
Gjerløw, Lilli, *Adoratio Crucis*, Oslo, 1961.
Studies:
Bishop, E., *Liturgica Historica*. Oxford, 1918.
Blake, N. F., *Caedmon's Hymn*. Notes and Queries 207, 1962, pp. 243–6.
Bonetti, I., *Le Stimate della Passione*. Rovigo, 1952.
von den Brincken, Anna Dorothee, *Marianus Scottus*. Deutsches Archiv fur Erforschung des M.A. 17, 1961, pp. 191–238.
Dubois, M.-M., *Aelfric, sermonnaire, docteur et grammarien*, Paris, 1943.
Förster, M., *Keltisches Wortgut im Englischen*. Halle, 1921.
Gougaud, L., *Christianity in Celtic Lands*. London, 1932.
Leclercq, J., *Monachisme et pérégrination du ixe au xiie siècle*. Studia Monastica 3, 1961, pp. 33–52.
Sisam, K., *Studies in the History of Old English Literature*. Oxford, 1953.
Whitelock, Dorothy, *The Audience of 'Beowulf'*. Oxford, 1951.

GODRIC OF FINCHALE

Study: Libellus de vita et miraculis S. Godrici, heremitae de Finchale, auctore Reginaldo monacho Dunelmensi. Adjicitur appendix miraculorum. Ed. by Joseph Stevenson. Surtees Society No. 20, 1847.
Article: Zupitza, J., "Cantus Beati Godrici," *Englische Studien*, II, 1888, pp. 401–32.

CHRISTINA OF MARKYATE

Study: The Life of Christina of Markyate, a twelfth-century recluse, ed. and trans. by C. H. Talbot. Clarendon Press, Oxford, 1959.
Article: Talbot, C., "Christina of Markyate—a monastic narrative of the Twelfth Century" in *Essays and Studies*, XV (1962), pp. 13–26.

AELRED OF RIEVAULX

Bibliography: Bibliotheca Aelrediana, by A. Hoste. (Instrumenta Patristica II.) Steenbrugge, 1962. There is a useful short bibliography in Hallier's work listed below.

Texts:

Latin works in PL 195. The *De vita eremitica (De institutis inclusarum)*, in PL 32, coll. 1451–74, among the works of Augustine.

Sermones inediti B. Aelredi Rievallensis, ed. by C. H. Talbot. Rome, 1952. (Scriptorum Sacri Ordinis Cisterciensis, I.)

The Mirror of Charity, trans. by Geoffrey Webb and Adrian Walker. Mowbray, London, 1962.

De Anima, ed. by C. H. Talbot. Warburg Institute Medieval and Renaissance Studies, No. 2. London, 1952.

De institutis inclusarum, ed. by C. H. Talbot. Analecta Sacri Ordinis Cisterciensis VII. Rome, 1951, pp. 167–217.

La vie de recluse (text and French trans.), ed. by C. Dumont. Sources Chrétiennes, No. 76. Paris, 1961.

L'amitié spirituelle (text with French trans.), ed. by J. Dubois, Bruges, 1948.

"L'Oraison pastorale de l'Abbé Aelred" *Revue Bénédictine*, XXVII, 1925, pp. 262 ff. Reprinted in *Auteurs Spirituels*, pp. 287–98.

Oratio Pastoralis of St. Aelred of Rievaulx, MS 34, ff. 97r–99r, Jesus College, Cambridge. Trans. *Prayer of a Superior*, pp. 231–5, *The Way*, July 1964.

The Pastoral prayer of St Aelred of Rievaulx. Trans. by a Religious of C.S.M.V. Dacre Press, London, 1955.

Quand Jésus eut douze ans (text and French trans.), ed. by A. Hoste and J. Dubois. Sources Chrétiennes, No. 60. Paris, 1958.

On Jesus at twelve years old, Meditations of St Aelred, trans. from the Latin by Geoffrey Webb and Adrian Walker. Fleur de Lys Series, No. 7. Mowbray, London, 1957.

The *Relatio de Standardo* in *The Chronicles of the reigns of Stephen*, etc., ed. by Richard Howlett. Vol. III, pp. 179 ff. Rolls Series, 1886.

The Sermon on the Saints of Hexham in *The Priory of Hexham*, ed. by James Raine. Vol. 1, pp. 173 ff., Surtees Society, 44. 1864.

St Aelred's letter to his sister, ed. and trans. by Geoffrey Webb and Adrian Walker. Fleur de Lys Series, No. 11. Mowbray, London, 1958.

Studies:

The Life of Ailred of Rievaulx, by Walter Daniel. Trans. from the Latin with introduction and notes by F. M. Powicke. Nelson, London, 1950.

St. Aelred of Rievaulx, by Thomas Edmund Harvey. Allenson, London, 1932.

Un éducateur monastique, Aelred de Rievaulx, by A Hallier. Gabalda, Paris, 1959.

T

Articles:

Ducey, L. M., "St. Ailred and the Speculum Caritatis," *Cath. Hist. Rev.*, XVII, 1931.

Sage, C. M., "The Manuscripts of St. Aelred," *Cath. Hist. Rev.*, XXXIV, 1949, pp. 437–45.

Wilmart, A., "L'Instigateur du Speculum Caritatis d'Aelred," *Rev. d'Ascétique et de Mystique*, XIV, 1933, pp. 369 ff., 429. With the text of Aelred's *Praefatio* and *Clausula*.

ANCHORESSES' GUIDE

Texts:

All the important English, French and Latin MSS are being edited for the E.E.T.S. The following have already appeared:

The Latin text of the Ancrene Riwle. Ed. by Charlotte d'Evelyn. O.S. 216, 1941. Reprinted 1957.

The French text of the Ancrene Riwle, B. M. Cotton MS. Vitellius. F. VII. Ed. by J. A. Herbert. O.S. 219, 1943.

The English text of the Ancrene Riwle. B. M. Cotton MS. Nero A XIV. Ed. by Mabel Day. O.S. 225, 1946. Reprinted 1957.

The English text of the Ancrene Riwle. Gonville and Caius College. MS. 234/120. Ed. by R. M. Wilson. With introduction by N. R. Ker. O.S. 229, 1948. Reprinted 1957

The English text of the Ancrene Riwle, B. M. Royal MS. 8.C 1. Ed. by A. C. Baugh. O.S. 232, 1949. Reprinted 1958.

The French text of the Ancrene Riwle, Trinity College Cambridge, MS. R.14.7. Ed. by W. H. Trethewey. O.S. 240, 1954.

Ancrene Wisse, Corpus Christi College, Cambridge, MS. 402. Ed. by J. R. R. Tolkien, with an introduction by N. R. Ker. O.S. 249, 1960.

The English text of the Ancrene Riwle. Ed. from Cotton MS. Titus D. XVIII by Frances M. Mack, together with the Lanhydrock fragment. Bodleian MS. Eng. Th. *c.* 70. Ed. by A. Zetterstein. O.S. 252, 1963.

Three other vols. are in preparation.

The Ancren Riwle: a treatise on the rules and duties of monastic life. Ed. and trans. from a semi-Saxon MS. of the thirteenth century, by James Morton. Camden Society, Old Series 57. 1853.

The Nun's rule. Being the Ancren Riwle modernised by James Morton. With introduction by Abbot Gasquet. Burns & Oates, London, 1905.

The Ancrene Riwle (the Corpus MS.: Ancrene Wisse). Translated into modern English by M. B. Salu with an introduction by Dom Gerard Sitwell, O.S.B., and a preface by J. R. R. Tolkien. Orchard Books. Burns & Oates, London, 1955.

The Ancrene Wisse, parts 6 and 7. Ed. with critical introduction, notes, bibliography and glossary by G. Shepherd. Nelson's Medieval and Renaissance Library, 1959.
Articles:
Kirchberger, Clare, "Some notes on the *Ancrene Riwle*," *Dominican Studies*, VII, 1954, pp. 215–38.
Samuels, M. L., "*Ancrene Riwle* Studies," *Medium Aevum*, XXII, 1953.

ADAM OF DRYBURGH

Texts:
Works in PL 198. Also, *De quadripartito exercicio celle* in PL 153, coll. 787–884.
Sermones fratris Ade Ordinis Praemonstratensis, ed. by W. de G. Birch. Edinburgh, 1901.
Ad viros religiosos. Quatorze sermons d'Adam Scot. Texte établi avec introduction et notes par F. Petit. Tongerloo, 1934.
Eden's fourfold river. An instruction on the contemplative life, written for the monks of Witham Charterhouse, Somerset, *c.* A.D. 1200. Ed. with an introduction by a monk of Parkminster. Burns & Oates, London, 1927.
Study: Adam of Dryburgh, by J. Bulloch. S.P.C.K., London, 1958.
Articles:
Wilmart, André, O.S.B., "Magister Adam Cartusiensis," *Mélanges Mandonnet*, 2, 1930, pp. 145–61.
Wilmart, André, O.S.B., "Maître Adam Chanoine prémontré devenu Chàrtreux à Witham," *Analecta Premonstratensia*, IX, 1933, pp. 209 ff.

STEPHEN OF SAWLEY

Texts:
Le Triple Exercise d'Etienne de Sallai, ed. by A. Wilmart in *Rev. d'Ascétique et de Mystique*, XI, 1930, pp. 355–74.
Les Méditations d'Etienne de Sallai, ed. by A. Wilmart in *Rev. d'Ascétique et de Mystique*, X, 1929, pp. 368–415.
Le Speculum Novitii d'Etienne de Sallai, ed. by E. Mikkers in Analecta O.C.R., 1946, pp. 3–32.
Study: "Stephen of Eston, Abbot of Sawley, Newminster and Fountains, by J. Macnulty. *Yorks. Archaeological Journal*, XXXI, (1934), pp. 49–64.

EDMUND OF ABINGDON

Texts:
Anglo-Norman text: *La Merure de Seinte Eglise*, ed. by H. W. Robbins. University Print Shop, Lewisburg, 1925.

English text:
Yorkshire Writers, Richard Rolle of Hampole, by C. Horstmann, Vol. 1, pp. 219–61.
The Mirror of St. Edmund. Trans. into modern English by Francesca M. Steek. With a preface by the Very Rev. Fr. V. McNabb. Burns & Oates, London, 1905; and an abridged version in *The Mediaeval Mystics of England.* Ed. with an introduction by Eric Colledge, pp. 123–40, Murray, London, 1962.
Latin text: *Bibliothecae Veterum Patrum et Auctorum Ecclesiasticorum,* ed. by M. de la Bigne. 3rd ed. Paris, 1610. Vol. 5, cols. 983–1004, and in a number of subsequent editions.

Studies:
St. Edmund of Abingdon. A study in Hagiography and History, by C. H. Lawrence. Clarendon Press, Oxford, 1960.
The Life of St. Edmund of Canterbury from original sources, by Wilfrid Wallace, O.S.B., Kegan Paul, London, 1893.
Edmund Rich, Archbishop and Saint, by M. R. Newbolt. S.P.C.K., London, 1928.
St. Edmund, Archbishop of Canterbury. His life as told by Old English writers, arranged by Bernard Ward. Sands, London, 1903.

PIERS PLOWMAN

Texts:
The Vision of William concerning Piers the Plowman in three parallel texts together with Richard the Redeless. Ed. from numerous manuscripts with preface, notes and a glossary by W. W. Skeat. 2 vols. Clarendon Press, Oxford, 1886. Reissued 1924.
Piers Plowman: the three versions. General editor George Kane. Athlone Press, London, 1960. Only the A text has so far been published.
The Book concerning Piers the Plowman. Trans. into modern English by Donald and Rachel Attwater. Dent, London, 1957 (Everyman's Library 571).
Piers the Ploughman. Trans. into modern English. With an introduction by J. F. Goodridge. Penguin Books, Harmondsworth, 1959.

Studies:
Piers Plowman as a fourteenth-century apocalypse, by Morton W. Bloomfield. Rutgers University Press, New Brunswick, 1962.
Piers Plowman, an interpretation of the A text, by T. P. Dunning. Talbot Press, Dublin, 1937.
Piers the Plowman and the Scheme of Salvation, by Robert W. Frank. (Yale Studies in English), 1936.

Piers Plowman and contemporary religious thought, by Greta Hort. S.P.C.K., London, 1938.

Back to Langland, by Stanley B. James. Sands, London, 1935.

Piers Plowman, an essay in criticism, by John Lawlor. Arnold, London, 1962.

Piers Plowman and Scriptural Tradition, by D. W. Robertson, Jr., and B. F. Huppé. Princeton, 1951.

Piers Plowman, an introduction, by Elizabeth Salter. Blackwell, Oxford, 1962.

Langland: Piers Plowman, by Nevill Coghill. Longmans, London, 1964 (Writers and their Work, 174).

Articles:

Dawson, C., *The Vision of Piers Plowman* in *Medieval Essays*. Sheed & Ward, London, 1953, pp. 239–71. This is a revised version of an essay which first appeared in *The English Way*.

Dunning, T. P., "The Structure of the B text of Piers Plowman," *Review of English Studies*, N.S., VII (1956), pp. 225–37.

Hussey, S. S., "Langland, Hilton and the Three Lives," *Review of English Studies*, N.S., VII (1956), pp. 132–50.

RICHARD ROLLE

Texts:

Writings ascribed to Richard Rolle, Hermit of Hampole, and Materials for his Biography, by Hope Emily Allen (Modern Language Assoc. of America, Monograph Series No. 3), London and New York, 1927.

English Writings of Richard Rolle, Hermit of Hampole, ed. by Hope Emily Allen. Clarendon Press, Oxford, 1931.

Yorkshire Writers, Richard Rolle of Hampole an English Father of the Church and his followers, ed. by C. Horstmann, 2 vols. Swan Sonnenschein, London, 1895–96.

Selected works of Richard Rolle, Hermit. Transcribed with an introduction by G. C. Heseltine. Longmans, London, 1930.

Selected writings of Richard Rolle, trans. and arranged by John G. Harrell. S.P.C.K., London, 1963.

English prose treatises of Richard Rolle de Hampole, ed. by George G. Perry. A new and revised text and glossary, two parts. E.E.T.S., O.S., 20, London, 1921.

The Form of Perfect Living, and other prose treatises. Rendered into modern English by Geraldine E. Hodgson. Baker, London, 1910.

Some minor works of Richard Rolle with the Privity of the Passion by S. Bonaventura. Trans. and ed. by Geraldine E. Hodgson. Watkins, London, 1923.

The Life of Richard Rolle; together with an edition of his English lyrics by Frances M. M. Comper. Dent, London, 1928.

Le feu de l'amour, le modèle de la vie parfaite, le pater. Traduits par M. Noetinger. Mame, Tours, 1929.

The Fire of love and the Mending of Life. The first English in 1435 from the *De Incendio Amoris,* the second in 1434 from the *De emendacione vitae* of R. Rolle by R. Misyn. Ed. by R. Harvey. E.E.T.S., O.S., 106, London, 1896.

The Fire of Love or Melody of Love and the Mending of Life or Rule of Living. Trans. by Richard Misyn from the *"Incendium Amoris"* and the *"De Emendatione Vitae."* Ed. and done into modern English by Frances M. M. Comper. With an introduction by Evelyn Underhill. Methuen, London, 1914, and 2nd ed., 1920.

The Officium and Miracula of Richard Rolle of Hampole. Ed. by Reginald M. Woolley. S.P.C.K., London, 1919.

The Mending of life, being an anonymous version of about A.D. 1400 from the "De Emendatione Vitae" of Richard Rolle of Hampole. Ed. in a modernised form from the Cambridge MS. Ff. V.40 (now first published) with an introduction and notes by Dundas Harford. H. R. Allenson, London, 1913.

The Amending of Life. Trans. with an introduction by H. L. Hubbard. Watkins, London, 1922.

Du péché à l'amour divin ou l'amendement du pecheur. Traduite et annoté par Léopold Denis, S.J. Desclée, Paris, 1926.

The Incendium Amoris of Richard Rolle, ed. by Margaret Deanesly. University Press, Manchester, 1915.

The Fire of love. Being a translation of the *Incendium Amoris,* by G. C. Heseltine. Burns & Oates, London, 1935.

The Melos Amoris of Richard Rolle of Hampole, ed. by E. J. Arnould. Blackwell, Oxford, 1957.

Studies:

The authorship of the "Pricke of Conscience," by Hope Emily Allen. Radcliffe College Monographs, No. 15, 1915.

The Sanity of Mysticism. A study of Richard Rolle, by Geraldine E. Hodgson. Faith Press, London, 1926.

Article: Wilmart, A., "Le Cantique d'amour de Richard Rolle," *Revue d'Ascétique et de Mystique,* XXI (1940), pp. 131–48.

THE MONK OF FARNE

Texts:

Meditaciones cuiusdam monachi apud Farneland quondam solitarii, ed. by Hugh Farmer, O.S.B. (Studia Anselmiana 41), 1957, pp. 141–245.

The Monk of Farne, ed. and introduced by Dom Hugh Farmer,

O.S.B., and trans. by a Benedictine of Stanbrook. Darton
Longman and Todd, London, 1962.
Article: Pantin, W. A., "The Monk-Solitary of Farne: A fourteenth-
century English Mystic," *Eng. Hist. Rev.*, 59, 1944, pp. 162–86.

WILLIAM FLETE

Texts: Manuscripts of the Latin text of *De remediis contra temptationes*
are in the Bodleian. (MSS. Bodley 43, Bodley Laud misc. 407),
Cambridge University Library (II.vi.30) and Trinity College,
Cambridge (R.14.1). The Middle English trans. is in the British
Museum (Harley 2409) and the Bodleian (MSS. Bodley 131).
Studies:
  Sainte Catherine de Sienne. Essai de critique des sources, par R. Fawtier.
  2 vols., Paris, 1921–30. 1, pp. 53–81; 2, pp. 212–5, 334–5, 368.
  Santa Caterina da Siena. Dottrina e fonti. Morcelliana, Brescia, 1953,
  pp. 274–99.
  English Austin friars in the time of Wyclif, by Aubrey Gwynn, S.J.
  O.U.P., London, 1940, pp. 139–210.
  William Flete, O.S.A. (c. 1325–1390) and St. Catherine of Siena, by
  Benedict Hackett, O.S.A. An unpublished Dublin National
  University of Ireland Ph.D. dissertation.
Articles:
  Fawtier, R., "Catheriniana" in *Melanges d'archéologie et d'histoire,*
  XXXIV (1914), pp. 40–93.
  Hackett, B., O.S.A., "The spiritual life of the English Austin Friars
  of the fourteenth century" in *S. Augustinus vitae spiritualis magister.*
  Rome 1959, vol. II, pp. 471–92.
  "William Flete and the 'De remediis contra temptaciones'" in
  Medieval studies presented to Aubrey Gwynn, S.J., Dublin, 1961,
  pp. 330–48.
  Laurent, M. H., O.P., "De litteris ineditis Fr. Willelmi Fleete
  (cc. 1368–1380)" in *Analecta Augustiniana,* XVIII (1942), pp. 303–27,

THE CLOUD OF UNKNOWING

Bibliography: There is a good bibliography in the 1958 reprint of
Phyllis Hodgson's E.E.T.S. edition of the Cloud.
Texts:
  The Cloud of Unknowing and the Book of Privy Counselling. Ed. by
  Phyllis Hodgson. E.E.T.S., O.S. 218, London, 1944. Reprinted
  with additions in 1958.
  *"Deonise Hid Divinite" and other Treatises on contemplative prayer
  related to the "Cloud of Unknowing."* Ed. by Phyllis Hodgson.
  E.E.T.S., O.S. 231, London, 1955.

The Cloud of Unknowing and other treatises by an English Mystic of the fourteenth century. With a commentary on the Cloud by Augustine Baker. Ed. by Justin McCann, O.S.B. Sixth and revised edition (Orchard Books). Burns & Oates, London, 1952. Reprinted in 1960. The original edition was in 1924.

A Book of contemplation the which is called the Cloud of Unknowing, in which a soul is oned with God. Ed. from the British Museum MS., Harl 674. With an introduction by Evelyn Underhill. J. M. Watkins, London, 1912. 2nd ed. 1934.

The Divine Cloud (with notes and a preface by Augustine Baker). Ed. by H. Collins. Richardson, London, 1871.

The Cloud of Unknowing (an interpretation written at Pendle Hill, Wallingford, Pennsylvania). Harper, New York and London, 1948.

The Cloud of Unknowing, introductory commentary and trans. by Ira Progoff. Rider, London, 1959.

The Cloud of Unknowing. Trans. into modern English by Clifton Wolters. Penguin Books. Harmondsworth, 1961.

Le Nuage de l'Inconnaissance. Trans. by Dom M. Noetinger. Mame, Tours, 1925.

Four of the minor treatises are included in *The Cell of self knowledge*. Ed. with an introduction and notes by E. G. Gardner. Chatto & Windus, London, 1910.

A Letter of Private Direction, rendered into modern English with an introduction by James Walsh, S.J. Printed for the friends of Burns & Oates [Verona], 1963.

Studies:

Sense and thought. A study in mysticism, by Greta Hort. Allen & Unwin, London, 1936.

Christian Dhyāna; or Prayer of loving regard. A study of "*The Cloud of Unknowing*" by H. V. H. Elwin. S.P.C.K., London, 1930.

Articles:

Gardner, Helen L., "Walter Hilton and the authorship of the 'Cloud of Unknowing,'" *Review of English Studies*, Vol. IX, 1933, pp. 129–47.

Review of *The Cloud of Unknowing*, ed. by P. Hodgson. *Medium Aevum*, XVI, 1947, pp. 36–42.

Hodgson, Phyllis, "Walter Hilton and the 'Cloud of Unknowing.' A problem of authorship reconsidered," *Modern Language Rev.*, L, 1955, pp. 395–406.

Knowles, David, "The Excellence of the Cloud of Unknowing," *Downside Rev.*, LII, January 1934, pp. 71–92.

McCann, Justin, "The Cloud of Unknowing," *Ampleforth Journal*, XXIX, 1924, pp. 192–7.

Noetinger, Maurice, "The Authorship of the Cloud of Unknowing," *Blackfriars*, 1924.

WALTER HILTON

Bibliography: There is a useful bibliography in the study by A. C. Hughes but it is marred by numerous misprints.

Texts:
The Scale of Perfection, trans. into modern English with an introduction and notes by Dom Gerard Sitwell, O.S.B. Orchard Books. Burns & Oates, London, 1953.

The Minor Works of Walter Hilton. Ed. by Dorothy Jones. Burns, Oates and Washbourne, London, 1929.

The Goad of Love, an unpublished translation of the Stimulus Amoris formerly attributed to St. Bonaventura, now edited from manuscripts by Clare Kirchberger (Classics of the Contemplative Life). Faber, London, 1952.

The Scale of Perfection. Newly edited from MS. sources with an introduction by Evelyn Underhill. J. M. Watkins, London, 1923.

The Ladder of Perfection. A new trans. with an introduction by Leo Sherley Price. Penguin Books, Harmondsworth, 1957.

Epistle on Mixed Life in Yorkshire Writers, Richard Rolle of Hampole. Ed. by C. Horstmann, Vol. 1, pp. 264–92.

The Scale (or Ladder) of Perfection, written by Walter Hilton. With an essay on the Spiritual Life of Mediaeval England by the Rev. J. B. Dalgairns. New edition. Art and Book Co., London, 1901.

Of the knowledge of ourselves and of God. A fifteenth-century spiritual florilegium (from Walter Hilton and Julian of Norwich). Ed. by James Walsh and Eric Colledge. Fleur de Lys Series 17. Mowbray, London, 1961.

Study: Walter Hilton's Direction to Contemplatives, by Alfred C. Hughes. Gregorian University, Rome, 1962.

Articles:
Russell-Smith, Joy M., "Walter Hilton and a tract in defence of the veneration of images," *Dominican Studies*, VII, 1954, pp. 180–214.

Colledge, Eric, "Recent work on Walter Hilton," *Blackfriars*, XXXVII, No. 435 (June 1956), pp. 265–70.

Gardner, Helen, "The Text of the Scale of Perfection," *Medium Aevum*, V (1936), pp. 11–30.

Sitwell, Gerard, O.S.B., "Contemplation in the 'Scale of Perfection,'" *Downside Review*, 67 (summer 1949), pp. 276–90; 68 (winter 1949), pp. 21–34; 69 (summer 1950), pp. 271–89.

JULIAN OF NORWICH

Bibliography: There is a detailed bibliography in Father Molinari's
book.

Texts:

The Revelations of Divine Love of Julian of Norwich. Trans. by James
Walsh, S.J. (Orchard Books). Burns & Oates, London, 1961.

Revelations of Divine Love shewed to a devout Ankress. Ed. from the
MSS. by Dom Roger Hudleston, O.S.B. With an introduction
by the same. Burns & Oates, London, 1927. 2nd ed., 1952.

A Shewing of God's Love. The shorter version of sixteen revelations
of divine love. Ed. and partially modernised from the fifteenth
century MSS. by Sister Anna Maria Reynolds, C.P. Longmans,
London, 1958.

XVI Revelations of Divine Love. Shewed to Mother Juliana of Norwich,
1373. With a preface by George Tyrrell, S.J. Kegan Paul, London,
1902, 2nd imp. 1920.

Comfortable words for Christ's lovers: being the visions and voices
vouchsafed to Lady Julian. Transcribed and ed. from the recently
discovered manuscript (B.M. addit. 37,790) by the Rev. Dundas
Harford. H. R. Allenson, London, 1911.

Revelations of Divine Love. A version from the MS. in the British
Museum ed. by Grace Warrack. Methuen, London, 1901,
14th ed. 1952.

Meditations on the Litany of the Sacred Heart of Jesus. Culled by F. A.
Forbes from the writings of Juliana of Norwich. Paternoster
Series, No. 9. Burns & Oates, London, 1920.

Studies:

Juliana of Norwich. An introductory appreciation and interpretative
anthology. By P. F. Chambers. Gollancz, London, 1955.

A Description of St. Julian's Church, Norwich, and an account of Dame
Julian's connection with it, by R. H. Flood. Norwich, 1937.

Julian of Norwich: the teaching of a fourteenth-century mystic, by Paul
Molinari, S.J. Longmans, London, 1958.

The Lady Julian: a psychological study, by R. H. Thouless. S.P.C.K.,
London, 1924.

Articles:

Reynolds, Sr. Anna Maria, C.P., "Some Literary Influences in the
Revelations of Julian of Norwich," *Leeds Studies in English*, 7 & 8,
1952, pp. 18–28.

Walsh, James, S.J., "God's homely loving. St. John and Julian of
Norwich on the divine indwelling," *The Month*, N.S.19, March
1958, pp. 164–72.

MARGERY KEMPE

Texts:

The Book of Margery Kempe. Ed. with introduction and glossary by Sanford Brown Meech with prefatory note by Hope Emily Allen, and notes and appendices by S. B. Meech and H. E. Allen. E.E.T.S., O.S. 212, 1940. Reprinted 1961.

The Book of Margery Kempe, 1436. A modern version by W. Butler-Bowdon. With an introduction by R. W. Chambers. Cape, London, 1936. Also included in the World's Classics Series. Oxford University Press, London, 1954.

Studies:

Margery Kempe, genius and mystic, by Katherine Cholmeley. Longmans, London, 1947.

The Apprentice Saint, by Louise Collis. Michael Joseph, London, 1964.

Margery Kempe: an example in the English Pastoral Tradition, by Martin Thornton. S.P.C.K., London, 1960.

Surprising mystics, by Herbert Thurston, S.J. Ed. by J. H. Crehan, S.J., Burns & Oates, London, 1955, pp. 27–37.

ST. THOMAS MORE

Bibliography:

St. Thomas More: a preliminary bibliography of his works and of Moreana to the year 1750; compiled by R. W. Gibson and J. Max Patrick. Yale U.P., New Haven, 1961. A revised edition will appear after the completion of the Yale edition of the *Complete Works.*

Moreana, 1478–1945. A preliminary check list of material by and about St. Thomas More, by Frank Sullivan and M. P. Sullivan. Rockhurst College, Kansas City, 1946.

Texts:

A definitive edition of the *Complete Works* in 14 volumes is being published by Yale U.P. The second volume, *Richard III* has already appeared. Yale are also publishing *Selected Works* in 7 volumes. *Selected Letters* and *Utopia* have already appeared.

The English works of Sir Thomas More, ed. with a modern version of the same by W. E. Campbell, 2 vols. Eyre & Spottiswoode, London, 1931.

Utopia and a Dialogue of Comfort. Introduction by John Warrington. Revised ed. (Everyman's Library, 461), Dent, London, 1951.

A Dialogue of comfort against tribulation. A modernised version ed. with an introduction by P. E. Hallett. Burns & Oates, London, 1937.

A Dialogue of comfort against tribulation. Ed. by M. Stevens. Sheed & Ward, London, 1951.

English prayers and Treatise on the Holy Eucharist. Ed. with an introduction by P. E. Hallett. Burns & Oates, London, 1938.

The four last things. Ed. by D. O'Connor. Burns & Oates, London, 1935.

St. Thomas More's History of the Passion. Trans. by his granddaughter. Ed. in modern spelling with an introduction by Mgr. P. E. Hallett. Burns & Oates, London, 1941.

Studies:

The Life and writings of Sir Thomas More, Lord Chancellor of England and martyr under Henry VIII, by T. E. Bridgett. Burns & Oates, London, 1891.

Thomas More, by R. W. Chambers, Cape, London, 1935. Re-issued with minor corrections in the *Bedford Historical Series* in 1948.

St. Thomas More, by E. E. Reynolds. Burns & Oates, London, 1953.

The Trial of St. Thomas More, by E. E. Reynolds. Burns & Oates, London, 1963.

Lives of St. Thomas More, by William Roper and Nicholas Harpsfield. Ed. with an introduction by E. E. Reynolds (Everyman's Library 19). Dent, London, 1963.

L'Univers de Thomas More, par G. Marc'hadour. J. Vrin, Paris, 1963. Some additions and corrections to this book are printed in *Moreana,* 2 (February 1964), pp. 71–82.

Articles:

Marc'hadour, G., "Obedient unto death: a key to St. Thomas More," *Spiritual Life,* 7 (Fall 1961).

Moreana, a periodical devoted to St. Thomas More is published by the Amici Thomae Mori and ed. by G. Marc'hadour from 29, rue Volney, Angers, France. The first issue appeared in September, 1963.

BENET CANFIELD

Bibliography: There is a useful bibliography in *Lexicon Capuccinum.* Rome, 1951, col. 193.

Texts:

Regula perfectionis; seu breve totius vitae spiritualis compendium. Paris, 1609. There were several later editions in the seventeenth century.

The rule of perfection contayning a breif and perspicuous abridgement of all the wholle spirituall life. C. Hamillion, Rouen, 1609. Another edition was printed for John Cousturier at Rouen, probably between 1630 and 1640. These translated the first and second parts of the *Regula perfectionis.* The third part was translated and published in England as *A brightstarre leading to and containing in Christ our Perfection*. By Giles Randall in 1646.

The holy will of God: a short rule of perfection. Trans. by Fr. Collins. Richardson, London, 1878.

The Christian Knight, by Sir William Wiseman. J. Leggat, London, 1609.

Studies:

Benoit de Canfield (1562–1610): Sa vie, sa doctrine et son influence, by Fr. Optat de Veghel, O.F.M.Cap. Institutum Historicum. Ord.Fr.Min.Cap., Rome, 1949.

The lives of Ange de Joyeuse and Benet Canfield, by Jacques Brousse. Ed. from Robert Rookwood's trans. of 1623 by T. A. Birrell. Sheed and Ward, London, 1959.

Histoire litteraire du sentiment religieux en France depuis la fin des Guerres de Religion jusqu'à nos jours, par Henri Bremond. II. *L'invasion mystique*, Bloud et Gay, Paris, 1916, pp. 152–68.

Article: Sheppard, L. C., "Benet of Canfield and his Rule of Perfection," *Downside Review*, LIX, 217 (Summer 1959), pp. 323–32.

AUGUSTINE BAKER

Texts:

Holy Wisdom or directions for the prayer of contemplation. With an introduction by Dom Gerard Sitwell, O.S.B. (Orchard Books). Burns & Oates, London, 1964.

Holy Wisdom or directions for the prayer of contemplation. Methodically digested by Serenus Cressy and now ed. from the Douay edition of 1657 by Abbot Sweeney. Burns & Oates, London, 1911.

The Confessions . . . extracted from a manuscript treatise preserved in the library of Ampleforth Abbey and ed. by Dom Justin McCann. Burns & Oates, London, 1922.

Studies:

The Life of Father Augustine Baker, O.S.B. (1575–1641), by Fr. Peter Salvin and Fr. Serenus Cressy. Ed. by Dom Justin McCann, O.S.B. Burns & Oates, London, 1933.

Memorials of Father Augustine Baker and other documents relating to the English Benedictines. Ed. by Justin McCann and Hugh Connolly. (Catholic Record Society, 33). London, 1933.

The Life and Spirit of Father Augustine Baker, by J. N. Sweeney, O.S.B. London, 1861.